POVERTY IN AFFLUENCE

Under the General Editorship of Robert K. Merton
Columbia University

The Social, Political, and Economic
Dimensions of Poverty
in the United States

POVERTY IN AFFLUENCE

EDITED BY

ROBERT E. WILL and HAROLD G. VATTER

Carleton College

HARCOURT, BRACE & WORLD, INC.

New York   Chicago   Burlingame

Library of Congress Catalog Card Number: 65–18384

Printed in the United States of America

To GUNNAR MYRDAL, *Social Scientist*

Like preventable disease, economic want persists as a social ill only because men do not desire sufficiently that it shall cease. There is still much mumbling of old commonplaces, and it has seemed worth while to emphasize anew this definite corollary of modern political economy, that the essential causes of poverty are determinable and its considerable presence unnecessary.

—*Jacob Hollander*

Preface

This book is about a pathological condition afflicting American society: poverty. It is an organized collection of writings from diverse sources discussing the causes, forms, and results of poverty, and the proposals that have been made for its abolition. The selections represent differing points of view, giving the reader a broad survey of the subject; the representative section of doctrinal background material is, so far as we know, unique.

Much useful and interesting material on poverty is available; the selections chosen are those which we believe will give the reader a comprehensive introduction to the subject. In addition, the analytical headnotes that begin each of the eight sections are not only a guide to the readings which follow, but a discussion of several concepts not included in the readings. The headnotes also often point up the relevant theoretical problems on each topic: the headnote for Section 8 outlines the underlying ideological issues of the policy controversies. The book thus gives the reader a body of ideas and information representative, we hope, of the best contemporary thought on poverty. We believe that new writings on the subject in the next few years will be largely an elaboration of the seminal concepts discussed here.

A book of this size cannot analyze any one aspect of poverty in depth, but the reader will get here a sound basis for more detailed study. We suggest that such further study might well start with the full texts from which these selections have been taken.

Although *Poverty in Affluence* is not confined to one approach, its editors are dedicated to the abolition of poverty in all its forms; they favor amelioration only as a transition policy until the social disease of poverty can be completely eradicated.

This book is for the student and for the nonprofessional reader who is interested in social problems in general and the problem of poverty in particular. It should be useful in adult education courses and in discussion groups. College and university courses in which it can be used include introductory sociology, economics, and political science; social science area or survey courses; economic problems and policies; American society and contemporary American social problems; and American studies. We hope that it may encourage the academic community to give more time to the study of poverty.

We wish to acknowledge the many constructive suggestions from Professor David Caplovitz, Columbia University; Professor Jacob J. Kaufman, Pennsylvania State University; and The Honorable Daniel Patrick Moynihan, Assistant Secretary of Labor. The final choice of materials is, of course, the responsibility of the editors. Many helpful ideas were conveyed to us by Dean William Kolb of Beloit College, and Professor Forbes Hays, Department of Government and International Relations, Carleton College. We are also deeply indebted to our wives for their numerous suggestions and copious time away from home and family and in conflict with their own intellectual activities. For typing and work requiring imaginative detail we wish to thank Mrs. Florence Scott, particularly, and Mrs. Evelyn Flom. We also extend thanks to the Carleton Library staff for its considerable research assistance. The Ford Foundation Fund for Research in Public Affairs, administered by Carleton College, is to be credited for a grant that helped defray our production costs.

Robert E. Will
Harold G. Vatter

Contents

8 POLICY 211

Governmental Programs and Their Critics

Poverty in Perspective

Introduction

Poverty as a social and economic problem has long been with us. For many of us today, however, it has been nearly invisible, our closest involvement being an occasional impersonal gift to a private charity or the more regular paying of taxes, a small part of which we know to be used for governmental relief and assistance. We may also be aware that the great bulk of our tax payments indirectly help alleviate poverty to an unknown degree by contributing to the maintenance of employment, income, and spending.

In the general prosperity of the 1960's, poverty, as a pathological condition, has finally recaptured the analytical attention of social scientists as well as the sudden concern of politicians in connection with President Johnson's "war on poverty." It is noteworthy that New York's governor W. Averell Harriman called for an "Attack on Poverty" in his annual message to the legislature in 1956. This broad new interest in the nature of poverty as a disease of society, and in the means for attacking it, provides us with an opportunity to take stock of our past experience with life for the many Americans who live at deplorable levels. We can take this opportunity to realize the possibilities of achieving, during the foreseeable future, a decent life for these large numbers of people whom Thorstein

Veblen, that brooding genius, included in his descriptive term "the underlying masses." Arising out of the interaction of ethical commitment in the religious community, scholarly and popular studies by the intellectual community, and responsible leadership in the political community is a determination to make this yet the century of the common man.

The attack on involuntary poverty throughout those major parts of the world where human misery and degradation still prevail may not have proved fully victorious when the century draws to a close, although here in the United States we know that poverty can be eliminated within two or three decades. The record can, and no doubt will, show that the good war has been escalated, that the good life is being increasingly shared by those rising out of poverty into at least a life of minimum health and decency.

Poverty, as this book shows, has many faces. It is an economic phenomenon of the material conditions of life, of psychic travail, of the multiproblem family and individual, of dysfunctional behavior. But perhaps above all, it is the first of these; as Carlyle so penetratingly stressed, "it is to live miserable we know not why; to work sore and yet gain nothing." William Dean Howells described it as "the fear and dread of want," and Franklin Delano Roosevelt condemned it eloquently a generation ago. While it is indeed true that poverty may be associated in specific cases with virtue and possibly happiness, yet twentieth-century humanism demands that such virtue or happiness in the general case arise from wellsprings other than poverty. Unlike the nineteenth and earlier centuries, the Twentieth-Century Enlightenment finds little that is good in the fact of a life lived in poverty.

The Industrial Revolution shattered the ages-old continuum of human poverty by ushering in the epoch of the abundant economy. It is true that the emergence of abundance as a fact of life for so many of us in the United States has so far only lightly touched most of the world's peoples, including a surprisingly large number here at home. Nevertheless, the historical discontinuity in the process of human and social evolution can be perceived. As the eminent geographer Erich Zimmerman has shown, with the Industrial Revolution mankind crossed the great divide separating past scarcity from present abundance, largely because of impressive technological achievements that have enlarged our physical resource base and vastly improved our efficiency in the use of human and machine skills.

It is appropriate that the first breakthroughs have occurred in those regions of the world where the Industrial Revolution was initially embedded and then extended. Today there are no technological constraints limiting the eradication of poverty in a large area of the Western world. It remains to be seen, however, to what extent the social structure will take advantage of these technological potentialities of our present high-capacity economy. It is a striking fact that a number of European countries have already gone far toward the complete elimination of poverty; in this respect they are ahead of the United States.

Dean John C. Bennett of Union Theological Seminary points out in the quotation below what a great divide also exists in the contemporary, as contrasted with the traditional, ethical attitude toward poverty and wealth distribution resulting from the emergence of abundant economies. In this connection he quotes in part the report of the Oxford Conference in 1937:

> The abolition of such poverty now seems to depend on the human organization of economic life, rather than on favors given in nature or on what might be called the inevitable constitution of every economic order. But the possibility of economic "plenty" has this moral importance, that to an increasing extent it makes the persistence of poverty a matter for which men are morally responsible. This possibility marks off our time from the period of the New Testament and from other periods in which Christian thinking about economic life has been formulated. In the light of it the direction of Christian effort in relation to the economic order should henceforth be turned from charitable paternalism to the realization of more equal justice in the distribution of wealth.

Today, also, in the materially less developed countries, even in remote corners of the globe, there is a revolution of rising expectations as more and more people determine to share the fruits of the technological revolution. Thus, an adequate perspective on the task of eliminating poverty requires both an historical and a cross-cultural appreciation of its nature and extent, an appreciation which can merely be suggested in the following pages.

Despite present technological potentialities, the history of poverty from the ancient lowly to the contemporary poor still reveals the continuity of this scourge. Sections 1 and 2 indicate the extent to which poverty remains a bitter reality faced daily by many of our countrymen, despite debatable changes in the distribution of income and wealth in recent decades.

Both a fatalistic acceptance of the inevitability of poverty and an optimistic anticipation of its extirpation have emerged, paradoxically, from its long continued presence. Many great minds of the past have influenced contemporary attitudes; it is, therefore, both fair and enlightening to explore some of these older perspectives, as is done in Section 3. It is only fair to acknowledge and learn what we can from these classic statements on poverty, written often when the full significance of the technological revolution was as yet unrecognized or at best seen through a glass darkly. It is enlightening to savor the grim prognostications and crude justifications of those who maintained poverty was inevitable and even desirable because they help us to see how far most of us have come in our own thinking since the last century. They also remind us how little many of us have updated our perspectives, as the letter-to-the-editor and the Gallup Poll results will reveal below.

Most of what follows in this book is designed to help the reader formulate or reassess his position on a major social issue, by means of examining the contemporary subculture of poverty in the United States. After an overview of this subculture in Section 4, the examination continues in terms of first, the spatial distribution of poverty in cities, farms, and depressed areas; second, the categorical distribution, among special groups, such as youth, the unemployed and underpaid, and minorities; and lastly, other cultural dimensions of poverty, such as overpopulation and political inarticulateness (Sections 5, 6, and 7).

The examination should provide an understanding of the many dimensions of poverty and a recognition of the difficulty of precisely defining it. Perhaps the most useful definition is a pragmatic one, based on standards of living relevant to the particular culture being studied. The pragmatic "line of poverty" approach, presently stated as an annual family income of $3,000 or less, has its historical roots in two groups of studies begun at the turn of the century, one seeking to establish minimum family budgets in real terms at different levels of living, and the other attempting to measure the cost of living. The concepts developed then have subsequently been refined, notably by the Heller Committee in California. There are now three distinguishable budget levels—minimum subsistence, minimum health and decency, and minimum comfort—and two less precise levels, at the extremes—insufficiency, and luxury.

At the same time the budgetary levels were being developed, economists and statisticians were expanding and improving techniques for measuring the cost of living and changes in it. When the price data provided by the extensive cost of living studies, undertaken today by the federal Bureau of Labor Statistics, are combined with each budget level, it is possible to determine the level of annual income at which a family can achieve a level of living providing minimum health and decency. The Bureau is presently developing a new minimum adequacy budget for the 1960's. Although it would be possible to distinguish different minimum incomes for families of various sizes, with different locations (that is, urban or rural, North or South), the current benchmark income, $3,000, is a valuable shorthand figure, roughly separating the poor from the rest of the nation.

While the many similarities of material living conditions and personal style of life among the poor permit us to consider them as a distinct subculture, that subculture includes diversity as well as uniformity. This diversity will become apparent to those who survey the nature of poverty in the pages that follow. Recognition of the heterogeneity of poverty in the context of a broad and deep homogeneous subculture is essential, in our view, to the development of adequate policy measures. We state frankly that even if the United States were to adhere to its established dedication to full employment and a "high" rate of economic growth, the many-faceted phenomenon of poverty would not be eliminated. Caught in the crossfire between those who find growth the all-encompassing policy panacea and those who stress the pockets-of-poverty approach, we take the eclectic view that growth at full employment is the essential condition, but that it is far from a sufficient condition for eliminating poverty. Neither is "education," however broadly advocated, a panacea. Nor does the record below show that we are already doing enough, as some observers aver. We believe it is a fantastic statistical exercise to assert that our country is currently spending "over $100 billion a year" to "attack poverty." On such grounds one may as well cite the entire gross national income as a measure of the contemporary antipoverty effort.

Our conclusion, consistent, we believe, with the facts, is that a many-pronged attack, systematically planned and persistently applied on both public (federal, state, and local) and private levels, is the only adequate program. Such a program must be addressed to the ill and incapacitated, the poverty-ridden child's peculiar personality, the delinquent, the politically alienated, the migratory, the immobile, the untrained, the impecunious retired, the under-motivated, the prejudiced, and the ignorant, if it is to succeed. Only an interdisciplinary approach that mobilizes the full intellectual resources of the sciences, the humanities, and the social sciences can shape the blueprint.

Certainly if any country in the world is equipped to make a national commitment to the complete elimination of poverty within its borders, the United States is that country. The United States may be behind a number of other countries in terms of formal commitment, but it is preeminent in its capacity to underwrite such a commitment. Our resources exceed our aggregate needs; the law of scarcity need not be the guide where such a relative plethora obtains. It will, perhaps, become appropriate to attempt to apply the economist's traditional principles of resource conservation and allocation insofar as the United States extends its antipoverty program on an extensive scale to the poorer nations, through foreign aid. On this scale, scarcity considerations become more operative.

Policy measures for carrying out our national commitment, at home and abroad, are presented and criticized in Section 8. Between the shadow and the reality, between commitment and program execution, lies the task of restructuring public attitudes toward the hungry two-thirds of the world, toward our own military spending, toward the nature of income itself, and toward our ethical position on poverty. These and other attitudes pose barriers that warn us, in the words of Bernard Nossiter, that "it will be a long war." The attitudinal obstacles to an antipoverty program revealed in many selections below are further discussed in our analytical headnote for Section 8. The heritage of the past, with its frequent stress on the inevitability of poverty and on rugged individualism, hangs heavy over the contemporary public mind. Perhaps the greater educational task in the good war lies here, rather than among the poor themselves. We hope this book will contribute to an understanding of the nature and causes of poverty as well as to the relevance and realism of the reader's attitudes toward poverty and its eradication.

1 / The Problem of Poverty Today

Mass involuntary poverty as extensive as that revealed in the selected passages from the *Economic Report of the President,* issued on the eve of the war on poverty, arouses more than humanistic sentiments and a consciousness of guilt. It also forces us to recognize the harsh reality of the nation's balance sheet: poverty represents huge social and private costs. Although there is no way to assess accurately the aggregate of these costs, their nature can be pointed out. In undertaking this task, Fred A. Mangum, Jr., reminds us that the costs of the war on poverty, whatever they may turn out to be in the long run, will be offset to an important degree by reductions in present uncoordinated and often only stopgap measures attempting to alleviate, and optimistically hoping to eradicate, poverty. The stock-taking represented in the selections in this section, although grim and harsh, as is any stock-taking in the sphere of human suffering, makes no pretense to be exhaustive or precise. Yet the fact remains that success in the good fight for the poor *will* contract the expenditure of resources now being channeled in various ways into this effort.

Small comfort can be taken in the estimate, advanced by President Johnson and explored in Robert J. Lampman's analysis, that the poor now comprise only one-fifth, rather than President Roosevelt's one-third, of the nation. Perhaps more comfort can be derived from Lampman's emphasis on the fact that the removal of poverty has been added to the array of humanistic national goals.

Poverty As a Way of Life

A family living [in poverty] must never spend a penny on railway fare or omnibus. They must never go into the country unless they walk. They must never purchase a halfpenny newspaper or spend a penny to buy a ticket for a popular concert. They must write no letters to absent children, for they cannot afford to pay the postage. They must never contribute anything to their church or chapel, or give any help to a neighbour which costs them money. They cannot save, nor can they join sick club or trade union, because they cannot pay the necessary subscriptions. The children must have no pocket money for dolls, marbles or sweets. The father must smoke no tobacco, and must drink no beer. The mother must never buy any pretty clothes for herself or for her children, the character of the family wardrobe, as for the family diet, being governed by the regulation, "Nothing must be bought but that which is absolutely necessary for the maintenance of physical health, and what is bought must be of the plainest and most economical description." Should a child fall ill, it must be attended by the parish doctor; should it die, it must be buried by the parish. Finally, the wage-earner must never be absent from his work for a single day.

If any of these conditions are broken, the extra expenditure involved is met, *and can only be met*, by limiting the diet; or, in other words, by sacrificing physical efficiency.

That few York labourers receiving 20s. or 21s. per week submit to these iron conditions in order to maintain physical efficiency is obvious. And even were they to submit, physical efficiency would be unattainable for those who had three or more children dependent

---

Poverty As a Way of Life: From *Poverty and Progress*, B. Seebohm Rowntree (New York and London: Longmans, Green and Co., 1941), p. 103.

B. Seebohm Rowntree (1871–1954). A leading English businessman and philanthropist as well as a prolific sociologist specializing in problems of income and wealth disparities.

upon them. It cannot therefore be too clearly understood, nor too emphatically repeated, *that whenever a worker having three children dependent on him, and receiving not more than 21s. 8d. per week, indulges in any expenditure beyond that required for the barest physical needs, he can do so only at the cost of his own physical efficiency, or of that of some members of his family.*

POVERTY REMAINS A BITTER REALITY

Council of Economic Advisers

There will always be some Americans who are better off than others. But it need not follow that "the poor are always with us." In the United States today we can see on the horizon a society of abundance, free of much of the misery and degradation that have been the age-old fate of man. Steadily rising productivity, together with an improving network of private and social insurance and assistance, has been eroding mass poverty in America. But the process is far too slow. It is high time to redouble and to concentrate our efforts to eliminate poverty.

Poverty is costly not only to the poor but to the whole society. Its ugly by-products include ignorance, disease, delinquency, crime, irresponsibility, immorality, indifference. None of these social evils and hazards will, of course, wholly disappear with the elimination of poverty. But their severity will be markedly reduced. Poverty is no purely private or local concern. It is a social and national problem.

But the overriding objective is to improve the quality of life of individual human beings. For poverty deprives the individual not only of material comforts but of human dignity and fulfillment. Poverty is rarely a builder of character.

Poverty Remains a Bitter Reality: From *Economic Report of the President, 1964,* Council of Economic Advisers (Washington, D.C.: U.S. Government Printing Office, 1964), pp. 55–57.

The poor inhabit a world scarcely recognizable, and rarely recognized, by the majority of their fellow Americans. It is a world apart, whose inhabitants are isolated from the mainstream of American life and alienated from its values. It is a world where Americans are literally concerned with day-to-day survival—a roof over their heads, where the next meal is coming from. It is a world where a minor illness is a major tragedy, where pride and privacy must be sacrificed to get help, where honesty can become a luxury and ambition a myth. Worst of all, the poverty of the fathers is visited upon the children.

Equality of opportunity is the American dream, and universal education our noblest pledge to realize it. But, for the children of the poor, education is a handicap race; many are too ill prepared and ill motivated at home to learn at school. And many communities lengthen the handicap by providing the worst schooling for those who need the best.

Although poverty remains a bitter reality for too many Americans, its incidence has been steadily shrinking. The fruits of general economic growth have been widely shared; individuals and families have responded to incentives and opportunities for improvement; government and private programs have raised the educational attainments, housing standards, health, and productivity of the population; private and social insurance has increasingly protected families against loss of earnings due to death, disability, illness, old age, and unemployment. Future headway against poverty will likewise require attacks on many fronts: the active promotion of a full-employment, rapid-growth economy; a continuing assault on discrimination; and a wide range of other measures to strike at specific roots of low income. As in the past, progress will require the combined efforts of all levels of government and of private individuals and groups.

All Americans will benefit from this progress. Our Nation's most precious resource is its people. We pay twice for poverty: once in the production lost in wasted human potential, again in the resources diverted to coping with poverty's social by-products. Humanity compels our action, but it is sound economics as well.

I SEE ONE-THIRD OF A NATION ILL-HOUSED, ILL-CLAD, ILL-NOURISHED

Franklin Delano Roosevelt

To hold to progress today . . . is more difficult. Dulled conscience, irresponsibility, and ruthless self-interest already reappear. Such symptoms of prosperity may become portents of disaster! Prosperity already tests the persistence of our progressive purpose.

Let us ask again: Have we reached the goal of our vision of that fourth day of March, 1933? Have we found our happy valley?

I see a great nation, upon a great continent, blessed with a great wealth of natural resources. Its hundred and thirty million people are at peace among themselves; they are making their country a good neighbor among the nations. I see a United States which can demonstrate that, under democratic methods of government, national wealth can be translated into a spreading volume of human comforts hitherto unknown, and the lowest standard of living can be raised far above the level of mere subsistence.

But here is the challenge to our democracy: In this nation I see tens of millions of its citizens—a substantial part of its whole population—who at this very moment are denied the greater part of what the very lowest standards of today call the necessities of life.

I see millions of families trying to live on incomes so meager that the pall of family disaster hangs over them day by day.

I see millions whose daily lives in city and on farm continue under conditions labeled indecent by a so-called polite society half a century ago.

I See One-Third of a Nation Ill-Housed, Ill-Clad, Ill-Nourished: From *Second Inaugural Address,* January 20, 1937, Franklin D. Roosevelt.

Franklin Delano Roosevelt. President of the United States from 1933 until his death in office in 1945.

I see millions denied education, recreation, and the opportunity to better their lot and the lot of their children.

I see millions lacking the means to buy the products of farm and factory and by their poverty denying work and productiveness to many other millions.

I see one-third of a nation ill-housed, ill-clad, ill-nourished.

It is not in despair that I paint you that picture. I paint it for you in hope—because the Nation, seeing and understanding the injustice in it, proposes to paint it out. We are determined to make every American citizen the subject of his country's interest and concern; and we will never regard any faithful, law-abiding group within our borders as superfluous. The test of our progress is not whether we add more to the abundance of those who have much; it is whether we provide enough for those who have too little.

If I know aught of the spirit and purpose of our Nation, we will not listen to Comfort, Opportunism, and Timidity. We will carry on.

Overwhelmingly, we of the Republic are men and women of good will; men and women who have more than warm hearts of dedication; men and women who have cool heads and willing hands of practical purpose as well. They will insist that every agency of popular government use effective instruments to carry out their will.

Government is competent when all who compose it work as trustees for the whole people. It can make constant progress when it keeps abreast of all the facts. It can obtain justified support and legitimate criticism when the people receive true information of all that government does.

If I know aught of the will of our people, they will demand that these conditions of effective government shall be created and maintained. They will demand a nation uncorrupted by cancers of injustice and, therefore, strong among the nations in its example of the will to peace.

Today we reconsecrate our country to long-cherished ideals in a suddenly changed civilization. In every land there are always at work forces that drive men apart and forces that draw men together. In our personal ambitions we are individualists. But in our seeking for economic and political progress as a nation, we all go up, or else we all go down, as one people.

To maintain a democracy of effort requires a vast amount of

patience in dealing with differing methods, a vast amount of humility. But out of the confusion of many voices rises an understanding of dominant public need. Then political leadership can voice common ideals, and aid in their realization.

THE GREAT UNFINISHED WORK OF OUR SOCIETY

Lyndon B. Johnson

We are citizens of the richest and most fortunate nation in the history of the world.

One hundred and eighty years ago we were a small country struggling for survival on the margin of a hostile land.

Today we have established a civilization of free men which spans an entire continent.

With the growth of our country has come opportunity for our people—opportunity to educate our children, to use our energies in productive work, to increase our leisure—opportunity for almost every American to hope that through work and talent he could create a better life for himself and his family.

The path forward has not been an easy one.

But we have never lost sight of our goal: an America in which every citizen shares all the opportunities of his society, in which every man has a chance to advance his welfare to the limit of his capacities.

We have come a long way toward this goal.

We still have a long way to go.

The distance which remains is the measure of the great unfinished work of our society.

The Great Unfinished Work of our Society: From *Message on Poverty*, March 16, 1964, Lyndon B. Johnson.
Lyndon B. Johnson. President of the United States, 1963—.

To finish that work I have called for a national war on poverty. Our objective: total victory.

There are millions of Americans—one fifth of our people—who have not shared in the abundance which has been granted to most of us, and on whom the gates of opportunity have been closed.

What does this poverty mean to those who endure it?

It means a daily struggle to secure the necessities for even a meager existence. It means that the abundance, the comforts, the opportunities they see all around them are beyond their grasp.

Worst of all, it means hopelessness for the young.

The young man or woman who grows up without a decent education, in a broken home, in a hostile and squalid environment, in ill health or in the face of racial injustice—that young man or woman is often trapped in a life of poverty.

He does not have the skills demanded by a complex society. He does not know how to acquire those skills. He faces a mounting sense of despair which drains initiative and ambition and energy.

Our tax cut will create millions of new jobs—new exits from poverty.

But we must also strike down all the barriers which keep many from using those exits.

The war on poverty is not a struggle simply to support people, to make them dependent on the generosity of others.

It is a struggle to give people a chance.

It is an effort to allow them to develop and use their capacities, as we have been allowed to develop and use ours, so that they can share, as others share, in the promise of this nation.

We do this, first of all, because it is right that we should.

From the establishment of public education and land grant colleges through agricultural extension and encouragement to industry, we have pursued the goal of a nation will full and increasing opportunities for all its citizens.

The war on poverty is a further step in that pursuit.

We do it also because helping some will increase the prosperity of all.

Our fight against poverty will be an investment in the most valuable of our resources—the skills and strength of our people.

And in the future, as in the past, this investment will return its cost many fold to our entire economy.

If we can raise the annual earnings of 10 million among the poor by only $1,000 we will have added 14 billion dollars a year to our national output. In addition we can make important reductions in public assistance payments which now cost us 4 billion dollars a year, and in the large costs of fighting crime and delinquency, disease and hunger.

This is only part of the story.

Our history has proved that each time we broaden the base of abundance, giving more people the chance to produce and consume, we create new industry, higher production, increased earnings and better income for all.

Giving new opportunity to those who have little will enrich the lives of all the rest.

Because it is right, because it is wise, and because, for the first time in our history, it is possible to conquer poverty, I submit, for the consideration of the Congress and the country, the Economic Opportunity Act of 1964.

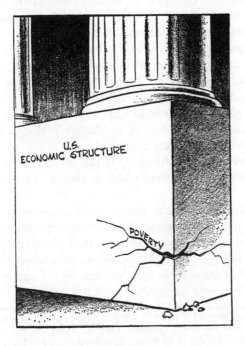

Flaw

Palmer in the Springfield, Mo., *Leader and Press*

WHAT ARE THE COSTS OF FAILURE TO ADJUST OUR HUMAN RESOURCES?

Fred A. Mangum, Jr.

Changes in technology and tastes are constantly altering the pattern of demand for labor in our economy. New industries appear and expand while old ones decline; job opportunities multiply in one region and disappear in another; new skills are required as old ones become obsolete. The more rapidly an economy grows and changes, the greater the flux in its labor markets.

Those who adapt to growth and change usually gain. For those who do not change with economic growth the costs are usually very great. Often, these costs are borne by the total society. We can view these costs under three headings: (1) higher costs to consumers for goods and services, (2) increased costs of social welfare programs, and (3) loss of productive resources represented by unemployed or underemployed workers.

Consumers have been fortunate in this country in having a wide variety of quality goods from which to choose. This has not been by accident.

In our economic system, profits are the motivating factor for industries. As profits increase, industries increase their investment, expand the size of their businesses, use their plants nearer to capacity outputs and put more of their income into research and development. All of these mean that Mr. and Mrs. Consumer are able to buy a wider variety of products of better quality and at less cost.

What Are the Costs of Failure to Adjust Our Human Resources?: From *People, Jobs, and Economic Growth,* Fred A. Mangum, Jr. (Ames, Iowa: Center for Agricultural and Economic Development, Iowa State University), pp. 5–6.

Fred A. Mangum, Jr. Extension Economist in Area Development, North Carolina State College, Raleigh, N.C.

Our manpower has been a major factor in the efficiency and profitableness of our economic system. Unless it continues to improve in quality and to adapt to changing needs, consumers will suffer in the form of higher prices for goods and services. Thus, failure to adjust our human resources represents a cost to every American.

The second cost of failing to adjust our human resources lies in increasing costs of our social welfare programs.

In 1957, Federal expenditures by the Department of Health, Education and Welfare were approximately 1.9 billion dollars. Five years later, in 1962, this expenditure had more than doubled to over 4.5 billion dollars. By 1980, this could be the most expensive item in our Federal budget except for defense spending.

In 1960, seven million families and individuals had personal incomes lower than $2,000. Part of this number is a result of temporary unemployment. A large number, however, remain poor in all periods of economic activity.

In Cook County, Illinois (Chicago), 87 percent of the persons applying for relief because of unemployment in the first three months of 1959 had not finished high school.

The cost of these relief programs and for assistance to families with insufficient earnings is borne by all of society. The only alternative to ever-mounting costs of social welfare is a growing dynamic economy and programs to equip our human resources for jobs as they develop. Society's investment in education and training reduces welfare costs and permits the human resource to have a more satisfying life and to make a greater contribution to economic growth.

The third cost of failing to adjust is a loss of productive resources represented by idle labor.

We hear a great deal about automation. Usually when a process is mechanized, it means a more efficient way of performing the operation. If, however, it leads to large scale unemployment, the cost to society may prove greater than the gain from using the machinery.

By the same token, the farmer who is only seasonally employed in producing his crops represents a loss of productive manpower. If his farm were of sufficient size, if he could obtain a part-time job or a full-time non-farm job, his income would likely improve and his contribution to economic growth would be greater.

ONE-FIFTH OF A NATION

Robert J. Lampman

In his State of the Union Message and again in a special message to the Congress, President Johnson called for a sustained and co-ordinated "war on poverty." And in his Economic Report, the President pointed out that "Americans today enjoy the highest standard of living in the history of mankind. But for nearly a fifth of our fellow citizens, this is a hollow achievement. They often live without hope, below minimum standards of decency. The per capita money income of these 35 million men, women and children was only $590 in 1962—against $1,900 per capita for the nation as a whole."

Mr. Johnson observed that in the Great Depression mass un-employment made poverty a common experience, that since 1947 the incidence of poverty has been reduced from one-third to one-fifth of the nation, but that the erosion of poverty slowed meas-urably after 1957. To speed the rate at which poverty is being reduced, the President said that "the tactics of our attack on this ancient enemy must be versatile and adaptable. For the sources of poverty vary from family to family, city to city, region to region."

President Johnson's statements on poverty have historic mean-ing. The President associates himself with those who deny the in-evitability of a mass of impoverished people. In the tradition of Jefferson and Jackson and Franklin Roosevelt, he affirms the hope and promise that wave after wave of Americans and their children can rise from deprivation to full participation in a land of opportu-nity for all.

At the same time, the "war on poverty" theme signifies a drama-

One-Fifth of a Nation: From *Challenge, The Magazine of Economic Af-fairs,* Robert J. Lampman. Published by the Institute of Economic Affairs, New York University. Vol. 12, No. 7 (April, 1964), pp. 11–12.

Robert J. Lampman. Professor of Economics, University of Wisconsin.

tic shift away from a particular characterization of the American economy which flourished in the 1950's and which represented it as having arrived at a classless, homogenized state of affluence. Many critics, impressed by the explosive expansion of the economy in World War II and the virtually uninterrupted growth in the post-war period, concluded that all serious economic problems were matters for historians. Others joined a chorus of self-congratulatory celebration which highlighted the "income revolution" which Harvard's Simon Kuznets found occurred during the war (involving a drop in the income share of upper income groups), and the coming of what New York University's Marcus Nadler christened "people's capitalism" (a widening participation in ownership of the nation's wealth).

Business journals heralded the conversion of millions of low-income families to membership in the vast and growing middle-income markets. Political writers evaluated the arrival of the "welfare state" and the dominance of the security ethic. Projecting a vision of rapidly vanishing poverty, even social workers and clergymen appeared to be turning away from concern for old-fashioned poverty as an important cause of human misery and toward the idea of a "new poverty" of maladjusted individuals, a type of poverty best dealt with by psychiatrists and specialists in community organization. In short, the poor became "invisible."

It would be an interesting study in itself to uncover the factors which caused Americans to once again consider the poverty in their midst. Among such factors one would have to count the 1957–58 recession which brought to the fore such problems as chronic unemployment, depressed areas and the severe adjustment problems associated with automation. Other factors include the harsh realities of an onrushing agricultural revolution which spilled millions of poor off the farms, increasing longevity which put a national spotlight on the economic problems of the aged, and the inspirational revolt of the Negro.

In addition, there was a new emphasis on human resource development as a way to economic growth, and a gradual change in the sense of urgency related to international, nuclear and space matters. All these changes seem to have paved the way for the criticisms of American society by such writers as John K. Galbraith, Michael Harrington, Leon Keyserling and James Baldwin, who evoked a response to the ordinary needs of ordinary people that have been left behind in the rush to national riches and power. They have dramatized the fact that the poor do, as Harrington puts it, constitute the "other America," having an alienated, separatist subculture. These people remain remarkably untouched by the New Deal welfare state measures such as old-age and unemployment insurance, and are well beyond the reach of unions and co-operatives and federal programs in farming, housing and urban renewal.

In any event, President Johnson has lent the weight of his office to the school of thought which says that we have a lot of unfinished business on behalf of the poor. He underscores the view that while the poor are still with us, there are encouragingly fewer of them than there used to be, but their numbers have been dropping at a discouragingly slow rate in recent years.

President Johnson's declaration of war on poverty is an exercise in national goal setting. It calls for a new measuring rod for assessing the performance of the economy. Along with the now traditional goals of "maximum employment, production and purchasing power" specified in the Employment Act of 1946, and the less official goals of reasonable price stability, a satisfactory rate of economic growth and equilibrium in our balance of payments, the President, in appraising our national economic achievement, would have us consider a rapid reduction in the number of persons living below a stated "poverty line." No specific rate of reduction is set down as a goal, but presumably our historic experience is a good basis for selecting a feasible one. Hence, one may refer to the fact that the net reduction has averaged about 700,000 persons per year in the postwar period, with a significant drop in the rate after 1956 to a low of about 500,000 per year.

For this purpose the precise income level selected to mark off poverty from nonpoverty is not critical, so long as it is unchanged over time, except for necessary adjustments relative to the prevailing price level. The actual level which underlies the President's statement that 35 million Americans are poor is $3,000 for multi-person families and $1,500 for single individuals. It is interesting that these incomes are near the median income for several Western European nations and represent a level of living attained by only a tiny minority of the world's three billion people. On the other hand, they seem painfully low compared to the $10,000 median family income which we should reach in about 20 years.

2 / Trends in Income, Wealth, and Poverty

Even before the decade of the great depression the American consensus had moderately but steadily raised the standards applied in drawing the poverty line. Substantially greater rises in the actual level of living have more than offset these rising standards, so that the application of today's consensus leaves a notably smaller percentage in the poverty class. Nevertheless, on the single basis of the "line-of-poverty" criterion of the Johnson Administration, there is still much unfinished business.

The extent of the progress we have made as well as the extent to which we have fallen short in the quarter-century since Franklin Roosevelt's *Second Inaugural Address* are suggested in the following analyses by writers on the distribution of income, wealth, and poverty. It is not too much to say that the statistical examination of such distribution occurs in a vast wilderness area. There are, as is generally the case in matters involving a combination of data and value judgments, at least two schools of thought as to whether distribution is becoming more or less even. The statistics, as collected, do not speak for themselves; hence the interested reader should undertake further research in depth later.

The "orthodox" view, that the distribution of income is becoming more even in recent times, is presented by Goldsmith; Miller, Reuther, and Kolko present opposing views. Miller and Reuther deal primarily with income. Miller's major concern is the distribution among occupations, skills, and geographical areas. Although Reuther stresses the alleged enrichment of the rich, his passing references to the distribution of capital gains and the effects of the tax cut of 1964 should not escape the careful reader who wishes to pursue further the whole distribution controversy. The federal government's tax discrimination between income and capital gains is, of course, but a small part of the knotty problem of government's distributive role in the economy, which can be barely touched upon in this work. Kolko's presentation deals with the closely connected distribution of wealth and claims to wealth, rather than with income patterns.

It seems reasonably clear that in terms of real, take-home income, the lowest brackets are, as a whole, absolutely better off now than they were before World War II. But it is debatable whether they are relatively better off. In this connection, the reader might wish to appraise Sumner Slichter's comment on Marx's doctrine of increasing misery, given in the Miller selection, with the extract from Marx's *Capital,* in Section 3, "Ideologies of Poverty." Furthermore, there are apparently substantial numbers of our citizens who are still little if any better off than their respective group was on the eve of World War II.

There is disagreement about whether the proportion of income going to those in the "highest" income bracket is rising rapidly, increasing slowly, remaining stable, or falling. However, the definition of the "highest" bracket makes a considerable difference. Goldsmith's top 5 per cent of consumer units is not comparable with Reuther's top 20 per cent of families, for example.

Admittedly, the approach to the dimensions of poverty by way of the criterion of income or wealth distribution, though an essential step, is only a first approximation and a partial treatment at best. Moreover, it is conceptually rooted in the limited line-of-poverty definition. A representative presentation of this concept, with all its statistical uncertainties and limitations, is found in the discussion below of "The Economics of a Subculture" (4), by the Council of Economic Advisers. In reading this the reader may develop an appreciation of the comparative usefulness of the $3000 cut-off point presently in official use, especially by relating it to the qualitative analyses of the many facets of poverty found elsewhere in these readings. It seems evident that we cannot dispense with the line-of-poverty concept despite its inadequacies if we wish to understand the nature of poverty and to develop, through governmental and private agencies, useful policies for alleviating and even eradicating this scourge.

INCOME DISTRIBUTION IN DEPRESSION, WAR, AND PEACE
Selma F. Goldsmith

Although there is some argument as to its exact magnitude, partly as a result of problems of appropriate deflation procedures, there is general agreement that there has been a very substantial increase in total and average real income over the past quarter century. In terms of the personal income series of the Office of Business Economics, total real income flowing to families and

Income Distribution in Depression, War, and Peace: From "Changes in the Size Distribution of Income," Selma F. Goldsmith, *American Economic Review Papers and Proceedings,* Vol. XLVII, No. 2, (May, 1957), pp. 504–11. Selma F. Goldsmith. Formerly economist, U.S. Department of Commerce.

unattached individuals increased between 1929 and 1955 at an average annual rate of approximately 3 or 2.5 percent a year, depending on whether income is measured before or after federal individual income taxes. The number of families and unattached individuals sharing in the income total has increased at an average rate of about 1.4 percent per year. Thus, real mean family income has risen at an average yearly rate of about 1.5 percent on a before-tax basis or slightly over 1 percent on an after-tax basis, from 1929 to 1955.

The increase in average real income has been reflected in a very substantial upward shift in the income-size distribution of consumer units (families and unattached individuals). For example, with family incomes expressed in terms of 1950 prices—and ignoring for the moment certain important problems of comparability of data—we find that the proportion of consumer units with before-tax incomes over $3,000 increased from one-third in 1929 to two-thirds in 1954. The proportion above $4,000 rose from one-fifth to one-half and the proportion above $5,000 from about 13 to 35 percent.

The income-size distributions available for selected intermediate years within the 1929–54 period indicate that a very large part of the upward shift in real incomes occurred between 1941 and 1944. For example, about one-half of the 1929–54 increase of 33 percentage points in the proportion of consumer units with real (1950 dollar) incomes over $3,000 took place between 1941 and 1944. However, the available price indexes do not reflect certain hidden price increases that occurred during the war so that the deflated figures overstate somewhat the wartime rise in real incomes and understate the increase in the early postwar years.

Of equal significance with the absolute income figures are estimates of the changes in relative income distribution over the past twenty-five years. . . .

The two statistical series on income-size distribution to which we can turn, present essentially the same pattern for the post-1929 period; namely, a marked decline in the percentage share of total income accruing to the top income group.

The first of these series, developed by Professor Kuznets, presents annual data on relative income shares received by successive top percentiles of the population; e.g., by the 5 percent of men, women, and children covered on those individual income tax returns reporting the largest per capita incomes in each year. The second series, developed by my colleagues and myself, is on a family rather than a population basis and covers the full range of family incomes for selected years. The top 5 percent in this series refers to families and unattached individuals having the largest family personal incomes in each year.

Starting with Kuznets' series, in 1929 the incomes received by the top 5 percent of the population amounted to about 32 percent of the total income receipts of all individuals (measured before income taxes and excluding net capital gains). In 1939, this relative share had dropped to 28 per cent, reflecting mainly a loss in relative share by the topmost percentile of the population. After 1939 declines were registered by all bands within the top 5 percent. By 1946, the relative share of this top group had fallen to 20 percent and in 1948 it is estimated at somewhat over 19 percent (Table 1). For the 1929–48 period as a whole, this represented a decline of 40 percent in the relative share of before-tax income received by the top 5 percent of the population. Kuznets has recently conjectured that this narrowing of relative income differences is part of a long-time secular swing that followed a period of widening income inequality during the second half of the last century.

The family income distributions show a similar though somewhat dampened post-1929 decline for the top income group. The relative share of the top 5 percent of consumer units is estimated at 30 percent in 1929 and at under 21 percent in 1944 and in the postwar period.

Both the Kuznets' and family income series represent before-tax incomes and in deriving both of them data from federal individual income tax returns represented the primary source material. The difference between them reflects a number of factors, such as differences in the basic unit of measurement (the family versus the person), in the concept of income, and in the adjustments that were made in the basic tax-return statistics by Kuznets, on the one hand, and by the various sets of persons who initially developed the family distributions for selected prewar and postwar years, on the other.

The family income distributions also tell us how the decrease in relative income share of the top 5 percent of the consumer units was spread among other income groups. Between 1929 and 1947, for example, the 9 percentage points of decline in the share of the

TABLE 1 Percentage shares of income received by top 5 percent, selected years

Year	Top 5 percent of population Kuznets			Top 5 percent of consumer units	
	Economic income variant	Disposable income variant	Economic income variant plus realized net capital gains	Family personal income	Income after federal individual income tax liability
	1	2	3	4	5
1929	32.2	33.8	34.8	30.0	29.5
1935–36	28.8	27.9		26.5	
1939	27.8	26.8	27.8	25.8	24.8
1941	25.7	23.0		24.0	21.5
1944	18.7	15.8		20.7	
1946	20.0	17.7	21.4	21.3	
1947	19.1			20.9	
1948	19.4				
1952				20.5	18.2
Percent decrease					
1929 to 1946	38	48	38	29	
1939 to 1946	28	34	23	17	
1929 to 1948	40				
1929 to 1952				32	38
1939 to 1952				12	27

SOURCES: Columns 1 and 2, which represent, respectively, before-tax income exclusive of capital gains, and income after federal individual income taxes but inclusive of realized net capital gains, from Simon Kuznets, *Shares of Upper Income Groups in Income and Savings* (National Bureau of Economic Research, 1953), pages 453, 635, 637 (with 1948 extrapolated by Kuznets' "basic variant" series, page 599). . . . Column 3 derived by adding to column 1 Kuznets' adjustment to include net capital gains (page 599, column 5 minus column 1) and subtracting his adjustment for unwarranted inclusions (page 622, column 4 minus column 1). Column 4, which represents personal income before income taxes flowing to families and unattached individuals and excludes capital gains and losses, for 1952 from "Income Distribution in the United States, by Size, 1952–55," *Survey of Current Business,* June, 1956; 1946 and 1947 from "Income Distribution in the United States, by Size, 1944–50," a supplement to the *Survey of Current Business* (1953); 1941, 1935–36 and 1929 from Selma Goldsmith, George Jaszi, Hyman Kaitz, and Maurice Liebenberg, "Size Distribution of Income since the Mid-thirties," *Review of Economics and Statistics,* February, 1954; 1939 derived by interpolation between 1935–36 and 1941 using column 1 as a basis. Column 5, which represents column 4 minus federal individual income tax liabilities other than those on net capital gains, for 1952 and 1941 derived from sources listed for column 4 for those years; 1929 and 1939 obtained by subtracting from amounts underlying column 4 federal individual income tax liabilities excluding liabilities on net capital gains, estimated from data in *Statistics of Income, Part 1, 1929 and 1939* (U.S. Treasury Department).

top 5 percent were offset by the following gains: 3½ percentage points by the lowest 40 percent of families and unattached individuals, 2¼ points by the middle quintile, 2¾ points by the fourth quintile, and ¾ points by the 15 percent of consumer units directly below the top 5.

A salient point is that for the lowest 40 percent of consumer units, the period of greatest relative gains was between 1941 and 1944. Since 1944, there has been little change in the relative distribution of family income according to the available figures.

Kuznets has also developed a series in terms of disposable income (i.e., income after federal individual income taxes and inclusive of capital gains). For the top 5 percent of the population, the relative share in total disposable income dropped from almost 34 percent in 1929 to well under 18 percent in 1946, the last year for which this series is available. This represented a decrease of 48 percent, 10 points more than the 38 percent drop in the before-tax income share from 1929 to 1946 (Table 1).

These decreases in relative income shares are reflected strikingly in the average income figures for the top income sector. Kuznets' per capita disposable income of the top 5 percent is about one-eighth lower in 1946 than in 1929, even in current dollars; i.e., before allowance for the higher prices prevailing in the latter year (Table 2). On a before-tax basis the current-dollar per capita income of the top 5 percent just about kept up with the rise in the consumer price index for the period 1929–46 but fell behind by 1948. However, attention must be called to the limited applicability of the consumer price index in this context. Not until we are able to develop differential cost-of-living indexes appropriate for the various income groups and can solve the problem of how to deflate the portions of income used for income taxes and saving, will we be in a position to measure with precision changes in the distribution of real income.

Several related statistical series lend support to the finding that there has been a reduction in relative income differences in the post-1929 and particularly in the post-1939 period. Confining our attention to the before-tax income measures, these include:

1. Changes in the relative importance of the various types of income in the personal income total. Since 1929 there has been a striking increase in the percentage that wages and salaries and transfer payments constitute of the personal income total flowing

TABLE 2 Average income of entire population and of top 5 per cent, selected years

| Year | Average Income Per Capita *Kuznets* | | | | *Consumer price index* 1947–49=100 |
| | Economic Income Variant | | Disposable Income Variant | | |
	Total population	*Top 5 per cent*	*Total population*	*Top 5 per cent*	
1929	$ 674	$4,339	$ 690	$4,666	73.3
1939	537	2,982	528	2,831	59.4
1941	700	3,594	664	3,052	62.9
1946	1,234	4,926	1,166	4,118	83.4
1948	1,400	5,421			102.8
Percent increase					
1929 to 1946	83	14	69	−12	14
1939 to 1946	130	65	121	45	40
1929 to 1948	108	25			40

SOURCES: Averages (see Table 1 for definitions) derived from Simon Kuznets, *Shares,* etc., pages 635, 637, 639, 641, 644 (with 1948 extrapolated from 1947 by Kuznets' "basic variant" series). Consumer price index from Bureau of Labor Statistics.

to families and unattached individuals. These payments together accounted for 61 percent of total personal income in 1929, 67 percent in 1939, and 73 percent in 1950–55 (Table 3). In contrast, there was a marked reduction in the shares of dividends and interest—types of income that are heavily concentrated in the upper end of the family income scale.

2. Changes in the relative distribution of the various types of income. By examining the shares of the top 5 percent in separate types of income, Kuznets found that the relative shares of this top group, based on data from tax returns, declined from 1929 to 1948 for wages and salaries, dividends, interest, and—to a lesser extent —for rental income. More recently, Herman Miller compared the wage and salary data reported in the last two Decennial Censuses of Population for detailed occupation and industry groups and found three factors making for a narrowing of income differentials within the wage and salary sector between 1939 and 1949: (*a*) decreases in relative income dispersion for men within practically all of the 118 occupations and 117 industries he studied; (*b*) rela-

TABLE 3 Percent distribution of family personal income by major types of income and relative importance of compensation of employees in national income, selected years

	1929	1939	1949	1950–55 Average
Family personal income:				
Wages and salaries and other labor income	59.6	63.3	64.8	67.5
Transfer payments	1.7	4.0	5.9	5.4
Subtotal	61.3	67.3	70.7	72.9
Business and professional income:				
Farm	7.1	6.1	6.4	5.2
Nonfarm	10.5	10.2	10.7	9.8
Dividends and interest	14.7	12.6	8.2	8.3
Rental income	6.4	3.8	4.0	3.8
Total	100.0	100.0	100.0	100.0
Compensation of employees as a percent of national income originating in:				
Economy as a whole	58.2	66.1	65.2	67.3
Ordinary business sector (corporations, partnerships, and proprietorships)	61.2	65.8	64.0	66.4
All other sectors	46.9	67.2	69.8	70.7
All nonfarm corporations	74.5	80.9	75.8	76.6
Manufacturing corporations	75	81	74	75

SOURCES: Upper bank derived by adjusting U.S. Department of Commerce personal income series from *Survey of Current Business,* July, 1956, as described on pages 17–18 and 67 of "Income Distribution in the United States, by Size 1944–1950," U.S. Department of Commerce, 1953. Lower bank, except last line, derived from Table 12 (and underlying data) of 1954 *National Income* supplement and July, 1956, issue of *Survey of Current Business.* Last line derived from *Survey of Current Business,* November, 1956, page 20.

tively greater gains in median wage and salary income for low-paid than for high-paid occupations and industries; and (*c*) an increase in the proportion of workers classified in occupations with comparatively little income dispersion. Unfortunately similar data are not available from the Census for 1929.

Of particular interest to those in the teaching profession is Miller's finding that when the industries are ranked by size of median wage or salary and grouped into deciles, the educational services industry dropped from the third highest decile in 1939 to the fourth from the bottom in 1949.

3. A narrowing of relative income differences, as measured by mean incomes, between the farm and nonfarm population. Because average incomes are lower for farm than for nonfarm consumer units—even with allowance for income received in kind—a narrowing in this differential, barring other changes, will work in the direction of reducing relative income differences in the over-all income distribution. Per capita income of persons on farms was 3 times as large in 1949 as in 1939—reflecting in part the relatively low level of farm income in the earlier year—whereas the corresponding ratio was 2½ for persons not living on farms. Despite the fall in farm incomes in the past few years, the ratio of per capita income in 1952–55 to that in 1939 is still substantially higher for farm residents than for nonfarm.

4. Another recent study that has bearing on the subject under discussion is the analysis of changes since 1929 in income distribution by states that has been made by members of the staff of the Office of Business Economics. As part of this study, per capita incomes in the various states for selected years are expressed as percentages of the national average, and these percentages are compared over time. Two major conclusions emerge.

First, "there has been a significant narrowing over the past quarter of a century in the relative differences in average-income levels among States and regions. . . . As shown by the coefficient of variation, relative dispersion in the State per capita income array was reduced by nearly 40 percent from 1927–29 to 1953–55."

Second, the period of greatest narrowing of state per capita incomes was that of the war years, 1942–44. Only a small part of the reduction in dispersion occurred in the prewar period, and "the regional differentials obtaining in 1944 were carried over with only moderate alteration into the postwar period and since then have tended to remain relatively stable in most regions."

These findings are remarkably consistent with those for the relative distribution of family income by size. As was noted earlier, the period of greatest gain in relative income share for the two lowest quintiles in the family income size distributions was between 1941 and 1944, and after 1944 the available data show little change in the relative distribution of family personal income by size. Of course, the narrowing of state differentials in average income does not of itself prove that there was a reduction in the relative dispersion of income by size, but it does lend credence to the finding that such a reduction took place.

WHAT'S HAPPENING TO OUR SOCIAL REVOLUTION?

Herman P. Miller

A myth has been created in the United States that incomes are gradually becoming more evenly distributed. This view is held by prominent economists of both major political parties. It is also shared by the editors of the influential mass media.

Arthur F. Burns, chief economist for the Eisenhower Administration, stated in 1951 that "the transformation in the distribution of our national income . . . may already be counted as one of the great social revolutions of history." Paul Samuelson, one of President Kennedy's leading economic advisers, stated in 1961 that "the American income pyramid is becoming less unequal." Several major stories on this subject have appeared in the *New York Times,* and the editors of *Fortune* magazine announced ten years ago: "Though not a head has been raised aloft on a pikestaff, nor a railway station seized, the U.S. has been for some time now in a revolution."

. . .

Despite the existence of much poverty in the United States, there is general agreement that real levels of living are much higher than they were only ten years ago and that the prospects for future increases are very good. Since conditions are improving you may wonder why it is important to consider the gap between the rich

What's Happening to Our Social Revolution?: From *Rich Man, Poor Man: The Distribution of Income in America,* Herman P. Miller (New York: Thomas Y. Crowell, 1964), pp. 37–51.

Herman P. Miller. Special Assistant, U.S. Bureau of the Census.

and the poor. Isn't it enough that the *amount* of income received by
the poor has gone up substantially? Why be concerned about their
share? Many who have thought about this problem seriously regard
the *share* as the critical factor. When Karl Marx, for example,
spoke about the inevitability of increasing misery among workers
under capitalism he had a very special definition of misery in mind.
Sumner Slichter, in summarizing the Marxian position on this point,
states: "Marx held that wages depend upon the customary wants
of the laboring class. Wages, so determined, might rise in the long
run. Hence, Marx conceded that real wages *might* rise, but not the
relative share of labor. Even if real wages rose, misery would grow,
according to Marx, since workers would be worse off relative to
capitalists."

Arnold Toynbee has approached the problem of income shares
in still another way. He notes that minimum standards of living
have been raised considerably and will continue to be raised in the
future, but he observes that this rise has not stopped us from "de-
manding social justice; and the unequal distribution of the world's
goods between a privileged minority and an underprivileged majority has been transformed from an unavoidable evil to an intolerable injustice."

In other words "needs" stem not so much from what we lack as
from what our neighbors have. Veblen called this trait our "pecu-
niary standard of living" and modern economists refer to it as the
"relative income hypothesis," but it all comes back to the same
thing. Except for those rare souls who have hitched their wagons
to thoughts rather than things, there is no end to "needs." So long
as there are people who have more, others will "need" more. If
this is indeed the basis for human behavior, then obviously the gap
between the rich and the poor cannot be ignored, however high
the *minimum* levels of living may be raised.

Although the figures show no appreciable change in income
shares for nearly twenty years, the problem is complex and there
is much that the statistics cannot show. It is conceivable, for example, that a proportional increase in everybody's real income
means more to the poor than to the rich. The gap in "living levels"
may have closed more than the gap in incomes. Even if exact com-
parisons are not possible, many believe that by satisfying the most
urgent and basic needs of the poor, there has been some "leveling
up" in the comforts of life.

Other examples of a similar nature can be cited. The extension of government services benefits low-income families more than those who have higher incomes—by providing better housing, more adequate medical care, and improved educational facilities. The increase in paid vacations has surely brought a more equal distribution of leisure time—a good that is almost as precious as money. Finally, improved working conditions—air conditioning, better light, mechanization of routine work—has undoubtedly reduced the painfulness of earning a living more for manual workers than for those who are in higher paid and more responsible positions.

When allowance is made for all of these factors, and for many others not mentioned, it may well be that some progress has been made during recent years in diminishing the inequality of levels of living. But it is hard to know how much allowance to make and our judgments could be wrong. Most opinions regarding changes in inequality, including those held by professional economists, are based on statistical measures of income rather than on philosophical concepts. With all their limitations, the income figures may well serve as a first approximation of changes in welfare. These figures show that the share of income received by the lower income groups has not changed for twenty years.

                    •   •   •

One of the most widely and strongly held misconceptions about income concerns the narrowing of the difference in earnings between skilled and unskilled workers. The prevailing view holds that the decrease in the earnings gap between the skilled and the unskilled in the United States is part of a historical process that has been going on since the turn of the century. The Department of Labor reports that in 1907 the median earnings of skilled workers in manufacturing industries was about twice that received by unskilled workers. By the end of World War I, it was only 75 percent greater, and by the end of World War II only 55 percent greater. Thus, during a forty-year period, this income gap was reduced by about 50 percent, an average of about 1 percent per year.

There was not too much variation among occupation groups in the rate of income growth during the entire twenty-two-year period [1939–61]. The average income for most of the occupations quadrupled. But an examination of the growth rates for two different periods, 1939–50, and 1950–61, reveals striking differences.

During the decade that included World War II, the lower paid occupations made the greatest relative gains in average income. Thus, laborers and service workers (waiters, barbers, janitors, and the like), two of the lowest paid groups among nonfarm workers, had increases of about 180 percent. The gains for craftsmen, who are somewhat higher paid, was 160 percent; professional and managerial workers, the highest paid workers of all, had the lowest relative gains—96 percent.

During the past decade the picture has been reversed. Laborers and service workers made the smallest relative gains, 48 percent; craftsmen had increases of 62 percent, and the professional and managerial workers had the greatest gains of all, 75 percent. The narrowing of the income gap between the skilled and the unskilled, the high-paid and the low-paid workers, which was evident up to and including the war years, has stopped during the past decade and the trend seems to be moving in the opposite direction.

The above figures are national, averages in which all industries and regions are combined. They are very useful for identifying major trends, but they can also be very misleading because they average together so many different things. It is important to examine the figures for a particular industry in a particular region to get a better understanding of the underlying trends. The primary and fabricated metals industries have been selected for this purpose. The same analysis was also made for about ten other major American industries and the results are generally the same as those presented below.

About 2,200,000 men were engaged in the production of metals or the fabrication of metal products in 1960. This employment was about equally divided between production and fabrication.

The production of primary metals consists of three major components: blast furnaces and steel mills with about 600,000 men; other primary iron and steel works (mostly foundries) with about 300,000 men; and primary nonferrous metal (mostly aluminum) plants, with about 300,000 men. The iron and steel industry is highly concentrated in the Northeast and North Central states and within these states it can be further pinpointed to the following areas: Pittsburgh-Youngstown, Cleveland-Detroit, and Chicago.

The fabrication industry has a similar geographic distribution. About one-third of the workers are employed in the Northeastern states and a somewhat larger proportion are in the North Central region. This industry is divided into several major components, two of which are dominant and account for about nine-tenths of the employment. The largest component manufactures structural metal products—a miscellany ranging from bridge sections to bins, metal doors, windows, etc. It employs 200,000 men. The second major category, called "miscellaneous fabricated metal products," makes everything from dog chains to missiles and employs 700,000 men.

An examination of employment in this industry shows that the total number of workers increased by 24 percent between 1950 and 1960. Professional, managerial, and other white-collar workers increased 62 percent; skilled and semiskilled production workers increased by about 20 percent, but unskilled laborers decreased 9 percent. Thus, despite the general rise in employment and output in this industry, there was a drop in the demand for unskilled labor.

In view of these changes in the demand for labor in this industry, what happened to earnings? The figures for the eight major metal-producing and fabricating states are shown in Table 1. The states are shown in order of the size of their employment in this industry. They accounted for nearly three-fourths of the entire employment in this industry in 1960. The actual dollar earnings for unskilled, semiskilled, and all other workers (largely craftsmen and white-collar workers) for 1939, 1949, and 1959 are shown in the first part of the table; percentage changes are shown in the second part. It is the latter figures that are of greatest interest because they show which groups made the greatest relative gains. There are some differences in the definition of earnings for each of the years shown, but they are not believed to create serious distortions in the figures for these workers.

In all states except Ohio and California, unskilled workers in this industry made greater relative gains than the semiskilled between 1939–49. Similar figures are not available for the higher paid "other" workers for 1939. Thus there was a tendency toward a narrowing of earnings differentials in this industry between 1939–49. But, during the decade 1949–59, the reverse was true. In every state there was a widening of differentials, with the highest paid "other" workers making the greatest relative gains, followed by the semiskilled workers and then the unskilled. In Pennsylvania, for example, laborers had a 63 percent increase in earnings between 1949–59, semiskilled operatives had a 66 percent increase, and professional, managerial, and other white-collar workers had a

TABLE 1 Regional differences in income of men in the metal industries in 1939, 1949, and 1959

	Amount of earnings							
	Laborers			Operatives			Other workers	
State	1939	1949	1959	1939	1949	1959	1949	1959
Pennsylvania	$ 947	$2,414	$3,939	$1,153	$2,767	$4,597	$3,220	$5,624
Ohio	1,006	2,403	4,077	1,091	2,841	4,885	3,367	5,920
California	1,056	2,411	4,136	1,231	2,814	5,002	3,639	6,866
Illinois	950	2,506	4,448	1,124	2,931	5,034	3,517	6,321
New York	918	2,503	3,940	1,060	2,703	4,458	3,318	5,796
Michigan	962	2,645	4,134	1,150	2,997	4,726	3,691	6,246
Indiana	1,074	2,526	4,054	1,286	2,918	4,897	3,454	5,792
Alabama	701	2,032	3,565	887	2,316	4,301	3,073	5,864

	Percent increase, 1939–49		Percent increase, 1949–59		
State	Laborers	Operatives	Laborers	Operatives	Other workers
Pennsylvania	155	140	63	66	75
Ohio	139	160	70	72	76
California	128	129	72	78	89
Illinois	164	161	77	72	80
New York	173	155	57	65	75
Michigan	175	161	56	58	69
Indiana	134	127	60	68	68
Alabama	190	161	75	86	91

75 percent increase. The same general pattern of wage movement was found in each of the other states shown.

THE DISTRIBUTION OF WEALTH

Gabriel Kolko

The pattern of inequality that we have seen in the distribution of income also prevails in the larger picture—the distribution of stock, real estate, savings, and all other forms of wealth. Once again, we find the heavy concentration of holdings at the top, the thin scattering at the bottom.

The arresting fact is that, as of 1953, the 9 percent at the top of the income groupings owned more than 46 percent of the nation's net private assets. And, in that same year, the wealthiest 11 percent of spending units—those having a net worth of $25,000 and up—owned 60 per cent of the private assets, according to the Survey Research Center. Half of this wealthiest 11 percent were also members of the income class earning over $7,500—a fraction that would be larger if there were not so many farmers included in the wealthiest asset group. (Farmers are not actually comparable to other wealthy spending units because of the latter's much larger and more profitable net worth in business and investment assets.)

And so it is evident that a tiny minority of the American people possess both the highest income and the greatest share of private assets.

Savings are a major instrument of economic power. They are distributed much more inequitably among the income-tenths than annual personal income, and this inequality has not been lessened with rising dollar and real incomes for the lower tenths. This is a logical result of the necessity for the lower-income segments to spend all their incomes—or more—to obtain the basic essentials of

The Distribution of Wealth: From *Wealth and Power in America,* Gabriel Kolko (New York: Praeger, 1962), pp. 46–51.

Gabriel Kolko. Social historian, Harvard University.

life. In each postwar year, one-third of all families and unattached individuals have been spending more than they earn. The red-ink proportion for 1950, as an example, ranged from 36 percent in the $0–$3,000 class to 13 percent in the $7,500-plus class. And even though lower- and middle-income spending units may save at some time, by the end of their earning career, they generally have accumulated very little. The expenses of raising a family and then retirement soon dissipate their savings.

There can be little dispute over which income classes have the highest savings-to-income ratio. Clearly, the higher the income the greater the savings.

•   •   •

Liquid assets—such as checking and savings accounts, shares in savings-and-loan associations and credit unions, and government savings bonds—are of decisive importance to low- and even middle-income families exposed to layoffs, unemployment, or medical and other emergencies. Often they represent the entire margin between security and the relief rolls.

However, since the end of World War II, an average of at least one-quarter of American families and unattached individuals have had no liquid assets whatsoever. In early 1960, for example, 24 percent of the spending units had no liquid assets, 27 percent had $1 to $500, and 63 percent had less than $1,000. Because the almost identical distribution existed in 1948, when money was worth more, there obviously has been an absolute decline in the financial security of Americans.

What are the correlations to this inability to save? By income: In early 1960, 52 percent of those in the poorest income-fifth had no liquid assets, as compared to 6 percent in the richest fifth. By age: In virtually any year, the greatest assets were found among spending units headed by persons aged fifty-five to sixty-four; the lowest assets were found among the group needing them most, the spending units headed by persons aged sixty-five years and over. By occupation: In 1960, no liquid assets were held by 51 percent of the spending units headed by unskilled or service workers, 28 percent of the semiskilled, and 19 percent of the skilled—as compared to 3 percent of the professionals.

•   •   •

Historical data on savings patterns strongly indicate that this concentration was not diminished by the New Deal. This is not a very controversial assertion among specialists on savings, for as one of them, Raymond W. Goldsmith, put it, "it is fairly clear . . . that the upper-income groups have always accounted for the major part of total personal savings. . . . This fact, of course, has been known from all investigations made of the distribution of saving."

Almost all the theorists who contend there has been a redistribution of wealth in America concentrate their attention on one form of assets—stock shares in corporations. In a characteristic statement, Ernest van den Haag writes: "Corporate ownership is no longer confined to the upper classes. An increasing proportion of industry, of the productive wealth of the country, is owned by the middle- and lower-income brackets. Their money is becoming indispensable for investment, because the rich no longer can save enough to provide for all the investment needs of the economy. This shift in the ownership of wealth may be described as a peaceful, but not slow, process of socialization of the means of production."

This idea of "people's capitalism"—the official and highly publicized concept of the New York Stock Exchange and the Advertising Council—is shared by too many social scientists who should know better. Popular economists, such as Adolf A. Berle, Jr., and Peter F. Drucker, have suggested that stock ownership has become very widely diffused and that there are no longer any sizable concentrations of stock held among individuals. In reality, stock ownership, like every other form of wealth and assets, is very highly concentrated. This conclusion is supported by every reliable study of stock distribution in the United States.

The fact is that the concentration of stock ownership has shown no appreciable change since 1929. In that year, 51,000 individuals received one-half the value of the cash dividends received by all individual shareowners; in 1933 and 1937, this number was 45,000 and 61,000, respectively. Also, in 1937, some 6.6 percent of the population owned stock; this figure dropped to 5.1 percent in 1956, and not until 1959 had it increased to 7.9 percent.

Within the already small minority of the population owning stock, a very small percentage has always controlled the bulk of the stock, no matter how large the total number of stockholders. . . . J. Keith Butters, in *Effects of Taxation—Investment by Individuals* (1953), estimates that in 1949, the spending units owning $100,000 or more in marketable stocks—who made up about one-fifth of 1 percent of the total national spending units and 2 percent of the stockholders—owned between 65 and 71 percent of all the marketable stock held by individuals.

These data unavoidably understate the concentration of stocks held by the wealthy few, for 36 percent of the total stock in 1937, and 33 percent in 1951, was owned by fiduciaries, foundations, etc., and these nonindividual shares are excluded from the stock distributions given above. However, even though these holdings are not listed by individuals, they remain largely controlled by top-bracket stockholders primarily interested in devising means for avoiding various taxes.

THE RICH GET RICHER
Walter Reuther

Not only have we failed to solve the problem of poverty in this country, but in the past 10 or 11 years we have permitted a state of affairs in which the relative share of the Nation's income going to the poorest families has declined, while the relative share going to the richest has increased. This has represented a reversal of the trend which persisted during the New Deal and the Fair Deal.

. . . Approximately one-fifth of the people in the United States can be classed as poverty stricken, and another one-fifth as deprived of many of the goods and services which most of us consider essentials. This corresponds roughly to the presentation of Department of Commerce income data, in which all families in the country are divided into five classes, each containing 20 percent of the total number, arranged by amount of family income.

The data show that in 1935–36 the 20 percent of families with

---

The Rich Get Richer: From statement of Walter Reuther, *Hearings on the Economic Opportunity Act of 1964,* Subcommittee on the War on Poverty, Committee on Education and Labor, House of Representatives, 88th Congress, 2nd Session, April 9, 1964, pp. 437–38.

Walter Reuther. President, United Auto Workers of America.

lowest incomes received in total 4.1 percent of all family income. By 1953, under New Deal and Fair Deal policies, their share had increased to 4.9 percent. Between 1953 and 1959, however, it shrank again to 4.6 percent, where it remained until 1961, the latest year for which data are available.

The second 20 percent of families, corresponding roughly to those just above the poverty line, received 9.2 percent of total family income in 1935–36. By 1953 their share had increased to 11.3 percent. Between 1953 and 1959 it fell again to 10.9 percent, and by 1961 it stood at 11 percent.

The wealthiest 20 percent of families, by contrast, received 51.7 percent of all family income in 1935–36, but by 1953 their share had fallen significantly to 44.7 percent. Between 1953 and 1959 it rose again to 45.6 percent, and by 1961 had again fallen slightly to 45.4 percent.

The entire change in distribution of income is summarized in the following table:

Share of total income going to each fifth of all families

[In percent]

Families ranked by income	1935–36	1953[1]	1959	1961
Lowest fifth	4.1	4.9	4.6	4.6
2d fifth	9.2	11.3	10.9	11.0
3d fifth	14.1	16.6	16.3	16.4
4th fifth	20.9	22.5	22.6	22.6
Highest fifth	51.7	44.7	45.6	45.4
Total	100.0	100.0	100.0	100.0

[1] Most of the change from 1935–36 to 1953 occurred between 1935–36 and 1944.

The inequality in income distribution is even greater than shown because capital gains income is not included in the above data. Capital gains income has been expanding rapidly in the postwar period and in 1961 amounted to about $15 billion. Concentrated overwhelmingly in the upper income brackets, capital gains contributed to further concentration of income in the hands of the few.

At the same time, the share of accumulated wealth of the richest families has been climbing. The share of all personally held wealth of the Nation's richest 1 percent of families rose steadily from 24 percent in 1953 to 26 percent in 1956 to 28 percent in 1961, according to Robert J. Lampman's study of wealthholding in the United States.

The number of millionaires rose from 27,000 in 1953 to 100,000 in 1961, according to Lampman. And the very rich—with holdings of $5 million or more—increased 500 percent, from 2,000 to about 10,000.

This increasing imbalance in the distribution of wealth has been in part a consequence of the fact that those in our economy who possess a large measure of freedom to appropriate more than their fair share of the fruits of economic growth have been persistently abusing that freedom—particularly the major corporations which dominate whole industries, and which have and use the power to set the prices of their products, and consequently their profits, at a level of their own choosing without being subjected to the pressures of competitive market forces. The abuse of this power has been reflected in the fact that dividends, which go largely to a relatively few wealthy individuals, together with undistributed profits and depreciation allowances retained in corporate treasuries have increased in the past 10 years far faster than the incomes of those whose work produces corporate wealth.

Thus, between 1953 and 1963, labor income (wages, salaries, and fringe benefits) rose from $204.1 billion to $324.9 billion, an increase of 59.2 percent. During the same years, however, dividends paid by corporations, chiefly to wealthy stockholders, rose from $9.2 billion to $17.8 billion, an increase of 93.9 percent. The retained profits and depreciation allowances of corporations increased from $19.7 billion in 1953 to $37.6 billion in 1963, an increase of 90.9 percent.

This imbalance will unfortunately be aggravated still more by the unbalanced distribution of this year's tax cut. Over half of that cut will go to corporations and to individuals with incomes over $10,000; less than half will go to low and moderate income families with incomes under $10,000. As Leon Keyserling, former Chairman of the Council of Economic Advisers, pointed out in testimony this year before the Joint Economic Committee, families with incomes up to $5,000 will enjoy an increase of 2 percent or less in their take-home incomes as a result of the tax cut, while a family with $200,000 will see its after-tax income increased by 16 percent.

It is a coincidence that the $11 billion estimated by the Council as the amount that would eliminate poverty is almost exactly the amount of the tax cut. It is deeply disturbing that we can use $11 billion to increase the incomes of corporations and of families who are nearly all above the poverty level, and that over half the sum will go to those who cannot possibly be described as "needing" it, when the same amount would raise the income of every poor person to a level at which at least the worst of poverty would be eliminated.

This is not to say, of course, that taxes should not have been cut. We in the UAW have for several years been urging the necessity for a tax cut, concentrated in the lowest income bracket, because taxpayers in that bracket do have real needs to be met, and because if they were enabled to meet those needs their increased spending would give the economy the stimulus it should have received years ago, and would help to stimulate the economic growth which is essential if we are to win the war on poverty. But we must not forget that there are still millions of Americans who are so poor that even such a tax cut would not directly help them, because they do not have enough income to be taxed. We must launch massive programs, of which the Economic Opportunities Act is but a small beginning, to give them the direct help they need. And we must adopt constructive, dynamic national policies, including wage and price policies, designed to correct the imbalances in income distribution of which the poverty of the poorest fifth of our Nation is only one facet.

3 / Ideologies of Poverty

Many leading social theorists of the past have been sensitive to the existence of poverty. But contact with poverty for them, unlike their counterparts in the contemporary United States, was blatantly intimate to their daily lives, even though they might belong to the upper social strata. Despite their intimate contact, what some of these theorists had to say about the subject was already obsolete in their own times. Others were ahead of their times. It is the task of today's student to sift and winnow these earlier doctrines in order to discover what may be appropriate in them for our own day. This section and some selections in other sections present a number of "classical" statements for the reader to evaluate.

Although our concern is with involuntary poverty, it is important to recognize that virtuous poverty, as conceived by St. Francis, may have become confused with (involuntary) poverty as a virtue, as in the latter-day conceptualizations of a Carnegie. This insidious conversion, no doubt abhorrent to the followers of St. Francis, has in more recent centuries been given powerful intellectual support by the subsistence doctrine, or "iron law," of real wages. According to this view, eminently represented by Malthus, it was the want of necessaries that induced the laboring poor to produce luxuries—indeed, to work at all.

Labor was therefore a sort of subhuman species that would work only if driven by Howells' "dread of want." Fortified by the Malthusian population postulate that poverty stimulated high birth rates and the spurious psychology that laborers had an innately high propensity toward indolence, the classical subsistence doctrine implied that all productive effort exerted by the working classes was the result of workers being forced to overcome their laziness by the need for the bare necessities of life. If labor as a class rose above the poverty level, indolence would reign supreme. Furthermore, the provision for subsistence by public policy (for example, by poor laws) or even by private charity would, by destroying the fear of want, destroy the incentive to work. So deeply rooted did these principles become, in the culture of the North Atlantic world at least, that they still represent the dominant orthodoxy of the twentieth century. Hence the "letter to the editor," the frighteningly large "lack of effort" group in the Gallup Poll, and the results of Robert E. Lane's scholarly survey probably express some important vestiges of the past still current in Western culture. This section gives the reader a chance to consider in the original some of the classic projections of the eighteenth and nineteenth centuries—projections which obviously remain a part of the often subconscious attitudes of many Americans in the 1960's.

The poor "deserve what they get," according to this traditional perspective, because of their own individual deficiencies. In all likelihood these deficiencies stem from the individual's *innate* defects. Such individuals are *inherently* unfit, perhaps even unfit to survive, as the Social Darwinist put it. On the less dismal side of this Horatio Alger coin were, of course, the fit, whose contrasting material achievements were in themselves a sufficient proof of fitness. The ruggedly individualistic presuppositions of the doctrine did contain a germ of truth—just enough to establish firmly in a dominant position the spurious validity of *laissez faire* and the concomitant principle of social irresponsibility for human deprivation. Self-help by the poor themselves came first, and the ministrations of the conscience-stricken well-to-do, in the form of individual, private charity, then entered as a last resort. In this orthodox view, the poor laws in any form were an infamous concoction of the devil, because they invoked the concept of social responsibility for the poor and deprived, the ill and incapacitated, the unemployed and destitute.

Perhaps the greatest deficiency on the part of the poor, according to the time-honored doctrines dominating the traditional view, was their presumed irrational propensity to proliferate. Indeed, this population "principle" was the guarantee of poverty for the masses. Endowed with the sanctity of a natural law, the principle asserted that poverty bred irrational proliferation (see footnote 1 to the Marx selection), and the latter assured the elimination of temporary material gains until the long-run equilibrium of a misery-level subsistence was again reestablished. In Malthus' *First Essay,* written in response to Godwin's equalitarian views as well as to the threat to the existing Establishment represented by the French Revolution, there was no hope for these poor, "irrational animals." As the threat dimmed, Malthus introduced the softer notion of the "preventive check" in later editions of the population essay.

John Stuart Mill, penetrating genius that he was, advocated a taste of higher levels of living for the laboring classes for an entire generation, to be planned and engineered by the state. Thus, Mill sensed what we now more strongly hold, that rising living levels introduce their own incentives to generate a smaller equilibrium family size among the wage-earning classes. This is why the germ of truth in Malthusianism may apply today only in the "vicious circle" cultures of the depressed areas and the less developed regions.[1] More will be

[1] Perhaps we should note that the emergence of affluent pockets in modern suburbia has possibly introduced another social law of large families, for indeed it is here that the large-sized average family is creating a new object of population study today.

said on the population matter below, but it is relevant and important to note here that the population argument was a cornerstone of the traditional view of the inevitability of mass poverty. It is of course apparent that there are inconsistencies in the value-system of the traditional doctrine, such as the belief that poverty was at once a virtue and a vice.

Contemporary enlightened views of these matters have in common with the socialists the notion that poverty is primarily an institutionally generated phenomenon, calling for a social approach for its eradication. The social-reform approach differs from the socialist, of course, in its acceptance of existing institutional arrangements. In the United States today it is extremely doubtful that a massive antipoverty program could lead to a political threat to the established order. Poverty may have represented such a threat early in the great depression of the 1930's, as many of the more frightened New Dealers believed. But today we are motivated to develop and expand our public and private antipoverty programs more from humanistic grounds than from fear. In addition, perhaps, we recognize that the world is watching our performance and comparing it with that of the Soviet bloc.

Poverty Wasn't Always a Curse

To the Editor: My how the years change things. In the latter part of the 19th century, Andrew Carnegie, "steel king," said, "Abolish poverty and what would become of the race? Progress and development would cease." Or listen to our 20th President James Garfield in the same era say, "The richest heritage a young man can be born to is poverty."

President Johnson of the 20th century says, "I declare unconditional war on poverty!"

Take your choice, but I believe the person who itches for more is poorer than the one who has too little. Sometimes I wonder if the Bible is wrong and we are right.—Leslie M. Nyberg, Minneapolis.

Poverty Wasn't Always a Curse: From Letters to the Editor, Minneapolis *Tribune*, May 1, 1964

OVERPOPULATION AND THE DISTRESS OF THE LOWER CLASSES

Thomas R. Malthus

The principal object of the present essay is to examine the effects of one great cause intimately united with the very nature of man; which, though it has been constantly and powerfully operating since the commencement of society, has been little noticed by the writers who have treated this subject. The facts which establish the existence of this cause have, indeed, been repeatedly stated and acknowledged; but its natural and necessary effects have been almost totally overlooked; though probably among these effects may be reckoned a very considerable portion of that vice and misery, and of that unequal distribution of the bounties of nature, which it has been the unceasing object of the enlightened philanthropist in all ages to correct.

The cause to which I allude is the constant tendency in all animated life to increase beyond the nourishment prepared for it.

． ． ．

It may safely be pronounced . . . that population, when unchecked, goes on doubling itself every twenty-five years, or increases in a geometrical ratio.

The rate according to which the productions of the earth may be supposed to increase, it will not be so easy to determine. Of this, however, we may be perfectly certain, that the ratio of their increase in a limited territory must be of a totally different nature from the ratio of the increase of population. A thousand millions

Overpopulation and the Distress of the Lower Classes: From *An Essay on the Principle of Population,* Thomas R. Malthus (New York: E. P. Dutton, 1914, Everyman's Library, No. 692; 1st pub. 1798), pp. 5–16.

Thomas R. Malthus (1766–1834). English economist, population theorist, and utilitarian moralist.

are just as easily doubled every twenty-five years by the power of population as a thousand. But the food to support the increase from the greater number will by no means be obtained with the same facility. Man is necessarily confined in room. When acre has been added to acre till all the fertile land is occupied, the yearly increase of food must depend upon the melioration of the land already in possession. This is a fund, which, from the nature of all soils, instead of increasing, must be gradually diminishing. But population, could it be supplied with food, would go on with unexhausted vigour; and the increase of one period would furnish the power of a greater increase the next, and this without any limit.

· · ·

The ultimate check to population appears then to be a want of food, arising necessarily from the different ratios according to which population and food increase. But this ultimate check is never the immediate check, except in cases of actual famine.

The immediate check may be stated to consist in all those customs, and all those diseases, which seem to be generated by a scarcity of the means of subsistence; and all those causes, independent of this scarcity, whether of a moral or physical nature, which tend prematurely to weaken and destroy the human frame.

These checks to population, which are constantly operating with more or less force in every society, and keep down the number to the level of the means of subsistence, may be classed under two general heads—the preventive and the positive checks.

The preventive check, as far as it is voluntary, is peculiar to man, and arises from that distinctive superiority in his reasoning faculties which enables him to calculate distant consequences. The checks to the indefinite increase of plants and irrational animals are all either positive, or, if preventive, involuntary. But man cannot look around him and see the distress which frequently presses upon those who have large families; he cannot contemplate his present possessions or earnings, which he now nearly consumes himself, and calculate the amount of each share, when with very little addition they must be divided, perhaps, among seven or eight, without feeling a doubt whether, if he follow the bent of his inclinations, he may be able to support the offspring which he will probably bring into the world.

· · ·

These considerations are calculated to prevent, and certainly do prevent, a great number of persons in all civilised nations from pursuing the dictate of nature in an early attachment to one woman.

. . .

The positive checks to population are extremely various, and include every cause, whether arising from vice or misery, which in any degree contributes to shorten the natural duration of human life. Under this head, therefore, may be enumerated all unwholesome occupations, severe labour and exposure to the seasons, extreme poverty, bad nursing of children, great towns, excesses of all kinds, the whole train of common diseases and epidemics, wars, plague, and famine.

. . .

In every country some of these checks are, with more or less force, in constant operation; yet, notwithstanding their general prevalence, there are few states in which there is not a constant effort in the population to increase beyond the means of subsistence. This constant effort as constantly tends to subject the lower classes of society to distress, and to prevent any great permanent melioration of their condition.

These effects, in the present state of society, seem to be produced in the following manner. We will suppose the means of subsistence in any country just equal to the easy support of its inhabitants. The constant effort towards population, which is found to act even in the most vicious societies, increases the number of people before the means of subsistence are increased. The food, therefore, which before supported eleven millions, must now be divided among eleven millions and a half. The poor consequently must live much worse, and many of them be reduced to severe distress. The number of labourers also being above the proportion of work in the market, the price of labour must tend to fall, while the price of provisions would at the same time tend to rise. The labourer therefore must do more work to earn the same as he did before. During this season of distress, the discouragements to marriage and the difficulty of rearing a family are so great that the progress of population is retarded. In the meantime, the cheapness of labour, the plenty of labourers, and the necessity of an increased industry among them, encourage cultivators to employ more labour upon their land, to turn up fresh soil, and to manure and improve more completely what is already in tillage, till ultimately the means of subsistence may become in the same proportion to the population as at the period from which we set out. The situation of the labourer being then again tolerably comfortable, the restraints to population are in some degree loosened; and, after a short period, the same retrograde and progressive movements, with respect to happiness, are repeated.

EXPLOITATION AND THE ACCUMULATION OF MISERY

Karl Marx

The relative surplus-population exists in every possible form. Every labourer belongs to it during the time when he is only partially employed or wholly unemployed. Not taking into account the great periodically recurring forms that the changing phases of the industrial cycle impress on it, now an acute form during the crisis, then again a chronic form during dull times—it has always three forms, the floating, the latent, the stagnant.

In the centres of modern industry—factories, manufactures, iron-works, mines, &c.—the labourers are sometimes repelled, sometimes attracted again in greater masses, the number of those employed increasing on the whole, although in a constantly decreasing proportion to the scale of production. Here the surplus-population exists in the floating form.

. . .

The consumption of labour-power by capital is, besides, so rapid that the labourer, half-way through his life, has already more or

Exploitation and the Accumulation of Misery: From *Capital,* Karl Marx (Moscow: Foreign Languages Publishing House, 1959; 1st pub. 1867), Vol. I, pp. 640–45.

Karl Marx (1818–83). Social philosopher, revolutionary leader, and founder of "scientific" socialism.

less completely lived himself out. He falls into the ranks of the supernumeraries, or is thrust down from a higher to a lower step in the scale. It is precisely among the workpeople of modern industry that we meet with the shortest duration of life. Dr. Lee, Medical Officer of Health for Manchester, stated "that the average age at death of the Manchester . . . upper middle class was 38 years, while the average age at death of the labouring class was 17; while at Liverpool those figures were represented as 35 against 15. It thus appeared that the well-to-do classes had a lease of life which was more than double the value of that which fell to the lot of the less favoured citizens." In order to conform to these circumstances, the absolute increase of this section of the proletariat must take place under conditions that shall swell their numbers, although the individual elements are used up rapidly. Hence, rapid renewal of the generations of labourers (this law does not hold for the other classes of the population). This social need is met by early marriages, a necessary consequence of the conditions in which the labourers of modern industry live, and by the premium that the exploitation of children sets on their production.

· · ·

The third category of the relative surplus-population, the stagnant, forms a part of the active labour army, but with extremely irregular employment. Hence it furnishes to capital an inexhaustible reservoir of disposable labour-power. Its conditions of life sink below the average normal level of the working-class; this makes it at once the broad basis of special branches of capitalist exploitation. It is characterised by maximum of working-time, and minimum of wages. We have learnt to know its chief form under the rubric of "domestic industry." It recruits itself constantly from the supernumerary forces of modern industry and agriculture, and specially from those decaying branches of industry where handicraft is yielding to manufacture, manufacture to machinery. Its extent grows, as with the extent and energy of accumulation, the creation of a surplus-population advances. But it forms at the same time a self-reproducing and self-perpetuating element of the working-class, taking a proportionally greater part in the general increase of that class than the other elements. In fact, not only the number of births and deaths, but the absolute size of the families stand in inverse proportion to the height of wages, and therefore to the amount of means of subsistence of which the different categories of labourers dispose. This law of capitalistic society would sound absurd to savages, or even civilised colonists. It calls to mind the boundless reproduction of animals individually weak and constantly hunted down.[1]

The lowest sediment of the relative surplus-population finally dwells in the sphere of pauperism. Exclusive of vagabonds, criminals, prostitutes, in a word, the "dangerous" classes, this layer of society consists of three categories. First, those able to work. One need only glance superficially at the statistics of English pauperism to find that the quantity of paupers increases with every crisis, and diminishes with every revival of trade. Second, orphans and pauper children. These are candidates for the industrial reserve army, and are, in times of great prosperity, as 1860, *e.g.,* speedily and in large numbers enrolled in the active army of labourers. Third, the demoralised and ragged, and those unable to work, chiefly people who succumb to their incapacity for adaptation, due to the division of labour; people who have passed the normal age of the labourer; the victims of industry, whose number increases with the increase of dangerous machinery, of mines, chemical works, &c., the mutilated, the sickly, the widows, &c. Pauperism is the hospital of the active labour-army and the dead weight of the industrial reserve army. Its production is included in that of the relative surplus-population, its necessity in theirs; along with the surplus-population, pauperism forms a condition of capitalist production, and of the capitalist development of wealth. It enters into the *faux frais* of capitalist production; but capital knows how to throw these, for the most part, from its own shoulders on to those of the working-class and the lower middle class.

The greater the social wealth, the functioning capital, the extent and energy of its growth, and, therefore, also the absolute mass of the proletariat and the productiveness of its labour, the greater is the industrial reserve army. The same causes which develop the expansive power of capital, develop also the labour-power at its

---

[1] "Poverty seems favourable to generation." (A. Smith.) This is even a specially wise arrangement of God, according to the gallant and witty Abbé Galiani. "Iddio af che gli uomini che esercitano mestieri di prima utilità nascono abbondantemente." (Galiani, l. c., p. 78.) "Misery up to the extreme point of famine and pestilence, instead of checking, tends to increase population." (S. Laing, "National Distress," 1844, p. 69.) After Laing has illustrated this by statistics, he continues: "If the people were all in easy circumstances, the world would soon be depopulated."

disposal. The relative mass of the industrial reserve army increases therefore with the potential energy of wealth. But the greater this reserve army in proportion to the active labour-army, the greater is the mass of a consolidated surplus-population, whose misery is in inverse ratio to its torment of labour. The more extensive, finally, the lazarus-layers of the working-class, and the industrial reserve army, the greater is official pauperism. *This is the absolute general law of capitalist accumulation.* . . .

Within the capitalist system all methods for raising the social productiveness of labour are brought about at the cost of the individual labourer; all means for the development of production transform themselves into means of domination over, and exploitation of, the producers; they mutilate the labourer into a fragment of a man, degrade him to the level of an appendage of a machine, destroy every remnant of charm in his work and turn it into a hated toil; they estrange from him the intellectual potentialities of the labour-process in the same proportion as science is incorporated in it as an independent power; they distort the conditions under which he works, subject him during the labour-process to a despotism the more hateful for its meanness; they transform his life-time into working-time, and drag his wife and child beneath the wheels of the Juggernaut of capital. But all methods for the production of surplus-value are at the same time methods of accumulation; and every extension of accumulation becomes again a means for the development of those methods. It follows therefore that in proportion as capital accumulates, the lot of the labourer, be his payment high or low, must grow worse. The law, finally, that always equilibrates the relative surplus-population, or industrial reserve army, to the extent and energy of accumulation, this law rivets the labourer to capital more firmly than the wedges of Vulcan did Prometheus to the rock. It establishes an accumulation of misery, corresponding with accumulation of capital. Accumulation of wealth at one pole is, therefore, at the same time accumulation of misery, agony of toil, slavery, ignorance, brutality, mental degradation, at the opposite pole, *i.e.,* on the sides of the class that produces its own product in the form of capital.

POVERTY PURIFIES SOCIETY

Herbert Spencer

The well-being of existing humanity, and the unfolding of it into this ultimate perfection, are both secured by that same beneficent, though severe discipline, to which the animate creation at large is subject: a discipline which is pitiless in the working out of good: a felicity-pursuing law which never swerves for the avoidance of partial and temporary suffering. The poverty of the incapable, the distresses that come upon the imprudent, the starvation of the idle, and those shoulderings aside of the weak by the strong, which leave so many "in shallows and in miseries," are the decrees of a large, far-seeing benevolence. It seems hard that an unskilfulness which with all his efforts he cannot overcome, should entail hunger upon the artisan. It seems hard that a labourer incapacitated by sickness from competing with his stronger fellows, should have to bear the resulting privations. It seems hard that widows and orphans should be left to struggle for life or death. Nevertheless, when regarded not separately, but in connection with the interests of universal humanity, these harsh fatalities are seen to be full of the highest beneficence—the same beneficence which brings to early graves the children of diseased parents, and singles out the low-spirited, the intemperate, and the debilitated as the victims of an epidemic.

There are many very amiable people—people over whom in so far as their feelings are concerned we may fitly rejoice—who have not the nerve to look this matter fairly in the face. Disabled as they are by their sympathies with present suffering, from duly regarding ultimate consequences, they pursue a course which is very injudicious, and in the end even cruel. We do not consider it true kind-

Poverty Purifies Society: From *Social Statics*, Herbert Spencer (New York: D. Appleton and Company, 1880; 1st pub., 1850), pp. 353–56.
Herbert Spencer (1820–1903). English social philosopher.

ness in a mother to gratify her child with sweetmeats that are certain to make it ill. We should think it a very foolish sort of benevolence which led a surgeon to let his patient's disease progress to a fatal issue, rather than inflict pain by an operation. Similarly, we must call those spurious philanthropists, who, to prevent present misery, would entail greater misery upon future generations. All defenders of a poor-law must, however, be classed amongst such. That rigorous necessity which, when allowed to act on them, becomes so sharp a spur to the lazy, and so strong a bridle to the random, these paupers friends would repeal, because of the wailings it here and there produces. Blind to the fact, that under the natural order of things society is constantly excreting its unhealthy, imbecile, slow, vacillating, faithless members, these unthinking, though well-meaning, men advocate an interference which not only stops the purifying process, but even increases the vitiation—absolutely encourages the multiplication of the reckless and incompetent by offering them an unfailing provision, and *dis*courages the multiplication of the competent and provident by heightening the prospective difficulty of maintaining a family. And thus, in their eagerness to prevent the really salutary sufferings that surround us, these sigh-wise and groan-foolish people bequeath to posterity a continually increasing curse.

Returning again to the highest point of view, we find that there is a second and still more injurious mode in which law-enforced charity checks the process of adaptation. To become fit for the social state, man has not only to lose his savageness, but he has to acquire the capacities needful for civilized life. Power of application must be developed; such modification of the intellect as shall qualify it for its new tasks must take place; and, above all, there must be gained the ability to sacrifice a small immediate gratification for a future great one. The state of transition will of course be an unhappy state. Misery inevitably results from incongruity between constitution and conditions. All these evils, which afflict us, and seem to the uninitiated the obvious consequences of this or that removable cause, are unavoidable attendants on the adaptation now in progress. Humanity is being pressed against the inexorable necessities of its new position—is being moulded into harmony with them, and has to bear the resulting unhappiness as best it can. The process *must* be undergone, and the sufferings *must* be endured. No power on earth, no cunningly-devised laws of statesmen, no world-rectifying schemes of the humane, no communist panaceas, no reforms that men ever did broach or ever will broach, can diminish them one jot. Intensified they may be, and are; and in preventing their intensification, the philanthropic will find ample scope for exertion. But there is bound up with the change a *normal* amount of suffering, which cannot be lessened without altering the very laws of life. Every attempt at mitigation of this eventuates in exacerbation of it. All that a poor-law, or any kindred institution can do, is to partially suspend the transition—to take off for awhile, from certain members of society, the painful pressure which is effecting their transformation. At best this is merely to postpone what must ultimately be borne. But it is more than this: it is to undo what has already been done. For the circumstances to which adaptation is taking place cannot be superseded without causing a retrogression—a partial loss of the adaptation previously effected; and as the whole process must some time or other be passed through, the lost ground must be gone over again, and the attendant pain borne afresh. Thus, besides retarding adaptation, a poor-law adds to the distresses inevitably attending it.

SURVIVAL OF THE FITTEST

William Graham Sumner

Many of them [the economists] seem to be terrified to find that distress and misery still remain on earth and promise to remain as long as the vices of human nature remain. Many of them are frightened at liberty, especially under the form of competition,

Survival of the Fittest: From "The Influence of Commercial Crises on Opinions About Economic Doctrines," William Graham Sumner, address before The Free Trade Club, New York City, May 15, 1879, in *Essays of William Graham Sumner,* ed. A. G. Keller and M. R. Davie (New Haven: Yale University Press, 1934), Vol. II, p. 56.

William Graham Sumner (1849–1910). Professor of Political and Social Science, Yale University.

which they elevate into a bugbear. They think that it bears harshly on the weak. They do not perceive that here "the strong" and "the weak" are terms which admit of no definition unless they are made equivalent to the industrious and the idle, the frugal and the extravagant. They do not perceive, furthermore, that if we do not like the survival of the fittest, we have only one possible alternative, and that is the survival of the unfittest. The former is the law of civilization; the latter is the law of anticivilization. We have our choice between the two, or we can go on, as in the past, vacillating between the two, but a third plan—the socialist desideratum—a plan for nourishing the unfittest and yet advancing in civilization, no man will ever find.

SURVIVAL OF THE UNFITTEST

Thomas H. Huxley

It strikes me that men who are accustomed to contemplate the active or passive extirpation of the weak, the unfortunate, and the superfluous; who justify that conduct on the ground that it has the sanction of the cosmic process, and is the only way of ensuring the progress of the race; who, if they are consistent, must rank medicine among the black arts and count the physician a mischievous preserver of the unfit; on whose matrimonial undertakings the principles of the stud have the chief influence; whose whole lives, therefore, are an education in the noble art of suppressing natural affection and sympathy, are not likely to have any large stock of these commodities left. But, without them, there is no conscience, nor any restraint on the conduct of men, except the calculation of self-interest, the balancing of certain present gratifications against

Survival of the Unfittest: From *Evolution and Ethics and Other Essays,* Thomas H. Huxley (New York: D. Appleton and Company, 1902; 1st pub. 1894), pp. 36–37.
Thomas H. Huxley (1825–95). English biologist and proponent of the theory of evolution.

doubtful future pains; and experience tells us how much that is worth.

CARING FOR THE UNFIT: THE POOR LAW

John Stuart Mill

It would be possible for the state to guarantee employment at ample wages to all who are born. But if it does this, it is bound in self-protection, and for the sake of every purpose for which government exists, to provide that no person shall be born without its consent. If the ordinary and spontaneous motives to self-restraint are removed, others must be substituted. Restrictions on marriage, at least equivalent to those existing [1848] in some of the German states, or severe penalties on those who have children when unable to support them, would then be indispensable. Society can feed the necessitous, if it takes their multiplication under its control: or (if destitute of all moral feeling for the wretched offspring) it can leave the last to their discretion, abandoning the first to their own care. But it cannot with impunity take the feeding upon itself, and leave the multiplying free.

To give profusely to the people, whether under the name of charity or of employment, without placing them under such influences that prudential motives shall act powerfully upon them, is to lavish the means of benefiting mankind, without attaining the object. Leave the people in a situation in which their condition manifestly depends upon their numbers, and the greatest permanent benefit may be derived from any sacrifice made to improve the physical well-being of the present generation, and raise, by that

Caring for the Unfit: The Poor Law: From *Principles of Political Economy,* John Stuart Mill, ed. W. J. Ashley (London: Longmans, Green and Company, 1909; 1st pub. 1848), pp. 365–66.

John Stuart Mill (1806–73). English social philosopher and economist.

means, the habits of their children. But remove the regulation of their wages from their own control; guarantee to them a certain payment, either by law, or by the feeling of the community; and no amount of comfort that you can give them will make either them or their descendants look to their own self-restraint as the proper means of preserving them in that state. You will only make them indignantly claim the continuance of your guarantee to themselves and their full complement of possible posterity.

On these grounds some writers have altogether condemned the English poor-law, and any system of relief to the able-bodied, at least when uncombined with systematic legal precautions against over-population. The famous Act of the 43rd of Elizabeth under-took, on the part of the public, to provide work and wages for all the destitute able-bodied: and there is little doubt that if the intent of that Act had been fully carried out, and no means had been adopted by the administrators of relief to neutralize its natural tendencies, the poor-rate would by this time have absorbed the whole net produce of the land and labour of the country. It is not at all surprising, therefore, that Mr. Malthus and others should at first have concluded against all poor laws whatever. It required much experience, and careful examination of different modes of poor-law management, to give assurance that the admission of an absolute right to be supported at the cost of other people, could exist in law and in fact, without fatally relaxing the springs of industry and the restraints of prudence. This, however, was fully substantiated by the investigations of the original Poor Law Commissioners. Hostile as they are unjustly accused of being to the principle of legal relief, they are the first who fully proved the compatibility of any Poor Law, in which a right to relief was recognised, with the permanent interests of the labouring class and of posterity. By a collection of facts, experimentally ascertained in parishes scattered throughout England, it was shown that the guarantee of support could be freed from its injurious effects upon the minds and habits of the people, if the relief, though ample in respect to necessaries, was accompanied with conditions which they disliked, consisting of some restraints on their freedom, and the privation of some indulgences. Under this proviso, it may be regarded as irrevocably established, that the fate of no member of the community needs be abandoned to chance; that society can and therefore ought to insure every individual belonging to it against the extreme of want; that the condition even of those who are unable to find their own support, needs not be one of physical suffering, or the dread of it, but only of restricted indulgence, and enforced rigidity of discipline. This is surely something gained for humanity, important in itself, and still more so as a step to something beyond; and humanity has no worse enemies than those who lend themselves, either knowingly or unintentionally, to bring odium on this law, or on the principles in which it originated.

THE ADVANTAGES OF POVERTY

Andrew Carnegie

I think it will be found that the best and greatest of Britain do not differ from the greatest and best of other lands. These have had a lineage which linked them to honor and to public virtue, but almost without exception the lineage of honest poverty—of laborious, wage-receiving parents, leading lives of virtuous privation, sacrificing comforts that their sons might be kept at school—lineage from the cottage of poverty, not the palace of hereditary rank and position. . . .

Poor boys reared thus directly by their parents possess such advantages over those watched and taught by hired strangers, and exposed to the temptations of wealth and position, that it is not surprising they become the leaders in every branch of human action. They appear upon the stage, athletes trained for the contest, with sinews braced, indomitable wills, resolved to do or die. Such boys always have marched, and always will march, straight to the front and lead the world; they are the epoch-makers. Let one select the three or four foremost names, the supremely great in every

The Advantages of Poverty. Reprinted by permission of the publishers from *The Gospel of Wealth,* Andrew Carnegie, ed. Edward C. Kirkland (Cambridge, Mass: The Belknap Press of Harvard University Press, Copyright 1962, by the President and Fellows of Harvard College), pp. 53–64.

Andrew Carnegie (1835–1919). American industrialist and philanthropist.

field of human triumph, and note how small is the contribution of hereditary rank and wealth to the short list of immortals who have lifted and advanced the race. It will, I think, be seen that the possession of these is almost fatal to greatness and goodness, and that the greatest and best of our race have necessarily been nurtured in the bracing school of poverty—the only school capable of producing the supremely great, the genius. . . .

This percentage [of dependent persons] for Britain is happily only about one fourth of what it has been, and its steady decrease is most encouraging. Good and charitable workers among the poor can best accelerate this decreasing process, until something like the American figure is reached, by instilling within the working-classes of Britain those feelings of manly self-respect and those habits of sobriety and thrift which distinguish their race here, and keep it almost free, not only from pauperism, but from want or extreme poverty, except as the necessary result (accident and sickness excepted) of their own bad habits. . . .

In these days of excitement and exaggeration, let it always be borne in mind that at no period in the history of the English-speaking race, wherever that race resides, has it been so easy as it is to-day for the masses not only to earn comfortable livelihoods, but to save and have money in bank for a rainy day. When they fail to do so, the true reformer looks more to their habits than to existing conditions for a satisfactory explanation. . . .

Millionaires make no money when compelled to pay low wages. Their profits accrue in periods when wages are high, and the higher the wages that have to be paid, the higher the revenues of the employer. It is true, and not false, therefore, that capital and labor are allies and not antagonistic forces, and that one cannot prosper when the other does not.

THE LOWER CLASSES DESERVE NO BETTER THAN THEY GET

Robert E. Lane

[The specific and general conclusions Lane draws in this selection are based on his intensive study of attitudes toward political, economic, and social issues held by a selected group of adults in an Atlantic seaboard community of 100,000 which Lane has called "Eastport."]

By and large those in the lower orders are those who are paid daily (not weekly) or are on relief; they live in slums or in public housing projects (but not middle-income projects); they do not live respectable lives; they have only grammar-school education; they may have no regular jobs. Closer to home, those slightly lower in status are people like "the lady next door who has a little less than I have," the man who can't afford to take care of his kids properly in the project, people who spend their money on liquor, the person with less skill in the same line of work.

The rationale for their lower status turns chiefly on two things: their lack of education, and therefore failure to know what they want or failure to understand lifesmanship, and their general indifference. It is particularly this "not caring" that seems so salient in the upper-working-class mind. This is consonant with the general view that success is a triumph of the will and a reflection of ability. Poverty is for lazy people, just as middle status is for struggling people. Thus, Ruggiero, a building maintenance man, accounts for poverty by saying, "There's laziness, you'll always have lazy people." DeAngelo, a factory operative, sees it this way:

> A guy gets married and, you know, he's not educated too well, he doesn't have a good job and he gets a large family and he's in bad shape, y'know what I mean. It's tough; he's got to live in a lousy rent—he can't afford anything better.

But DeAngelo takes away some of this sympathy the next moment when he goes on to say:

> But then you get a lot of people who don't want to work; you got welfare. People will go on living on that welfare—they're happier than hell. Why should they work if the city will support them?

In general, there is little sympathy given to those lower in the scale, little reference to the overpowering forces of circumstance, only rare mention of sickness, death of a breadwinner, senility, factories moving out of town, and so forth. The only major cause of poverty to which no moral blame attaches is depression or "unemployment"—but this is not considered a strikingly important cause in the minds of the Eastport men. They are Christian in the sense that they believe "The poor ye have with you always," but there is no trace of a belief that the poor are in any way "blessed."

. . .

If the Eastport common man is unmoralistic, he is not amoral; if he thinks more easily in terms of error than of evil, he does not forget about good and bad; if he is slow to blame, yet he knows what blame is. He has a moral code that he follows—and applies to the situations confronting him.

In a lower-middle stratum of the population one can reach upward and engage the behavior of the ruling classes in a moral grip, or downward and prick out the violations of the moral code of the unrespectable, the *outré,* the failures. There is gratification to be had either way, but Eastport's common man chooses to moralize downward, not upward. He spends more time condemning the failures of the poor than in condemning the extravagance, the sinful living, the exploitative behavior of the rich. The poor are under his nose, while the rich are not; but the activities of the rich are reported, while those of the poor receive less public notice. (Yet it is true that the misbehavior of the stars of the entertainment world attracts a kind of lip-licking moralistic attention.)

It is the *economic* failure of the poor that occasions comment, not their loose living or indulgence or self-gratification. This economic criticism cannot be made of the rich, for they are successes. On the other hand the rich might be criticized for their shady practices, their exploitation, their monopolistic controls, their conspiracies against the people, their withholding from labor the fruits of its effort, and their deliberate organization of recessions. These things are said, but they are said infrequently—more as explanations than as moral judgments. No, the relief chiseler is morally worse than the price fixer; the person unable to hold a steady job is worse than the landlord who does not fix his broken railings. In general the moral defections of the upper-status groups are more tolerable in Eastport than the moral defections of the poor and lowly.

The relation between morality and success may assume many shapes in men's minds; one of them, greatly feared by Tocqueville, is that men will, upon seeing a successful man, "impute his success mainly to some of his vices." This has the grave consequence that "an odious connection is thus formed between the ideas of turpitude and power, unworthiness and success, utility and dishonor." In spite of the widespread recognition of corruption in government, Eastport does not make this "odious connection"—on the contrary, there is a tendency to believe that men in high places deserve the power and honor and responsibility; otherwise they wouldn't be there. They deserve it, it is true, because of talent, not virtue—but had they been notably unvirtuous they would have been found out. At the other end of the social scale, those who are notably unsuccessful are indeed thought to have failed, in considerable part, because of "playing the ponies," drink, laziness, or shiftlessness. The net consequences of this framework of relationships is a reinforcement of the moral idea: it pays to be good, a premise they follow out in their own lives. Of course, here we speak of the majority; three or four believe, in some degree, that it is otherwise, and have themselves sought to shade the moral code in business dealings where it was too restrictive.

TWO BASICALLY DIFFERENT VIEWS HELD ON CAUSES OF POVERTY

George Gallup

President Johnson's legislative attack on poverty must take account of two basically different views: one, that poverty is primarily due to circumstances beyond an individual's control; the other, that poverty is due to lack of individual effort.

Views on this subject go deep to the roots of the political philosophy of American voters. If you hold the belief that poverty is primarily due to lack of individual effort, you are more likely to be a Republican than a Democrat. If you believe it is due more to circumstances, then you are more likely to be a Democrat than a Republican.

Gallup Poll reporters asked this question of persons across the country:

"In your opinion, which is more often to blame if a person is poor—lack of effort on his own part, or circumstances beyond his control?"

Here are the nationwide findings:

Cause of Poverty?

Lack of effort	33%
Circumstances	29
Equal	32
No opinion	6

When those who could not make up their mind or could make no choice between the two are excluded, the results are as follows:

Cause of Poverty?

Lack of effort	54%
Circumstances	46

Two Basically Different Views Held on Causes of Poverty: From *Gallup Poll Report,* Spring 1964.

George Gallup. Director, American Institute of Public Opinion.

The rather sharp difference between Republicans, Democrats and Independents on this subject of poverty is shown as follows, excluding those who did not make a choice between the alternatives.

Cause of Poverty?

	Republicans	Democrats	Independents
Lack of effort	64%	47%	62%
Circumstances	36	53	38

Among those persons with income of $10,000 and over, more blame lack of effort than blame circumstances.

Among those persons with incomes under $3,000, more cite circumstances as the cause of poverty than blame lack of effort.

Those persons with the most education, who perhaps have had better opportunities, tend to cite lack of effort as the major reason for a person being in poverty.

4 / Poverty as a Subculture

The subculture concept of poverty emphasizes the shared life —the conditions, attitudes, sufferings, and behavior patterns— of the poor. It thus contributes to the definition of poverty itself. Social science research has stressed that the material conditions of experience are primary in identifying those who are the poor, pointing out at the same time that both subjective and behavioral aspects are also essential to the nature of poverty. This section can of course only suggest briefly the complex subculture of the poor.

The main purpose of the following selections is to provide the reader with a sense of how the outside world, as well as his own world, appears from the viewpoint of a poverty-stricken person. Unfortunately, the poor themselves have been more silent on this than have sympathetic outsiders (small wonder!), but they have often been reasonably well represented by middle-class spokesmen. A commendable sensitivity will be found in Robert Coles's discussion of the hiatus between the world of the middle-class professional and that of the poor

(Section 6). Perhaps the hiatus is much like that experienced between the voter registration corps from the North, that is fighting so nobly in this decade, and the southern Negroes with whom they are working. There is cooperation, but a vast chasm between viewpoints remains.

Frank Riessman's "Portrait of the Underprivileged" should be required reading today for all persons genuinely interested in the many-sided problem of poverty. It is most of all an objective treatment of several of the subjective features of the subculture. It appears eminently clear that the poor are a most self-conscious stratum. In a society ostensibly dedicated to vertical, occupational, income, and spatial mobility, as well as to full political participation of every citizen, we find, in fact, among the poor a conscious recognition, indeed almost a complete acceptance, of their own low status, which seriously inhibits the fulfillment of the individual's role. Readers who have all their lives been surrounded by good books, for example, will appreciate the barriers never crossed by those whose barren early environment induced either no taste for reading or the taste for trash or, all too often, even a functional inability to read.

The poverty subculture has its economic foundations. The roots of poverty in the inadequacies of earned income are highlighted in the selection from the *Economic Report of the President, 1964*. Our attempt to compensate for these inadequacies through public or private assistance payments is shown to be equally insufficient. Finally, the captive market in which the poor as consumers find themselves trapped is well portrayed by Caplovitz. He describes the little-known deviant marketing system of the subculture, a system that provides "compensatory consumption" for those faced by poverty of opportunity with respect to personal accomplishments in other areas of life. This selection concludes the introduction to the nature of that subculture. Having enlarged our understanding of some of the homogeneous elements of this subculture, we can then go on to examine the heterogeneity of poverty.

To Live Miserable We Know Not Why

William Dean Howells said to me recently, after I had told him of a visit to Tolstoy: "It is wonderful what Tolstoy has done. He could do no more. For a nobleman, with the most aristocratic ancestry, to refuse to be supported in idleness, to insist upon working with his own hands, and to share as much as possible the hardship and toil of a peasant class, which, but recently, was a slave class, is the greatest thing he could do. But it is impossible for him to share their poverty, for poverty is not the lack of things; it is the fear and the dread of want. That fear Tolstoy could not know." These remarks of Mr. Howells brought to mind the wonderful words of Thomas Carlyle: "It is not to die, or even to die of hunger, that makes a man wretched; many men have died; all men must die. . . . But it is to live miserable we know not why; to work sore and yet gain nothing; to be heart-worn, weary, yet isolated, unrelated, girt in with a cold, universal Laissez-faire." To live miserable we know not why, to have the dread of hunger, to work sore and yet gain nothing,—this is the essence of poverty.

There are many people in the world who believe that the provisions of charity are in the present day so generous and varied that no one need suffer; but, even if this were true, it would not materially lessen the sorrow of the poor. To thousands and thousands of working-men the dread of public pauperism is the agony of their lives. The mass of working-men on the brink of poverty hate charity. Not only their words convey a knowledge of this fact, but their actions, when in distress, make it absolutely undeniable. When the poor face the necessity of becoming paupers, when they must apply for charity if they are to live at all, many desert their families and enter the ranks of vagrancy; others drink themselves insensible; some go insane; and still others commit suicide. Recently a man who had been unable to find work and in despair committed suicide, left a note to his wife, saying: "I have gone forever; there is one less in the world to feed. Good-by. God help you to care for Tony; don't put her away." This is the fear and dread of pauperism; "don't put Tony away" is the last thought of the man whose misery caused him to take his own life.

To Live Miserable We Know Not Why: From *Poverty,* Robert Hunter (New York: Macmillan, 1912), pp. 1–2.

Robert Hunter (1874–1942). American sociologist and social worker, noted for early analyses of urban social problems, including poverty.

A PORTRAIT OF THE UNDERPRIVILEGED

Frank Riessman

He is traditional, "old fashioned" in many ways, patriarchal,[1] superstitious, somewhat religious, though not so religious as his wife.

He reads ineffectively, is poorly informed in many areas, and is often suggestible, although, interestingly enough, he is frequently suspicious of "talk" and "newfangled ideas."

While there are numerous areas about which he is confused and lacking in opinion (e.g., a high percentage of "no answer" and "don't know" on public opinion polls), there are important spheres in which the deprived person has definite, intense convictions and, indeed, is difficult to move. His beliefs about morality, punishment, custom, diet, traditional education (in contrast to progressive education, which he firmly rejects), the role of women, intellectuals, are illustrative here. Many of these attitudes are related to his traditional orientation and they are held unquestioningly in the typical traditional manner. They are not open to reason and they are not flexible opinions.

Frequently, the deprived individual feels alienated, not fully a part of society, left out, frustrated in what he can do. This alienation is expressed in a ready willingness to believe in the corruptness of leaders, and a generally antagonistic feeling toward "big shots."

The average underpriviliged person is not individualistic, intro-

[1] The deprived culture is essentially male-centered, with the exception of a major section of the Negro sub-culture which is matriarchal.

A Portrait of the Underprivileged: From pages 26–30, *The Culturally Deprived Child* by Frank Riessman. Copyright © 1962 by Frank Riessman. Reprinted with the permission of Harper & Row, Publishers, Inc.

Frank Riessman. Professor of psychology, Albert Einstein College of Medicine, Yeshiva University.

spective, self-oriented, or concerned with self-expression. It is unlikely that he will embrace an outlook that prefers moderation, balance, seeing all sides of an issue.

He holds the world, rather than himself, responsible for his misfortunes; consequently, he is much less apt to suffer pangs of self-blame, and can be more direct in his expressions of aggression.

Since he sees problems as being caused externally rather than internally, he is more likely to be a poor patient in psychotherapy.

While desiring a better standard of living, he is not attracted to a middle-class style of life, with its accompanying concern for status, prestige, and individualistic methods of betterment. A need for "getting by" rather than "getting ahead" in the self-realization and advancement sense is likely to be dominant. He prefers jobs that promise security to those that entail risk. He does not want to become a foreman because of the economic insecurity resulting from the loss of job seniority.

He is not class conscious, and while he is somewhat radical on a few economic issues, he is distinctly illiberal on numerous matters, particularly civil liberties and foreign policy. He is not interested in politics, does not vote a good deal of the time, and generally belongs to few organizations.

With regard to democracy, he seems to have two sets of attitudes which, on occasion, conflict. He tends to favor the underdog and his relationships to people are marked by an equalitarian, outspoken informality.[2] He is strongly anti-communist, but he does possess a number of traits that have authoritarian potential: he likes strong leaders; he is prejudiced and intolerant; he is less likely to see the need for having dissident opinions.

He sets great store by his family and his personal comforts.

He has an informal, human quality of easy, comfortable relationship to people where the affectionate bite of humor is appreciated. The factory "horseplay," the ritualistic kidding, is part of this pattern. He emphasizes personal qualities. It is the man, not the job, that is important.

The neighbor who gets ahead is expected "not to put on airs"; he should continue to like the "old gang" and accept them despite his new position. An individual is expected to transcend his office.

---

[2] He is not equalitarian in his relationship to women as his culture is predominantly patriarchal. In the portion of the Negro sub-culture which is matriarchal, the male-female relationships seem more equalitarian.

A foreman is an S.O.B., not because he is subject to stresses and demands on the job that force him to act harshly, but because of his personal qualities. Contrariwise, one of the top executives is frequently regarded as one who would help the rank-and-file if he had the chance because he is "a nice guy."

At the political level, the candidate as a decent, human person is more important than the platform.

The deprived individual likes excitement, likes to get away from the humdrum of daily life. News, gossip, new gadgets, sports, are consequently attractive. To some extent, his desire to have new goods, whether television sets or cars, is part of this excitement dimension. The excitement theme is often in contradiction to the traditional orientation.[3]

He is pragmatic and anti-intellectual. It is the end result that counts. What can be seen and felt is more likely to be real and true in his perspective. His practical orientation does not encourage abstract ideas. Education, for what it does for one in terms of opportunities, may be desirable, but abstract, intellectual speculation, ideas that are not rooted in the realities of the present, are not useful, and indeed may be harmful. On the other hand, he may have an exaggerated respect for the ability of the learned. A person with intellectual competence in one field is frequently thought of as a "brain," with ability in all fields.

The anti-intellectualism of the underprivileged individual is one of his most significant handicaps. It is expressed in his feeling that life is a much better teacher than books—theory is impractical, "most big ideas that look good on paper won't work in practice," "talk is bull," intellectuals are "phony eggheads." This anti-intellectualism seems to be rooted in a number of the traits that characterize him: his physical style, alienation, antagonism to the school, defensiveness regarding his gullibility, and his generally pragmatic outlook.

The deprived individual appears to learn in what Miller and Swanson describe as a much more physical or motoric fashion. "Some people can think through a problem only if they can work on it with their hands. Unless they can manipulate objects physi-

[3] It is perhaps worth noting that different sub-groups may favor one theme rather than another. Thus, younger groups, and especially juvenile delinquents, are probably much more attracted to the excitement theme, are more alienated, and less traditional.

cally, they cannot perform adequately. Other people (symbolic learners) feel more comfortable if they can get a picture of the task and then solve it in their heads. They may be handicapped in attacking problems that require a motoric orientation."

This difference in approach or style of life is expressed in many areas. In religion, for example, the deprived individual is much more likely to enjoy physical manifestations of emotions such as hand clapping and singing, in contrast to the more dignified sermon. Miller and Swanson note also that when the deprived individual becomes mentally ill, he is more likely to develop symptoms such as conversion hysteria and catatonia, which involve malfunctions of the voluntary muscles. Middle-class individuals, by contrast, more often develop symptoms such as obsessions and depressions, which are characterized by inhibition of voluntary movements and by ruminative attempts to figure out solutions to conflict.

Another reflection of the physical orientation is to be found in the deprived individual's admiration for strength and endurance, two of his principal economic assets. His great interest in sports, and admiration for prize fighters and baseball heroes, is one reflection of his attitude toward physical prowess. This interest may stem, in part, from a way of life that calls for considerable "ruggedness." The man who stands up well under these difficult conditions of life is well thought of. Furthermore, the status-giving attribute of strength is not easily usurped by other groups. This represents one possible line of achievement respected to some extent by other classes, although perhaps for different reasons.

Closely related to this physical bias is the emphasis on masculinity. The underprivileged boy's emphasis on masculinity derives, in part, from his patriarchal culture where the father is the "tough boss" of the home, and his authority is backed up by physical force. Even in the Negro sub-culture, the mother frequently plays a strong, masculine type of role, and is prone to stress and utilize physical force.

Talk, reading, and intellectualism in general are viewed as unmasculine—the opposite of action. Moreover, the school is often imaged as a "prissy" place dominated by women and female values.

THE ECONOMICS OF A SUBCULTURE

Council of Economic Advisers

Poverty is the inability to satisfy minimum needs. The poor are those whose resources—their income from all sources, together with their asset holdings—are inadequate. This section considers why those in poverty lack the earned income . . . and transfer payments to meet their minimum needs.

Why do some families have low earned incomes? Some are unemployed or partially unemployed. High over-all employment is a remedy of first importance. It would provide earned income for those unemployed who are able to accept jobs and greater earnings for many presently working part-time. Yet it is clear that this is only a partial answer. Even for those able and willing to work, earnings are all too frequently inadequate, and a large number of the poor are unable to work. An analysis of the incidence of poverty helps one understand the reasons for low earnings.

The incidence of poverty for any specified group of families is the percentage of that group with incomes below $3,000. For all families, the incidence in 1962 was 20 per cent. An incidence for a particular group higher than 20 percent, or higher than the rates for other similar groups, suggests that some characteristics of that group are causally related to poverty. The basic cause may not be the particular characteristic used to classify the group. But an examination of groups with high incidence should throw light on the roots of poverty. . . .

Table 1 shows that the incidence of poverty is 76 percent for families with no earners. From other data, it appears that the incidence rate is 49 percent for families headed by persons who work

The Economics of a Subculture: From *Economic Report of the President, 1964,* Council of Economic Advisers (Washington, D.C.: U.S. Government Printing Office, 1964), pp. 62–67 and 68–69.

TABLE 1   Incidence of poverty, by characteristics relating to labor force participation, 1962

Selected characteristic	Incidence of poverty (percent)
ALL FAMILIES	20
EARNERS IN FAMILY:	
None	76
One	20
Two	10
Three or more	8
LABOR FORCE STATUS OF HEAD:[1]	
Not in civilian labor force	50
Employed	12
Unemployed	34
AGE OF HEAD:	
14–24 years	31
25–54 years	13
55–64 years	19
65 years and over	47
SEX OF HEAD:	
Male	17
Wife in labor force	9
Female	48

[1] Status relates to survey week of March 1963.

NOTE.—Data relate to families and exclude unrelated individuals. Poverty is defined to include all families with total money income of less than $3,000; these are also referred to as poor families. Incidence of poverty is measured by the percent that poor families with a given characteristic are of all families having the same characteristic.

SOURCES: Department of Commerce and Council of Economic Advisers.

part-time. A family may be in either of these situations as a result of age, disability, premature death of the principal earner, need to care for children or disabled family members, lack of any saleable skill, lack of motivation, or simply heavy unemployment in the area.

The problem of another group of families is the low rates of pay found most commonly in certain occupations. For example, the incidence of poverty among families headed by employed persons is 45 percent for farmers, and 74 percent for domestic service workers. . . .

The chief reason for low rates of pay is low productivity, which in turn can reflect lack of education or training, physical or mental disability, or poor motivation. Other reasons include discrimination, low bargaining power, exclusion from minimum wage coverage, or lack of mobility resulting from inadequate knowledge of other opportunities, or unwillingness or inability to move away from familiar surroundings.

The importance of education as a factor in poverty is suggested by the fact that families headed by persons with no more than 8 years of education have an incidence rate of 37 percent (Table 2).

TABLE 2   Incidence of poverty by education, color, and residence, 1962

Selected characteristic	Incidence of poverty (percent)
ALL FAMILIES	20
EDUCATION OF HEAD:[1]	
8 years or less	37
9–11 years	20
12 years	12
More than 12 years	8
COLOR OF FAMILY:	
White	17
Nonwhite	44
RESIDENCE OF FAMILY:	
Farm	43
Nonwhite	84
Nonfarm	18

[1] Data relate to 1961, and money income in 1962 prices.
SOURCES: Department of Commerce and Council of Economic Advisers.

Nonwhite and rural families show an even higher incidence of poverty. The heads of these families are typically less well educated than average. For example, nonwhite family heads have completed a median of 8.7 years of school, compared to 11.8 for whites. In 1959 the median education of all males over 25 with incomes below $1,000 and living on a farm was slightly above 7 years in school; those with incomes above $5,000 had completed over 10 years in school.

. . . The incidence of poverty drops as educational attainments rise for nonwhite as well as white families at all ages. The high frequency of poverty for nonwhites is not, however, fully explained by their educational deficit. . . . The incidence of poverty among nonwhites is almost invariably higher than among whites regardless of age, family type, or level of educational attainment. . . . Nonwhites earn less than whites with the same education even when they practice the same occupation.

Some families are forced into poverty by society's own standards. Their potential earners, otherwise able to hold a job, cannot free themselves from the family responsibilities which they must fulfill. Such is the case, for example, with families headed by women with small children.

Customary or mandatory retirement at a specified age also limits earnings by some healthy, able-bodied persons. However, retirement is often associated with deteriorating health, and poverty among the aged is greatest at ages over 70 or 75 and for aged widows—persons for whom employment is not a realistic alternative.

· · ·

Poverty would be more prevalent and more serious if many families and individuals did not receive transfer payments. In 1960, these payments (those which are not received in exchange for current services) constituted only 7 percent of total family income, but they comprised 43 percent of the total income of low-income spending units. At the same time, however, only about half of the present poor receive any transfer payments at all. And, of course, many persons who receive transfers through social insurance programs are not poor—often as a result of these benefits.

Transfer programs may be either public or private in nature and may or may not have involved past contributions by the recipient. Public transfer programs include social insurance—such as Unemployment Compensation, Workmen's Compensation, and Old-Age, Survivors', and Disability Insurance (OASDI); veterans' benefits; and public assistance programs, such as Old Age Assistance (OAA) and Aid to Families with Dependent Children (AFDC).

Private transfer programs include organized systems such as private pension plans and supplementary unemployment benefits, organized private charities, and private transfers within and among families.

· · ·

The Federal-State unemployment insurance system covers only about 77 percent of all paid employment and is intended to protect workers with a regular attachment to the labor force against temporary loss of income. Benefits, of course, are related to previous earnings.

While the largest transfer-payment program, OASDI, now covers approximately 90 percent of all paid employment, there are still several million aged persons who retired or whose husbands retired or died before acquiring coverage. Benefits are related to previous earnings, and the average benefit for a retired worker under this program at the end of 1963 was only $77 a month, or $924 a year. The average benefit for a retired worker and his wife if she is eligible for a wife's benefit is $1,565 a year.

Public insurance-type transfer programs have made notable contributions to sustaining the incomes of those whose past earnings have been adequate, and to avoiding their slipping into poverty as their earnings are interrupted or terminated. These programs are of least help to those whose earnings have never been adequate.

Public assistance programs are also an important support to low-income and handicapped persons. Money payments under OAA average about $62 a month for the country as a whole, with State averages ranging from $37 to about $95 a month. In the AFDC program the national average payment per family (typically of 4 persons) is about $129 a month, including services rendered directly. State averages range from $38 a month to about $197 a month.

Private transfers within and between families are included in the total money income figures used in this chapter only to the extent that they are regular in nature, e.g., alimony or family support payments, and are excluded when they take the form of casual or irregular gifts or bequests. While data are lacking on the value of such gifts, they are clearly not a major source of income for the poor.

Private pensions, providing an annuity, are additional resources for some persons and families. In 1961 the beneficiaries of such plans numbered about 2 million (as against about 12 million receiving OASDI benefits), and total benefits paid were about $2 billion. While the combination of OASDI and private pensions serves to protect some from poverty, most persons receiving OASDI receive no private pension supplement. In any case, benefits under private pension plans range widely, and since they are typically related to the individual's previous earnings, they are low when earnings have been low.

Thus, although many families do indeed receive supplements to earnings in the form of pensions, social insurance benefits, and incomes from past saving, those families with a history of low earnings are also likely to have little of such supplementary income. And since most poor families have small amounts of property, they cannot long meet even minimum needs by depleting their assets.

THE POOR PAY MORE

David Caplovitz

The problems of low-income consumers stem from the same set of forces that have created that special system of sales-and-credit— the quasi-traditional economy—catering to their wants. Any program of action must therefore take into account the conditions that have brought this system into being.

. . . This marketing system is in many respects a deviant one, in which unethical and illegal practices abound. Nevertheless, it can persist because it fulfills social functions that are presently not fulfilled by more legitimate institutions. The system's paramount function is to allow those who fail to meet the requirements of the impersonal, bureaucratic economy to become consumers of products costing substantial sums. Families with almost no claim to credit—the welfare family, for example—are nevertheless able to buy major durables in this market. . . . The poorest risks are shunted to a special class of merchants who are ready to accept great risk. A close association probably exists between the amount

The Poor Pay More: Reprinted with permission of The Free Press of Glencoe from *The Poor Pay More* by David Caplovitz. Copyright © 1963 by The Free Press of Glencoe, a division of the Macmillan Co., pp. 179–82. David Caplovitz. Senior Study Director, National Opinion Research Center.

of risk that merchants in this system are willing to accept and their readiness to employ unethical and illegal tactics. It may even be that under the present marketing arrangements in our society, unethical practices are an inevitable consequence of serving the wants of the poorest risks. Society now virtually presents the very poor risks with twin options: of foregoing major purchases or of being exploited.

Of course, the poor risks are always free to do without the goods that are available to them only in this special system of marketing. But—and this is as much a part of the misfortune of the low-income consumer as the exploitative merchant—consumption in our society, as in many others, is more than a matter of getting and having material conveniences. Equally important, Americans in all walks of life are trained to consume *in order to win the respect of others and to maintain their self-respect.* These social pressures to consume are perhaps inevitable in a society characterized by a rising standard of living. As was observed by the French economist, Emile Levasseur, more than half a century ago:

> In fact the [American] laborer does spend more than [the laborer] in France. But it is because he desires to, and because he must adjust his life to a higher standard of living *in order not to be looked down upon by his fellows.*

Compounding the force of a rising standard of living is the fact that most low-income families (many of which belong to minority racial and ethnic groups) have little opportunity to base their self-respect and the respect granted them by others on occupational, educational, or other accomplishments. And this poverty of opportunity may only reinforce the significance of consumption in that pattern which we have called "compensatory consumption."[1]

The power of this special marketing system rests on more than its readiness to give credit to poor risks. The local merchants and

[1] Apart from these general conditions inducing low-income families to consume beyond their means, it is possible that the transitional character of their neighborhoods intensifies the problems of the consumers we have studied. As Cloward and Ohlin have pointed out, urban renewal programs result in high turnover of population and thus weaken local social organization. Social norms, which in stable communities regulate the behavior and impulses of their members, tend to break down in such areas. This loosening of social constraints might contribute to greater irresponsibility in the use of credit. See Richard A. Cloward and Lloyd E. Ohlin, *Delinquency and Opportunity* (New York: The Free Press of Glencoe, 1960), pp. 208–210.

peddlers—unhampered by bureaucratic procedure—are able to personalize their services. This has particular importance for those low-income families who come from more traditionalistic cultures and are consequently intimidated by the impersonality that pervades the major downtown stores. When they do venture into the more bureaucratic marketplace, some of these consumers, because of their manners, dress, and language problems, find themselves greeted with suspicion rather than with carefully contrived courtesy. By catering to the traditionalism of their customers, the local merchants and peddlers undoubtedly attract many who meet the formal credit requirements of the more legitimate economy but who find its social atmosphere cold, remote, and repelling. Their attention to social relations, as well as accepting great risk, help the neighborhood merchants to develop their "captive markets."

The consumer's traditionalism also makes for the *dys*functions of the system. The local merchants not only cater to traditional values, they exploit them for their own ends by imposing upon their naive customers terms of exchange that are far worse than those they could obtain if they knew where and how to shop.

Courses of action directed at the dysfunctions of the low-income marketing system will be effective only if they take account of the functions of that system. Two correlative kinds of action must be considered: changing the consumer through education and changing the marketing system through legislation.

5 / Spatial Distribution of Poverty

An analysis of the geography of poverty tells us much about its causes and about the probable effectiveness of policy alternatives for reducing or eliminating it. The use of geographical classifications—urban and rural, regional, depressed area, spatially diffused—cuts across other features of the phenomenon under study here such as education, unemployment, and so forth, which are discussed in Section 6. The predominant locational form, urban poverty, for example, is usually more or less concentrated in the slums and ghettos found largely in central cities. This reminds us at once that we are dealing in part with persons lacking earned income, working in low-income occupations, or suffering minority status, such as Negroes and Puerto Ricans in New York City and other metropolitan centers. We know also that these metropolitan concentrations are associated with substandard housing, dilapidated schools, and other physical blights that characterize much of the material environment of the urban poverty subculture as a whole. The fact that this subculture in the metropolis typically exhibits a localized spatial concentration and is indeed shaped precisely by such concentration, is important for the attack on poverty, as the New Haven program, outlined in Section 8, will dramatically demonstrate.

It seems also to be the case that the tendency for cyclical, structural, and frictional unemployment to be focused in the blue-collar stratum of the labor force produces spatial concentration in megalopolis and in working-class districts within megalopolis. The poverty-stricken slum youth is the inevitable accompaniment of these juxtaposed forces of occupation, minority status, and unemployment. This configuration is found in the metropolis of all regions.

The regional distribution of poverty is of interest largely in connection with the economy of the South. This is the most impoverished large region in the country, although its *average* income is more and more approaching the national figure. The explanation for the South's historical lag in economical development is beyond the scope of this book, although that lag goes far to explain poverty in the South today. In a more contemporary sense, Southern poverty is the product of the conjunction of low-wage industries, extractive industries whose resources have been largely depleted, the lowly status of the great Negro minority, a poor educational system, the small number of major cities, and overpopulation relative to employment opportunities.

The Southern region is also plagued with large depressed areas, most notable among these being Appalachia. The depressed area is the end result of declining or departed economic activities, coupled with insufficient outmigration of people. Although this condition may readily occur with highly developed activities such as manufacturing or transport, it is also widely found where exhaustible natural resources have been worked to practical depletion or reproducible natural resources have been "mined" rather than replenished. Appalachian coal illustrates the former case; Appalachian forests the latter. Other depressed natural resource areas are found in the cut-over forests of Northern Michigan and Wisconsin, the depleted iron ore deposits of the Lake Superior states, and the many areas of soil exhaustion and erosion that pock the face of rural America.

History has been whittling down the agrarian sector of U.S. society for many decades, reducing the absolute incidence of rural poverty in the country as a whole and generating, through migration, the rural in-migrant of the city slums. This type is likely to contribute an exacerbated degree of semi-illiteracy and social alienation to the melting pot of urban poverty. The rural in-migrants comprise the largest of Michael Harrington's "three poverties" (the other two include the holy poverty of the beatnik community and the destitute alcoholics of skid row).[1]

The overall declining number of the poor in the farm and rural areas has left substantial residues in certain regions and areas. These recalcitrant pockets of low income farming will be harder to treat in the years ahead than they were in the past. The hard-core nature of rural poverty is exacerbated by the inferior educational facilities in rural districts and the related lower levels of attainment and aspiration among farm youths. The spread of the larger, capitalistically organized corporate and noncorporate farm firm, replacing the family farm, has entailed the rise of the farm wage earner, and more particularly Edward R. Murrow's "harvest of shame"—the migratory farm worker. Farm migrants comprise an especially disadvantaged, underpaid, and poverty-stricken group. Their economic and political disfranchisement, persistent in the face of both long-term growth and short-run cyclical vicissitudes, is attested to by their continued exclusion from the Federal minimum wage law, to say nothing of social security and various private health and pension systems.

Finally, the diffused poverty of Barbara Carter's jalopy nomads calls attention to a particular group that is trapped by a maze of antiquated residence laws that limit its political participation and the eligibility for public welfare assistance.

[1 Michael Harrington, *The Other America: Poverty in the United States* (New York: Macmillan, 1962), pp. 82–83 *et seq.*]

Perhaps for the problems of this group a high rate of economic growth is the best single answer.

Poverty on the Lower East Side:
6 Live "Heavy Life" on $1 a Day

As the rain splashed in the grimy courtyard outside his apartment yesterday afternoon, Marcello Perez searched for the words that could describe his poverty.

"It's heavy, this life, you know?" he said.

Mr. Perez is 47 years old. For the last two months he has been feeding and clothing himself, his wife and their four young children on $1 a day. In all of 1963 he had $537 to spend on the essentials of life exclusive of rent, gas and electricity.

Mr. Perez is one of the 30 million Americans who live in families with yearly incomes of $2,000. Conservative estimates put the number of poverty-stricken New Yorkers at 815,000.

Both President Johnson and Mayor Wagner have declared their intention of mounting full offensives against poverty.

Mr. Perez agrees with the President and the Mayor. If he were Mayor he would make poverty his prime concern, he said.

"You have money, I have money, we can make something," he observed yesterday. "But this way is no good. They should let us live."

Mr. Perez lives with his 42-year-old wife and four children ranging in age from 7 to 11 in five small rooms on Rivington Street. He gets the apartment rentfree for acting as janitor of the seven-story building.

He also gets free gas and electricity and $30 a month for his services. Until November he supplemented his income by working as a trucker's helper for a company that manufactures clothing. During good weeks he got 10 hours of work at $1.25 an hour; during bad weeks he got no work at all. He was laid off two months ago.

Mr. Perez would like to collect unemployment insurance, but does not because his former employer told him not to apply. "I don't want the boss to be angry with me and not give me the job back sometime," he explained.

Mr. Perez receives no help from the Welfare Department. He considered applying a few years ago but got impatient with the details and decided against "signing the paper." He wants to make

"Poverty on the Lower East Side: 6 Live 'Heavy Life' on $1 a Day": From New York *Times,* January 10, 1964, p. 17. Copyright © 1964 by The New York Times Company. Reprinted by permission.

Paul Montgomery. Reporter, the New York *Times.*

some money and buy a nice home in Puerto Rico and he figures he cannot make much money if he gets on welfare.

His wife, a plump, jolly woman, keeps their apartment neat and clean. Mr. Perez painted it himself—white with blue trim.

The living room, about 10 feet square, contains the only furniture Mr. Perez has bought—blue couch and two orange chairs. He bought them seven years ago from the heirs of a tenant who died. They are covered with clear plastic to protect the upholstery. "The plastic cost $1.10 a yard," Mr. Perez said. "Every week I bought a yard until it was finished."

The three bedrooms are barely big enough to contain their double beds. A metal filing cabinet in one room serves as a chest of drawers. The room shared by the boys—Henry 8, and Angelo, 7—has no window. They receive compensation, however, by having the only bed with sheets on it.

The girls—Estella, 11, and Betty, 9—have three changes of clothing between them. The one that is not in use that day is hung neatly on the doorknob of their room. Mr. Perez owns two pairs of pants but one pair is at the cleaners and he has no money to retrieve it.

The kitchen—containing a sink, gas stove, refrigerator and a bare cupboard—is the largest room. The bathroom, off the kitchen, is the size of a large closet and has a bathtub and a toilet.

Mr. Perez thinks the apartment has certain advantages. There is always heat and hot water. The rats come only at night.

For breakfast yesterday the family had bread and milk. For supper there was rice and beans. The children get free lunch at school and Mr. and Mrs. Perez skip the midday meal. "We wait for night," Mr. Perez said.

The total outlay for the day's food was 50 cents for two quarts of milk, 15 cents for a loaf of bread, 25 cents for two pounds of rice and 10 cents for a half-pound of beans.

The last article of clothing Mr. Perez can remember buying was a pair of shoes for Henry "about a year ago." The family has gotten most of its clothing from a Catholic church nearby.

The family gets free medical care from the clinic at Bellevue. The three youngest Perez children were born there, the eldest in Puerto Rico.

For entertainment there is an old television set, given to Mr. Perez by his brother-in-law, that sometimes works, and a radio. There is no money for newspapers or books.

"If I see a paper on the street I pick it up and read it," Mr. Perez said. Movies are out of the question. Once a year the family goes to Coney Island.

Last spring the nearby House of Hospitality of the Catholic Worker movement, having nowhere else to turn, asked Mrs. Perez if she could put up a destitute old woman for a night.

The woman, who had psychopathic tendencies, had been ejected

from city and charitable institutions. Mrs. Perez readily agreed,
and housed and fed the woman for three months.

SPATIAL INCOME PATTERNS:
AN ANALYTICAL VIEW

Eugene Smolensky

I take it to be beyond dispute that the national size distribution
[of income] is, to a very considerable extent, a reflection of the
spatial pattern of economic growth. Von Thunen long ago and
Theodore Schultz more recently have argued convincingly that
location rents constitute the difference between high- and low-
income agriculture. But clearly the "backwash effects" of economic
growth afflict groups other than those on the farm. The aged,
women, Negroes, the uneducated, and those afflicted with the
tragic trinity of semi-skill, middle-age, and declining industry are
the flotsam and jetsam of economic backwash. Indeed, the unre-
lenting pressure on agricultural workers has now pushed their
numbers down to the point where relative poverty is no longer an
overwhelmingly rural problem. In the next decade we shall see the
shift of the bulk of poverty back to the large urban areas of the
industrial belt, after two decades of it being, very largely, a pox
on the rural population. Relative poverty is slowly returning to
what I would guess most of us think of as its natural habitat—the
urban slum. I do not believe that has already occurred, although
it may seem so, with all the fanfare over the enactment of distressed-area legislation. (I am quite certain that the major recipients of distressed-area money will be the rural counties of the
Southeast.) At any rate, surely in the next decade we can expect

Spatial Income Patterns: An Analytical View: From "Recent Developments
in the Study of Income Distribution," Eugene Smolensky, American Statistical Association, *Proceedings,* 1961, pp. 348–49.

Eugene Smolensky. Economist, Lilly Faculty Research Fellow, University of
Chicago.

the shift largely to happen as the farm population continues to dwindle.

This new course of the spatial growth pattern raises a host of questions concerning what we can anticipate to be the future course of income inequality. In particular, will income inequality continue to decline as the growth process becomes, in virtually all regions, an almost entirely urban matter? In the past, or at least since 1850 in this country, one had a reasonably good rule-of-thumb guide to the course of income inequality. If workers were leaving the farm and if agricultural income per worker was rising relative to non-agricultural incomes, then one could be reasonably certain that the trend was toward greater equality. This being so, it was possible to proceed further and to view the reduction of income inequality as part of the upward spiral of growth symbolized by the withering away of the agrarian sector. So, if we look at spatial income differentials in the United States the most impressive single fact is that almost any factor which one thinks of as associated with poverty exists in the Southeast to a disproportionate extent. If you look at trends in the spatial distribution of income in the U.S. in recent years, and at the factors that determined those trends, the most striking fact is that most of the underlying determinants are pushing the distribution in the same direction at the same time. It is rare indeed, that there is one trendmaker riding over a sea of factors which bubbles stochastically below. Clearly, many of the variables which we take to be independent in our studies are not independent at all, but reflect growth by industrialization, within the constraints placed by prior history.

For a while I thought that some insight into the future course of income distribution might be garnered by speculating on forecastable differences in urban industrial structure. We are beginning to get a theory of urban industrial structure, relating this variable to the size distribution of cities. But, industrial earnings differentials excluding agriculture are not likely to grow large enough ever to explain more than a small part of variations in income. The recent studies on income distribution in New York City iced the cake. Myers found New York City poverty to be totally unrelated to any special aspects of city life. Rather, the New York City distribution is the outcome of the proportion of family heads non-white, poorly educated, aged, and female. If only there could be more farmers in New York City, the analogue to national results could be complete.

But I do feel that the difference between the national-size distribution in 1960 and in 1980 will largely reflect growth differences among urban centers between now and then. The source of these differences will rest not so much on industrial structure as on the differences in mean income around which the industrial structure will erect a reasonably common variance. The differences among means, in turn, will depend upon growth rates and upon differences in demographic characteristics. The challenge is to forecast age structures, proportion of household heads that will be female, and so on, by class of city.

That is, the income distribution of the nation will largely depend upon the proportion of the national population having easily identifiable debilitating socio-economic characteristics. But the distribution will be modified by the geographic distribution of such individuals, for aggregate demand will differ among the various urban labor markets. That is, were Negroes clustered disproportionately at the bottom of the income scale in Newburgh, Washington, and Los Angeles, the aggregate size distribution would nevertheless differ with different distributions of this group among these three areas. The vital question is: Will the future spatial distribution of those traditionally caught in the backwash continue to trap them in low growth areas, in low growth industries, at low incomes with consequent low levels of aspirations, education, continuing high fertility rates and unstable family relations, or can we count on a break in this vicious circle? What possibility is there, for example, of Negroes being at the bottom of the income scale in Seattle, and Denver, and Washington in 1980, but having higher incomes than similarly skilled whites in Scranton, and Pittsburgh? If this can happen, and if the distribution of non-whites can become concentrated disproportionately in high growth cities, then the economic impact of racial discrimination can be blunted and a dramatic closing of the national distribution can occur.

SLUMS AND POVERTY

Conference on Economic Progress

Poverty and deprivation are responsible for the fact that millions of people still live in urban and rural slums because they do not earn enough to live better. Meanwhile, the slums help to perpetuate poverty and deprivation, because they are hurtful to health and morale, and generate many social aberrations which impede family and individual economic progress. In addition, the high economic cost to the Nation of carrying the overhead of slum living consumes resources which otherwise might be devoted to eradicating poverty.

There are now about 9½ million seriously deficient dwelling units in the United States, or about one-sixth of the total of 58 million units. This includes about 5 million units in metropolitan areas, and about 4½ million units elsewhere. In addition, some 6.2 million units need repair and alterations including modernization, beyond ordinary maintenance requirements. There is also a quantitative shortage of more than a million adequate dwellings.

There is no litmus paper test of whether housing is standard or substandard. The Housing Census uses a variety of tests, solely or in combination, including dilapidation, lack of sanitary facilities, and inadequacies of light and ventilation. Whether the more precise substandard figure is the 9½ million seriously deficient units, or the more than 15½ million including the units needing substantial repair or modernization, depends upon the criteria used.[1]

---

[1] Prior to the 1960 Census, the concept of substandard was somewhat generally agreed upon as including all dilapidated dwellings, those lacking certain major facilities, and some of those in substandard blocks. The estimates of serious deficiencies in 1960 are considerably more restrictive than the estimates of substandard for 1956 and earlier years.

Slums and Poverty: From *Poverty and Deprivation in the U.S.—The Plight of Two-Fifths of a Nation,* Conference on Economic Progress (Washington, D.C.: Conference on Economic Progress, 1962), pp. 66–70.

Of the 9½ million seriously deficient units today, about 4.3 million units might be improved sufficiently by rehabilitation. But 5.2 million units are estimated to require replacement, dividing almost equally between metropolitan and other areas.

In New Orleans, according to one study, 44 percent of the incidence of tuberculosis was concentrated in slum sections covering only 25 percent of the residential area of the city. In Newark, the incidence of tuberculosis and infant mortality was found to be 2⅔ times as high in slum areas as in public housing areas, and of communicable diseases among children under five years of age 2½ times as high. In Louisville, Cleveland, Philadelphia, and many other large cities, studies establish a juvenile delinquency rate several times as high in bad housing areas as in other areas.

Los Angeles has found that blighted areas, compared with better developed areas, cost the city 87 percent more per capita in police services, 67 percent more in fire department services, and 125 percent more in health services—while yielding only 38 percent as high a rate of tax revenues.

According to data from the U.S. Census Bureau's 1956 National Housing Inventory, more than half of the rented dwelling units occupied in that year by families with incomes below $2,000, and almost a third of those rented by families with incomes between $2,000 and $4,000, were substandard. Only 10 percent of the rented housing occupied by families with incomes between $6,000 and $8,000 were substandard, and lesser percentages at higher income levels. In owner-occupied housing, the high correlation between low incomes and substandard conditions was similar. Stated differently, close to 80 percent of all the substandard housing in 1956 was occupied by families with incomes below $4,000.

Percent of Various Income Groups Living in Substandard Housing

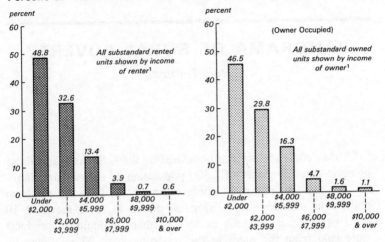

[1] Income shown is total money income before taxes, of occupying family or individual. Data: Bureau of the Census, National Housing Inventory, 1956.

Percent of Substandard Housing Occupied by Various Income Groups

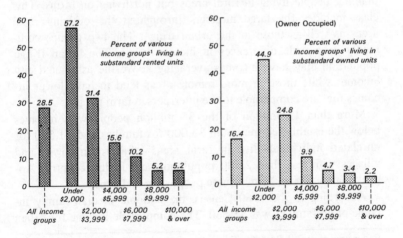

[1] Income shown is total money income before taxes, of occupying family or individual. Data: Bureau of the Census, National Housing Inventory, 1956.

PANORAMA OF RURAL POVERTY

Buis T. Inman

Urban people are arbitrarily defined by the U.S. Census as those living in cities or places of 2,500 population or more. Rural families are divided into rural nonfarm and rural farm. Rural farm population includes those living on places in rural areas of 10 acres or more, if as much as $50 worth of agricultural products were sold from the place in the reporting year. Those living on rural places of less than 10 acres are also included, if as much as $250 worth of agricultural products were sold from the place in the reporting year. Thus, farm people include not only full-time farm operators and their family members, but also part-time farmers, and farm laborers. Rural nonfarm population includes the remaining people living in rural areas but not living on farms. This class includes the large numbers throughout the outlying rural areas as well as those in the urban fringe. The two groups commonly have wide differences in income levels. The urban fringe population may have incomes averaging above the associated city incomes while those in more remote areas tend to have lower incomes that are comparable to the interspersed farm people.

More than 15 million of the 35 million people with incomes below the established minimum $3,000 for families and $1,500 for unrelated individuals live in rural areas—that is, in towns and villages with less than 2,500 population and in the country. Approximately 5¼ million of these people live on farms.

According to the 1960 Census, the national median family income of all families was $5,660. The comparable income for urban

Panorama of Rural Poverty: From *Rural Poverty: Cause, Extent, Location and Trends,* Buis T. Inman (Washington, D.C.: U.S. Department of Agriculture, 1964), pp. 1–6.

Buis T. Inman. Agricultural Economist, Resource Development Economics Division, Economic Research Service, U.S. Department of Agriculture.

families was $6,166; for rural nonfarm, $4,750; and for farm families, $3,228. From these data, one can see that the average income of farm families was about one-half that of city families. Recent studies show that, although the income of each of these groups is increasing, the spread between farm and nonfarm family incomes is increasing.

Rural poverty is centered in the South and border areas. . . . Other areas not closely associated with the South are in the northern portion of the Lake States, northern Missouri, scattered areas in the Northern Plains, portions of the Southwest, and scattered areas in the Northwest. . . . However, let's not forget that there are substantial amounts of poverty throughout the country.

Let us now look at the larger segments of our rural population that make up the poor. Of the approximately 5 million rural Negroes enumerated by the 1960 Census, more than half of the families had annual incomes under $2,000.

Because their families are one-third larger than white families, the Negro per capita income problem is even more serious. According to Department of Commerce data, there are about 1.6 million nonwhites living on farms. These people are classed as poor by the current definition. Their number has declined rapidly in the post war period. The last Census of Agriculture in 1960 enumerated only 285,000 nonwhite farm operators in the South, 121,000 of which were sharecroppers. The Negro rural poor have heaviest concentrations in the Coastal Plains from Virginia to Texas and in the Mississippi Delta.

A second large area concentration of poor rural people is composed of the whites in the Appalachian Mountain area, extending from northern Alabama to West Virginia, including some 3 million people. A smaller concentration is in the Arkansas-Missouri-Oklahoma Ozarks. In the early days, these people worked in mines, on the timber harvest and lumber manufacture, or they farmed. Because of the decline in employment in the two nonfarm industries and the difficulty of adjusting the farms to modern techniques, these people have experienced grave problems. Heavy outmigration of young people is occurring in these areas.

A third major poor rural group is the Spanish-Americans located principally in Arizona, California, Colorado, New Mexico, and Texas. They have not become fully assimilated into the national economy. They make up 25 percent of the migrant farm labor.

A fourth rural poverty group is the American Indian. In 1960, 72 percent of all Indians lived in rural areas. The rural number was 378,000. They lag far behind the national level in income and level of living.

Many factors are recognized as influencing the low-income positions of rural families. The persistence of the problem for farm families is associated with conditions of entry and exit of individual farms and of resource transfers in and out of agricultural production. Generally, agriculture in low-income areas has developed around enterprises and types of farming that in earlier periods tended toward small-scale operations and low capital requirements for entry.

Early settlement of many of these low-income rural areas was rather sparse at first and development did not keep pace with other areas. Development in these areas was intensified by such nonfarm activities as mining, harvest of timber, and construction of the railroads, particularly from 1880 to 1910. This combined expansion in economic activity provided employment for a rapidly expanding population. In terms of living conditions and considering the technology available, farming and such other occupations as lumbering and mining furnished incomes that appear to have been fairly comparable to those received elsewhere. Following the climax in these nonfarm activities, land was cleared and farm units were established. The rapidly declining sources of nonfarm income could not be offset by expansion in farming. Also, agriculture in these areas declined in importance as more productive farming areas with greater comparative advantages were opened and settled. The marked decline in the physical resource base and the relatively high birth rates brought about considerable population pressure on resources. During World War I, an exodus from these areas began and has continued to a marked degree.

As early as the 1930's, this low-income problem among farm people was recognized and some effort was made to identify areas of concentration and indicate the extent of the problem. The areas thus delineated overlap many of those delineated today, indicating the chronic and persistent nature of the problem.

The basic determinant of an individual's level of living is the ability to command a job and receive the resultant income. Studies of farm and nonfarm families in eight selected low income rural areas show that such characteristics of individuals (particularly the family head) as age, education, physical capabilities, and individual preferences are major determinants of income. The low-income areas studied were characterized by high proportions of people above 45 years of age and below 19 years, with fewer in the 20–44 year age group, and with a low level of educational attainment. This was largely the result of heavy outmigration of the younger working age groups with the higher level of education. The selectivity of outmigration also resulted in a relatively high proportion of physically handicapped persons of working age. These percentages of family heads with physical disabilities that affected employment ranged from 21 percent to 26 percent.

Rural individuals in general receive less formal education than do urban residents. Although this discrepancy has narrowed in recent years, the differences are still considerable. Median school completion in rural counties for those over 25 is only 9.2 years as compared with 10.6 years for urban counties with major centers of from 25,000 to 50,000 population. Moreover, there continues to be a considerable body of rural adults who are functionally illiterate, which means that they have had less than 5 years formal school completion and are likely to have little capacity to follow written instructions.

A recent study of farm youth in the Midwestern, Southern and Western States indicates that the farm population has less in comparative educational attendance than the urban population. Only approximately 58 percent of farm operators and 55 percent of their children 15 to 21 years old had completed 8 grades of school. Among the factors which account for this were heavy concentrations of low incomes, limited financial resources to provide adequate facilities and services for high school and technical and vocational training.

In summary, for all the rural families included in the areas studied, both farm and nonfarm, with net money incomes below $2,000 in the study areas, approximately three-fourths of the family heads had one of the following characteristics: the family head was 65 years of age or over, a female under 65, a male under 65 but with a physical handicap, or a male under 65 with less than 5 years schooling and no physical handicap.

The rural population suffers from a lack of local demand for labor relative to its supply when compared to the Nation as a whole. Rural adults who seek to improve their personal economic position through outmigration face many difficulties. In general, a rural migrant can claim a job in an urban area only as a residual claimant in a plant. In other words, the migrant tends to be employed only after persons who have had previous experience in the plant or agency, but have been laid off, have had an opportunity for re-employment. The rural migrant also generally lacks information as to opportunities for urban employment. This tends to restrict opportunities for the rural migrant to the least attractive jobs. Jobs are commonly rationed on the basis of such "quality" factors as age and education. There is evidence that persons who rank low in income relative to the national average can make significant improvements in their relative standing only during periods of high rate of national economic growth. During periods of high employment, as during the Second World War, factors such as age and education are not such deterrents.

The largest problem for underemployed rural males or those earning low income is among men between 45 and 64 years of age. It is recognized that both geographic and occupational mobility are much more limited for these people than for younger age groups. These older persons do have more and stronger social and economic ties to their rural communities. These ties may be their relatives and neighbors, their church, their lodge, or the real estate they own. The Council of Economic Advisors shows that non-whites typically earned less than 80 percent as much as whites with similar qualifications.

Agriculture in the Southeast, where low-income farms are most prevalent, is characterized by the production of cotton and tobacco. Cotton in this region is characteristically produced on small acreages, with mechanization only partial. In contrast, cotton in the West is produced largely on irrigated land, highly mechanized equipment is used, and per acre yields are higher than in the Southeast.

Tobacco is still produced on small acreages per farm and currently requires large amounts of hand labor in planting, cultivating, harvesting and preparing the leaf for market. This year-round demand for labor usually prevents operators from obtaining off-farm employment.

Another major area where farming adjustments are slow is the southern fringe of the Corn Belt.

APPALACHIA:
THE PATH FROM DISASTER

Harry Caudill

America has recently discovered that a sub-nation of paupers is hidden within its opulent structure. During the past year television commentators, newspaper reporters and photographers, sociologists and assorted government agents have swarmed through the Kentucky mountains, and have beamed a panorama of misery into practically every living room in the country. To a man, the invaders have been baffled by the huddled ugliness and want that scar the landscape.

The Cumberland Plateau of Eastern Kentucky is the hard, bleak core of Appalachia, and Appalachia is a huge region of stagnation that extends through parts of nine states from Pennsylvania to Alabama. It is the largest and the best known of the islands of poverty that endure, and grow, in the United States.

In the Kentucky hills, dozens of drab little towns and mining camps and thousands of dilapidated shacks stretch up a maze of creeks and hollows. Heaps of junked automobiles clutter the roadsides and incredible quantities of trash and garbage clog the silted streams.

The roads are little more than ribbons of mud which wind through countless communities that travelers on the main highways never see. The schools fall so far short of national standards that the high school graduate generally possesses little more learning than an eighth grader in more fortunate parts of the country. The housing, if the word can be applied without irony to many of the shacks, is so poor that in November, President Kennedy

Appalachia: The Path From Disaster: From "Appalachia: The Path From Disaster," *The Nation,* Harry Caudill, Vol. 198, No. 11 (March 9, 1964), pp. 239–41.

Henry Caudill. Attorney, of Whitesburg, Kentucky; author of *Night Comes to the Cumberland.*

ordered an emergency program to preserve the health of the people until spring. Grants of up to $1,000 per family were extended for flooring, roofing, shingles and other essential repairs.

Amid this squalor dwells a people so thoroughly pauperized that at least 50 percent of them are dependent upon the dole and public-assistance grants for their daily bread. The reduction of this land, once so rich in natural resources, to such shabby dejection is one of the tragedies of history. The region never had good schools because the frontiersmen who settled it six generations ago were almost entirely out of contact with formal education, and the state government never required that good schools be built. Industrialists were able to buy up the mineral wealth for a pittance long before its value was recognized by the mountaineers, and, in effect, the region was placed at the mercy of a few score absentee corporations.

.   .   .

Until after the Second World War the coal industry was a mass employer of men. Abundant investment capital and advancing technology threw 100,000 American coal miners into abrupt obsolescence at almost the same moment in history as the Kentucky log forests played out and the worn mountain farms became so exhausted that crops were no longer worth the planting. The mountaineer's agricultural methods have always been extremely primitive, and his continual search for "new grounds" brought the soil to almost total ruin.

When this alarming situation was reached fifteen years ago, the nation made a grave decision, though not a conscious one. It determined that the mountaineer, though scarcely worth rehabilitating, was none the less an American and could not be permitted to starve to death. Half the population was put on the dole, receiving monthly issues of rations out of the scandalously large national stores of agricultural commodities. After fifteen years of "mollygrub," idleness, frustration and bewilderment the mountaineer is so demoralized that outsiders who see him almost invariably throw up their hands and flee back to the cities to tell the awful story. No one in this ingenious age has offered a real solution for his difficulties and at least one gentleman, long an adviser to Kentucky's governors, has remarked that the problems of the Kentucky mountains are past solution.

This attitude is ridiculous. If we would help the Kentucky mountaineer, we must look at him frankly, disabuse our minds of old and erroneous notions, and start a rehabilitation program geared to the needs of the man and his land.

Government programs thus far have been geared to teaching the mountaineer to farm, and year after year they have come to naught. The mountaineer is not a farmer. Few of these highlanders have farmed for a living in the last generation and most of them have been out of touch with the soil for more than half a century. They are in the main industrial workers and to them the earth is scarcely more than an expanse of dirt covering quantities of coal. Historically, it has been practically impossible to convert industrialized or urbanized people back to the land, and the Kentucky mountaineer has been no exception to this rule.

If he is to work again, it must be for industry. The immediate question is: "What can the mountaineer produce that the nation needs in large quantities?" When the nature of his land is considered, the answer is inescapable: electricity.

The Appalachian coal field is within less than a thousand miles of practically all the nation's great population centers, with the exception of Los Angeles. . . . Thus the Appalachian coal field sits in the middle of a great and rapidly growing power market.

The corrugated landscape is streaked by swift-flowing and filthy creeks. Thousands of acres of mountainous terrain have been turned upside down by strip miners gouging out the coal. Forty-five to fifty inches of rainfall strikes this tortured earth each year, lashing the region's towns and scattered hamlets with ferocious flash floods. In eastern Kentucky alone, more than 3 billion tons of coal lie unmined.

The land and people cry out for a Regional Authority comparable to the TVA and charged with a mandate to develop the total resources of the region for the nation's benefit. A modernized version of the TVA could restore the region to beauty and usefulness without any ultimate cost to the taxpayers. As in the valley of the Tennessee it should invoke that mighty trinity: water, electric power and fertilizer. An investment of approximately $1 billion could restore eastern Kentucky to productivity and, by present standards, to prosperity.

· · ·

The region is presently dying for lack of revenue for investment in schools and other public facilities. Congress should charge the corporation with the stern duty to plow back into regional development in the impoverished counties at least one mill per kilowatt-hour produced. Such an investment in schools, roads, libraries, health facilities, reforestation and land reclamation could work a genuine miracle in transforming the whole face of the land. Most of the expenses of the authority could be paid out of the proceeds of power sales. However, it should not be expected to pay the entire cost of regional renaissance from income. . . . An unavoidable duty to our posterity should impel us to set many of the idle mountaineers to work reforesting the hillsides so that the multitudes who will crowd into the country on our own departing footsteps will find this tattered region in a state fit for their occupancy.

Obviously this scheme cannot work unless it is hedged with certain safeguards. Most urgently needed is an act of Congress to prohibit the strip mining of coal in the steep Appalachian Mountains. This atrocious practice is transforming vast areas of forest land into desert, silting up countless miles of public waterways, rendering the countryside hideous to look at, and wasting immense quantities of coal—coal that can never be mined by any presently known method of recovery.

A national agency is the appropriate device. The water and mud pouring down from the highlands cross state lines, as do the coal shipments. Similarly the region's problems are being transmitted at a quickening tempo to the nation's cities, so that the tragedy of Appalachian deterioration forces itself upon the mind and conscience of the entire country. Unless national solutions for its ills are found, Appalachia will become a rotting corpse nauseating our national system.

The authority must be vested with power to discipline the inhabitants into acceptance of normal social standards. The dumping of trash and garbage into waterways ought to be sternly suppressed. Sanitary trash disposal centers should be established and the unsightly junkyards should be swept away from the roadsides.

·   ·   ·

In April, 1963, President Kennedy appointed a committee—the President's Appalachian Regional Commission—to make a careful study of the woes of Appalachia and recommend remedial legislation for submission to the Congress. Under the chairmanship of Franklin D. Roosevelt, Jr., the group conscientiously and zealously tackled its task. In protracted tours of the Appalachian backlands its members acquired an excellent grasp of the problem. As might have been expected, they found a monumental lack of interest in several state houses. In some states effective political machines have been constructed on the servile support of a "kept" population of "welfare voters." Local political pressures thus enforce the *status quo* and are exerted strongly upon state officials.

The commission's . . . recommendations are excellent—as far as they go. They contemplate an investment of about $1 billion in east Kentucky in an effort to lift it to the threshold of a self-supporting economy. Principally, this capital investment would go for education, highways, airports, recreational and flood-control lakes, reforestation of private lands and the establishment of a huge new national forest. All these are essential objectives.

The difficulty with the report is threefold: it contemplates a weak state-federal agency to sponsor regional renaissance, it omits any provision for utilization of the immense coal beds, and it does not contemplate any effective effort to upgrade the schools to normal national standards. The suggested development corporation would divide responsibility between Washington and the state capitals. It would thereby place in the hands of dozens of potent county political machines the indirect power to veto or cripple any undertaking deemed too disturbing to the ultraconservative courthouse cliques.

THE JALOPY NOMADS

Barbara Carter

It's too bad, in a way, that "pockets of poverty" has become such a useful phrase, for it suggests that poverty is confined to fixed spots—such as the city slums or tenant farms or distressed areas along the Appalachian chain. Poverty, however, is not a static

The Jalopy Nomads: From "The Jalopy Nomads," Barbara Carter, *The Reporter,* May 7, 1964, pp. 31–33.
Barbara Carter. Writer on the staff of *The Reporter.*

thing. It wheels along the highways, too. The war on poverty, which generally is centered on local communities, overlooks the fact that thousands of newly uprooted people are circling our cities today in search of work. These are not migrant workers but a growing new class of nomads who have pulled up stakes and taken to the road. Some are in search of more than work, a new way of life perhaps. Some are simply in flight from reality. Their number is increasing, but scant attention has been paid to their shifting and erratic travel. We know far more about the migration routes of birds.

Near Chattanooga, for example, a tenant farmer, his wife, and three children have been traveling from place to place for several months, looking for odd jobs. At night, they usually sleep in roadside parks, with the father and the two boys stretching out on the wooden picnic tables so that the mother and daughter can have the car. They cook on roadside grills, and when they need to change or wash their clothes, they avail themselves of service-station rest rooms.

In Kansas City not long ago, a laid-off steelworker from West Mifflin, Pennsylvania, had to ask the police for help. With his wife and nine-year-old son, he was on his way back to Pennsylvania after a fruitless trek to San Francisco in search of work. For several nights the family had been living in their car parked a few blocks from the Kansas City post office, where the steelworker hoped an unemployment check would be forwarded to him. He had turned to the police for help because his wife, ill with a toothache and upset at discovering their son begging for a hamburger in a nearby café, had gone for a walk and not returned.

Some of the modern Okies are totally uninformed about the job possibilities before them. They are in trail of a rumor, or a will-o'-the-wisp. They think they may find work in Detroit, or Chicago, or maybe in San Francisco, only to find their chance for a job there no better than in the place they left, except for one difference: they are now "outsiders" and the surroundings are hostile.

·   ·   ·

Begging begins in a moment of crisis and little by little turns into a way of living. Welfare authorities, if involved at all, are able only to move the nomads on or send them back where they came from, with no follow-up to see if they arrive. Finally, dependent largely on the generosity of gas-station attendants, they move from handout to handout in an endless trip to nowhere. Children grow up in the back seats of cars and never see the inside of a schoolroom.

The new Okies are made up of many groups. They are Southern tenant farmers who have been pushed off the land by mechanization; skilled and semi-skilled workers displaced by automation; families from distressed areas such as parts of Pennsylvania, West Virginia, and the mountains of Kentucky; teen-age school dropouts hitchhiking across the country; abandoned young mothers with children looking for relatives to help them; occasional schizophrenics who have been released from hospitals under the new drug therapy—in short, any of various combinations of the unemployed, the unskilled, and the unwanted. Many of them are Negro, and many are illiterate.

No one really knows how many there are. The National Travelers Aid Association has come across "hundreds of thousands" in recent years, even though the organization's facilities are, for the most part, located in airports and bus and train stations, not on the highways, and even though it has few bureaus, except in California, west of the Rockies, where an unprecedented migration is taking place. As its director, Mrs. Savilla Millis Simons, points out, "We are just touching the surface." . . .

Scattered statistics from its various bureaus show the striking change in the organization's case work within the last decade: from Oklahoma City, a five hundred percent increase in cases involving employment problems, a 213 percent increase in migrant cases; from Jacksonville, Florida, eighty percent of the case load is uprooted people from the highway seeking work; from Chattanooga a similar pattern, though ninety percent of them are married men with families; from Los Angeles, the case load in a ten-day period up forty percent over the year before, the proportion of families up 144 percent; and from the director of the Travelers Aid bureau in Texarkana, Arkansas, this description: "As we view the travel here on five major highways, it seems that much . . . represents erosion of resources, possessions, self-assurance, and even the ability to plan. Some of our callers seem all but hypnotized by the . . . endless road and mirages of plenty; gasoline seems the most important thing in the world and the day's goal, rather than work."

There has been almost no research into the problem, but in the one survey made, by the National Study Service, of the small triangular area connecting Albany, Schenectady, and Troy, New

York, it was discovered that far more strangers than expected were turning from the highways to the communities for help—some 2,300 a month, in fact. (Spot checks made near Pittsburgh and Charleston, West Virginia, revealed a similar pattern.) Most of the people were turning to gas-station attendants for help, and these new philanthropists, along with the clergy to whom the second largest number turned, were found to be giving an estimated $40,000 a year in handouts to strangers in this small area alone. . . .

Compared to the slum dwellers, say, or the tenant farmers who cling to the land, the uprooted poor are doubly in jeopardy, for their tattered odyssey can render them stateless as well as homeless. Without legal residence, they are without claim for public aid. Voluntary agencies concern themselves for the most part only with the problems of residents, feeling that this gives them more than enough to do. While city missions will provide a few nights' shelter for the homeless, the emphasis is to get them to move on. The Salvation Army also provides shelter and occasionally case work, but Travelers Aid is the only organization dealing solely with people on the move.

Only two states, Connecticut and Hawaii, have no residence requirements for either Federal aid (under the Social Security Act) or local aid. More than forty states, however, require the maximum allowed of one year's residence to qualify for Federal aid to dependent children, and many avail themselves of the five years' maximum allowed for the three other categories of Federal aid—to the aged, to the blind, and to the totally disabled. In most states, then, the new arrivals must seek local rather than Federal aid, and this varies widely in a chaotic criss-cross of laws. Though local aid can be given for emergencies, it all depends on the availability of funds, the willingness of the states to reimburse the localities, and the disposition of county commissioners. Usually, it is formally stipulated that local aid to nonresidents can be given only to return them where they came from. Rarely is any provision made to help them settle down.

The results of such strictures are often grotesque. Not only are nonresidents denied assistance but frequently newcomers who have been able to find work are set on the road again.

Residence can be as easy to lose as it is hard to gain. In two states, local assistance can be denied after six months' absence, while in others it takes five years' residence to qualify. Even so, the laws fail to protect the community from an "influx of outsiders." States with high residence requirements but attractive to newcomers, such as California, Florida, and Arizona, still have the high immigration rates that motivated the enactment of those requirements, while other states with few or no requirements have comparatively few newcomers on their relief rolls. Do the lawmakers suppose that migrants in search of work spend time poring over the various states' residence requirements?

The laws accomplish little beyond permitting the states to dodge responsibility for newcomers. Instead, they often boomerang. One painful example is provided by the gaunt, coughing old man who was found in a bus station. X-rays confirmed the suspicion that he had active tuberculosis. Though hospitalization was recommended immediately, public facilities were closed to nonresidents. Welfare funds could be given only to return him to his place of residence, and he had no legal residence anywhere. What did he do? After a few days' rest in a flophouse he found a job as a short-order cook.

The states' residence requirements stem from the English Poor Law of 1601, when feudal estates were breaking up and vagrancy loomed as a problem to be dealt with harshly. The British, of course, have long since modified their laws and now help uprooted people to settle down. A number of our states, on the contrary, prefer to remain strikingly Elizabethan. In Vermont, to take what may be an extreme example, if a nonresident asks the same township's overseer of the poor for help more than once during the year, he may be fined or clapped in jail or both.

Except for the efforts of Travelers Aid, what is being done to help these people? Attempts in Congress to lower residence requirements for Federal aid have died in committee. Suggestions that the Federal government step in with aid where the states fail to act have fallen flat. Nothing has been done, unless one counts the forthcoming contribution of the AFL-CIO, which will present two mobile units this month to Travelers Aid so as to enable it, as part of a new pilot program, to get onto the highways where the trouble lies. Even the war on poverty offers little hope, for as President Johnson said, "This program . . . [is] based on the fact that local citizens best understand their own problems, and know best how to deal with those problems."

MIGRATORY FARM WORKERS

Lenore Epstein

Migratory workers are among those having serious problems of income, of health, and of education. The domestic migrant work force, according to the Department of Agriculture, numbers almost 500,000. In addition, about 450,000 foreign agricultural workers enter the country each year, mostly from Mexico. There are three major migrant streams for domestic migrants. The largest, followed by about 250,000 workers, is the mid-continent movement made up largely of Texas-Mexicans, whose home base is in South Texas. About 100,000 workers follow the Western States migrant stream, which moves from Southern California northward through the Pacific Coast States. The East Coast migrant stream attracts almost 100,000 workers—Southeastern Negroes, Puerto Ricans, and some Texans. This stream moves north from Florida to North Carolina to New York State and then back to Florida.

In 1960 about 317,000 domestic migrants worked on a farm, for wages, for 25 days or more. During the year they worked, on the average, 157 days and had earnings of $1,016. Almost two-thirds of all migrants earned less than $1,000 from farm and non-farm work combined. About 40 out of every 100 experienced some involuntary unemployment; about 1 out of 10 were out of work for at least half the year.

One reason the problem of the migrant worker families is so serious is the number of children in these families—350,000–450,000. About 225,000 travel with their parents, and about a third of this group work. More than half the migrant children lag

Migratory Farm Workers: From "Unmet Need in a Land of Abundance," Lenore Epstein, *Social Security Bulletin*, Vol. 26, No. 5 (May, 1963), pp. 10–11.

Lenore Epstein. Division of Program Research, Office of the Commissioner, Social Security Administration.

behind other children in their school work by 1–4 years. Usually they do not get past the fourth grade. Seven States have established summer schools for the migrant children—generally for periods of 4–6 weeks—and eight States have enacted legislation relating to the education of migrant children.

Among the migrants aged 20 or over, about 2 out of every 3 have not completed the eighth grade. Almost 3 out of 10 would be classified as functionally illiterate, with less than 5 years of school, and only 14 percent had completed high school. The low educational status of the migratory farm laborers has persisted since 1940, and the low educational level is especially marked for workers aged 45 and over and for the nonwhite migrants.

6 / Poverty Among Specific Groups

This section examines the heterogeneity of the poverty subculture, a subculture which is chiefly urban. Our study of the anatomy of poverty thus far has revealed the statistical outlines of those who comprise the poor in contemporary America. In the readings that follow, the human features in all their intricate texture are more fully exposed to view. One-third of the poor are children under eighteen. As a statistical fact, this is serious enough, but it becomes much more significant when we recognize that low income limits educational opportunity, motivation, and attainment, and, in turn, the lack of education leads to low income. Because of the importance of this poverty-linked characteristic and its incidence among young people, we have included a generous selection of studies pertaining to the culturally deprived child, the unique aspects of personality and ideology formation in the poverty subculture, the school dropout, the role of the school, educational deprivation in particular, the draft rejectee, and juvenile delinquency. Many of these are linked characteristics among the youth. The typical draft rejectee, for example, is an unemployed or under-employed high school dropout deficient in both training and aspiration. There is also a too-high correlation between drop-outs and delinquency. It is reasonable to say that if we can resolve the problems of poor children and youth, we shall go far in winning the war on poverty.

These studies of the early years in the life of the deprived may help the reader understand why the subculture creates in the individual a unique way of perceiving and reacting to the world—a way that is all too inaccessible to the middle class teacher, counsellor, psychologist, psychiatrist, social worker, government official. As Bernard Asbell put it (*Redbook,* October 1963), ". . . the slum child is a child of another world. Our laws do not bind him, our standard middle-class ambitions do not inspire him, our IQs do not measure him and, most of all, his teacher is not reaching him." We are beginning to see ever more emphatically that this great mental chasm must be understood and bridged if an attack in depth on poverty is to be mounted.

As we move chronologically into adulthood, we see that many of the ills besetting the multiproblem adult family or individual—the poor are typically multiproblem people—appear at an early age. This is true in the public and private "welfare subculture," where we find the emergence of unemployment, combined with delinquency and lack of education. Hence, in turning to the problem of unemployment in relation to poverty, we do not leave the youth behind and address ourselves exclusively to the adult poor. Indeed, the special concentration of unemployment in the younger, as well as in the over-fifty-four age bracket, is notorious. Age distinctions provide vital clues to proper unemployment policy, for even should aggregate demand in the economy as a whole be adequate, the policy focus for youth needs to be upon both motivation and training to compensate quantitatively and structurally for the displacement associated with accelerated automation. With advancing age the focus becomes less a matter of motivation and more a matter of training, spatial mobility, good health and the development of more sympathetic employer attitudes toward the older worker.

The poverty group includes not only those outside the labor force and those unemployed but still in the labor force. It also covers those who are underpaid and those who are underemployed. "Underpaid" here does not refer to the imputed productivity of the worker, but to extra-market valuations respecting standards of living. A literature relevant to the underpaid, probably almost as enormous as that pertaining to unemployment, can be found in the empirical and theoretical treatment of the problems of the minimum wage.

If one-third of the poor are children, another and overlapping third are members of minority groups. By and large, the problems of minorities are directly or indirectly related to their poverty. The overlap between minority status and the other types of poverty is again very great; therefore, here, as in the section on the spatial distribution of poverty, we highlight whatever can legitimately be viewed as peculiarly stemming from minority status. That such status exacerbates the problems of sheer poverty, through discrimination and segregation, there can be no doubt. The Fayette County story, like the grim human interest material found in today's newspaper reports on the civil rights struggle, will drive this home to readers in both North and South. To the chasm between the well-off and the poor, we must add the white-nonwhite chasm.

The numerically largest minority by far in the United States is of course the Negro. This is not fully reflected in the section on the minority poor, below, in terms of pages devoted to the Negro minority. However, through such overlap as the later discussion of the effectiveness of the Negro vote (Section 7), the problems of the greatest minority receive due attention.

Old age and sickness, conjoined with poverty, are heart-rendingly widespread in our society. These are the most acute cases. But even when the three are not found together in the same family or individual, it is clear that we confront very special problems that are not readily amenable to the economic growth panacea. Health programs and measures uniquely addressed to the aged poor will be persistently called for in the years ahead in a necessarily many-faceted war on poverty, deprivation, and destitution. The importance of this social group has been increasing because of the unusual rise in the proportion of our population over sixty-five, coupled with that group's strong disposition to live alone.

A campaign to raise levels of both physical and mental health will of course have to comprehend all age groups. In the case of mental treatment, resources devoted to the youthful poor would forestall maladjustment in later years and thus minimize the costs of the campaign. That this will be no easy task is indicated clearly by the selection on psychiatrists and the poor.

The necessary complexity of a fruitful attack on poverty is again emphasized by the analysis of linkage among several poverty characteristics found in single families or individuals; a good example is that of Homer Burleigh. The interrelationships among poverty causes and results suggest a higher degree of coordination and planning than the war on poverty has as yet received.

The Young

Never to Be Employed

Anthony Rocha, 17, of Atlanta, Ga., is a small, slight youngster who exudes a nail-chewing nervousness; he is a high-school dropout; he has never had a real job. Of average intelligence, but two years behind his class because of illness and accidents, Rocha quit Atlanta's Fulton High School two weeks before Christmas while in the ninth grade, against his parents' wishes.

Dressed in a white shirt and tan, tight-legged trousers, lounging on a couch in his modest home, he tried to explain why. "Some people find an interest in school, but I just didn't. [So] me and a friend of mine decided we would just quit and get us a job. I

Never to be Employed: From *Newsweek,* April 1, 1963, p. 60.

didn't realize it would be so hard to find one. I've tried to get jobs at service stations, a bakery, and all the grocery stores out here, but there just aren't any jobs for a person like me."

There were other reasons, of course, for his leaving school. Anthony's stepfather, who never finished high school himself, is a warehouse stockman who earns only $62.50 a week, with which he must support a family of five.

"All I wanted to know when I quit school," adds Rocha, "was that I could support myself and stop mooching on my mother and father. I realize now I definitely made a mistake."

But the wisdom came too late, as it frequently does. That's the main reason there are more than 500,000 unemployed teen-agers in the U.S. today, more than 10 per cent of the unemployed. These figures are even more chilling in view of Labor Department predictions that of the 26 million youngsters who will enter the work force during the 1960s, 7.5 million will be high-school dropouts, ill-equipped for space-age work. "What can a kid do about unemployment," asks Wirtz, "pick up his phone and call his congressman?"

EFFECTS OF LOW INCOME ON CHILDREN AND THEIR FAMILIES

Lenore Epstein

To be a child in a family with inadequate income often means to be a child deprived of the kinds of food he needs to grow to healthy adulthood. It often means living in overcrowded quarters, with no decent place to play; going without preventive health care; and having little chance for more than a high school education. For about 1 in 4 it means that there is no father in the home; the mother is likely to work while the child is still very young.

Effects of Low Income on Children and Their Families: From "Some Effects of Low Income on Children and Their Families," Lenore Epstein, *Social Security Bulletin*, Vol. 24, No. 2 (February, 1961), pp. 12–17.

INCIDENCE OF LOW INCOMES

A discussion of the effects of inadequate income implies the existence of a standard of adequacy. There is, however, no single accepted standard of adequate family income, although on certain cut-off points there is little or no argument.

Robert Lampman, in a study paper prepared in 1959 for the Joint Economic Committee, estimated that in 1957 about one-fifth of the children in the United States were in families that had low incomes. Lampman defined a "low-income person" as "one with an income equivalent to that of a member of a four-person family with total money income of not more than $2,500 in 1957 dollars." In 1957 purchasing power this is the same as the $2,000 in 1947 that a congressional subcommittee on low-income families adopted as a minimum income figure for study purposes in 1949.

By another criterion, it is estimated that in 1959 almost one-fifth of the families, with nearly one-fourth of the Nation's children, had low incomes. These are families with incomes below the taxable limit under present Federal income tax laws—that is, less than $1,325 for a mother and child and less than $2,675 for a married couple with two children and $4,000 for a family of six.

That this is a conservative gauge of low income is evident from the fact that an income below the taxable limit is generally not much more than twice the amount needed for an adequate diet at low cost, according to the food plan issued by the U.S. Department of Agriculture. The average family actually spends about one-third of its income for food. Moreover, the food plan makes no allowances for "snacks," for meals eaten out, or for serving guests. It assumes that the housewife is a skillful cook, a good manager, and a careful shopper who will choose the most nutritionally economical foods from those in season.

The estimate that about 16 million children under age 18, or one-fourth of the total, are in families with incomes below the taxable limit was developed from the Bureau of the Census income distributions for families classified by number of related children, which are summarized in table 1. For the purposes of these estimates it was assumed that each family contained two adults in addition to the number of children specified. In fact, 20–25 percent of the families with children under age 18 contained at least three adults, and about 5 percent contained only one adult. Cut-off points for the taxable incomes assume the standard 10-percent deduction, although many families have larger deductions. As a result of these assumptions the number with incomes below the taxable limits is probably underestimated. Any overstatement of the number of

TABLE 1   Distribution of families by total money income in 1959, by number of children under age 18

Total money income (dollars)	Families with specified number of children					
	1	2	3	4	5	6 or more
Number (in thousands)	8,858	8,432	5,182	2,389	1,103	1,030
Percent	100.0	100.0	100.0	100.0	100.0	100.0
Less than 1,000	4.6	3.6	4.1	4.7	4.1	8.4
1,000–1,999	6.4	4.9	4.7	7.4	9.8	13.6
2,000–2,999	9.1	6.3	7.1	8.3	9.1	13.7
3,000–3,999	11.4	9.3	8.9	10.5	12.8	12.3
4,000–4,999	11.3	13.2	12.7	13.7	13.4	13.3
5,000–5,999	13.4	15.5	15.7	14.7	14.0	12.2
6,000–7,999	20.2	23.4	22.2	21.1	17.5	17.0
8,000–9,999	11.1	12.3	11.5	9.4	9.5	5.5
10,000 or more	12.5	11.7	13.0	10.0	9.7	4.1
Median income	5,534	5,833	5,792	5,367	5,048	4,136

SOURCE: Bureau of the Census, *Current Population Reports,* P-60, *Consumer Income,* No. 35.

families with small incomes that results from the tendency of respondents in field surveys to forget small or irregular receipts is thus probably more than offset.

Incomes vary both from family to family and for the same family at different stages in its life cycle, but year after year certain groups of families tend to have lower incomes than the population as a whole. Prominent among these groups are nonwhite families generally, families where the head does not work full time throughout the year, and broken families—especially those headed by women. Subfamilies—that is, families that do not maintain their own household but make their home with a relative—are also likely to be found in the low-income group.

The differences in income between families in which both parents are present and those with only the mother present are particularly striking. At the latest count, about 1 in every 12 children (more than some 5 million in all), were living in homes with only the mother present. Special tabulations of Census Bureau data for 1956 indicate, however, that about one-fourth of the children in families with incomes below the taxable limit had no father in the home. These data show also that the average income of families consisting only of a mother and children was about one-third the average received when there were two parents and children but no other persons in the family.

EFFECTS ON LIVING CONDITIONS

Low income characteristically means poor nutrition, poor housing, little or no preventive medical care. The facts hardly need documentation, but the extent of deprivation suffered by low-income families has been made clear in various studies.

A clear relationship between family income and the quantities of nutrients provided by the diet of nonfarm families was found by the Department of Agriculture in its 1955 Household Food Consumption Survey. For the 8 million or more children on farms, where income typically is lower than it is in cities, adequacy of diet is less closely related to income. In seasons of the year when homegrown and homepreserved fruits and vegetables have generally been used up, however, farm diets provide less vitamin A and vitamin C—important nutrients for children—than do city diets.

There are many examples of the inverse relationship between income and overcrowding and the direct correlation between income and the physical qualities of housing, the extent of conveniences, the quality of the neighborhood, and so on. Moreover, broken families whose incomes tend to be low are likely to share the home of relatives. In 1959, almost a fourth of the one-parent families but only 2 percent of the married couples with children lived in a relative's home.

The fact that overcrowded housing in rundown neighborhoods—with lack of privacy at home and lack of proper play space—may have unfortunate effects on children needs no underlining.

The National Health Survey, like previous surveys, found that the amount of medical care received by a family was related to the family income. The frequency of visits to the dentist provides not only a measure of the amount of dental care received but an index of ability to obtain preventive health care in general. It is therefore significant that there are substantial variations with family income in the number of dental visits by children. Among children aged 5–14, for example, those in families with incomes of $4,000 or more visited a dentist three times as often as did the children in families with incomes of less than $4,000. The variations would be more apparent if data were available for finer income intervals.

Children in families with incomes of $4,000 or more also visited physicians more frequently than those in lower-income families. The differences are most striking at the younger ages—0–4 and 5–14—where children in the higher-income families saw a doctor one and one-half times as often as children in lower-income families.

It is clear from the Survey that the difference does not reflect variations in need for medical care. The amount of family income —using the same broad income classification—was not related to the number of days missed from school because of illness or the number of days of restricted activity or days spent in bed because of disability.

EFFECTS ON EDUCATION

Children in homes with inadequate income are less likely to go to college than those whose families are better off. When they do go, they are less likely to stay to graduate.

An Office of Education study, published in 1958, reported lack of financial resources as a major cause of transfer or of dropping out of college completely. For students who stayed to graduate, the median income of the families was $1,000 higher than for students who dropped out by the end of the first term, and it was almost $500 higher than for all nongraduates. Students' ability, however, as measured by placement tests, bore almost no relationship to family income.

A sample survey just completed for the Office of Education by the Michigan Survey Research Center shows a sharp correlation between family income and actual or expected college attendance. Of the children aged 20–29 in 1960, for example, the proportion that had attended or were attending college was about five times as large when family income exceeded $7,500 as when it was less than $3,000, as shown below.

1959 income of family	Percent
Less than $3,000	12
$3,000–4,999	25
$5,000–7,499	28
$7,500–9,999	55
$10,000 and over	65

It is interesting that for younger children there is a similar relationship between parents' income and plans for the child to attend college. The younger the child, however, the more likely his family is to be planning for his college education.

A recent report by the Bureau of Labor Statistics compares the experience of high-school graduates in seven communities with that of students who dropped out of high school or who graduated but did not go on to college. It shows that economic need was not a major reason for dropping out of high school, if the phrase is interpreted to mean that the family could not supply the child with the necessities for school attendance. A study of two Louisiana parishes (counties), where information was obtained on the occupation of the father, suggests, however, that dropouts are much less common among the upper socio-economic groups. The parents' interest in education seemed to be related to their socio-economic status.

The study by the Bureau of Labor Statistics provides telling evidence of lower earning power and higher unemployment rates among dropouts. Undoubtedly, further evidence exists that young people who drop out of school early have only limited choice of jobs and lower earnings potential and that, as a result, the unfavorable economic situation in which they grow up tends to be perpetuated for them and for their children.

EFFECTS ON EMPLOYMENT OF FAMILY MEMBERS

Despite the large number of married women who now work—many from choice—it is still true that the smaller the husband's earnings the more likely the mother is to work. Among mothers with preschool children (under age 6) the proportion in the labor force in 1959 was more than three times as large when the husband earned less than $3,000 than when his earnings exceeded $10,000.

Mothers are also much more likely to work when there is no father in the home to share family responsibilities than when he is present. In March 1959, the proportion of mothers in the labor force varied as follows with the age of the children and the presence of the father:

[Percent]

Age of children in years	Married, husband present	Widowed, divorced, or separated
Total under 18	28	57
6–17, none younger	40	66
Under 6	19	45
None under 3	25	53
Some under 3	16	40

The Children's Bureau has just released a report summarizing what is known and what is not known about the effects of a mother's employment on the development and adjustment of the individual child and also on family structure and functioning. The evidence, though incomplete and inconclusive, suggests "that the quality of the family life influences the effects of a mother's outside employment more than her employment influences the quality of the family life."

Woefully little is known about the quality of substitute care, which can be crucial for a child's development and adjustment if the mother does work. There is no doubt, however, that total lack of care is hazardous. A national survey undertaken in 1958 by the Bureau of the Census for the Children's Bureau showed that 1 in 13 of the children under age 12 whose mothers worked full time were left to take care of themselves. A study made by the Bureau of Public Assistance of families receiving aid to dependent children in late 1958 shows that 1 in 9 of the children under age 12 whose mothers worked full time were left on their own. The difference suggests that lower incomes are associated with less adequate arrangements for care. Moreover, about one-third of the relatives taking care of the child, when arrangements for care were reported, were under age 18. Because of their age, it seems likely that they were older siblings who might be out of school for the purpose.

There is some evidence that teenagers are brought into the labor force when the father loses his job. A special survey of unemployment in Utica, N.Y., shows that when men aged 45–54 become unemployed the number of family members (other than the wife) in the labor force increases from 4 out of every 10 to 7 out of 10.

Low earnings may cause a man with heavy family responsibilities to "moonlight"—to take on a second job—a course that surely has an effect on family life and the children's relationship to the father. A recent report by the Bureau of Labor Statistics shows that in December 1959, for example, 6.5 percent of the married men held two or more jobs simultaneously. This was about twice as high a proportion of multiple jobholders as for other men and three times as high as for women.

Information is lacking on the extent to which need or opportunity leads a worker to take a second job. It is noteworthy, however, that 40 percent of the men with more than one job reported the occupation in their primary jobs as farmer, laborer, service worker, or factory operative—typically low paid. On the other hand, professional and technical men led all others in the rate of dual jobholding—presumably because their experience and skill open opportunities for extra work, and some, such as teachers, strive for a level of living higher than their salaries provide.

It is impossible even to outline in this summary report the hazards for child life when a family follows the migratory stream. The evidence is clear that it is a very low earning potential that creates our migratory labor force, and that the children of migrant workers have the least opportunities for proper development. In many cases they themselves work at a very young age, and many of them do not have the advantage of even an elementary school education or minimal health protection.

EFFECTS ON FAMILY STABILITY

As already suggested, poor and overcrowded housing and pressure for earnings to supplement or substitute for those of the father may affect family life unfavorably.

There is relatively little direct evidence on the relationship between income level and divorce and separation rates. Paul Glick's analysis of Census data for 1950, however, shows the rates of separation for women (standardized for age) varying inversely with years of school completed, which is one of the best indicators of socio-economic status. Divorce rates were found lowest for women with 4 or more years of college and highest for those with 1–3 years of high school (the problem dropout group), but the rate for those who had no secondary schooling was also relatively low. When divorce and separation rates for women aged 15–54 are combined, it seems clear that family disruption is associated with low economic status, as shown below.

Years of school completed	Divorce and separation rates per 1,000 women (standardized for age)		
	Combined	Divorce	Separation
Total	8.7	4.1	4.6
Elementary 0–8	10.7	3.8	6.9
High school 1–3	9.9	4.9	5.0
4	7.0	4.0	3.0
College 1–3	7.1	4.7	2.4
4 or more	5.4	3.4	2.0

A special study of 1950 data for Philadelphia shows that divorce as well as desertion tends to be inversely correlated with occupational levels. These findings raise a question on the validity of the cliché that desertion is the poor man's divorce—one that is supported, however, by Dr. Glick's finding that divorced men had higher incomes than men separated from their families. In any case, much more research is needed on the relationship between family stability and economic status.

The impact that family breakdown has on children may be inferred more directly from the way the proportion of families with children under age 18 that include only one parent—usually the mother—varies according to the education of the family head. In March 1959 the 2.2 million one-parent families (including those with a widowed parent) represented 9 percent of the Nation's 25 million families with children. The percentage of families that contained only one parent varied according to the education of the family head, as shown in the tabulation that follows:

Years of school completed	Percent
ELEMENTARY	
0–8	11.7
HIGH SCHOOL	
1–3	9.5
4	8.2
COLLEGE	
1–3	6.3
4 or more	2.9

These data suggest that when the family head has a college degree the child has four times as good a chance of living in a home with two parents as when the head never went beyond elementary school. Some but certainly not all of the difference reflects the fact that widows are older and therefore tend to have less education.

No evidence is available on the relationship of illegitimate first conceptions and economic status. Certainly it is clear that the well-to-do have a better chance than the poor of avoiding and of concealing an illegitimate birth. Moreover, it probably would not be disputed—though factual evidence is sparse—that multiple illegitimate births generally occur to women in the lowest socio-economic groups.

NEGRO YOUTHS IN THE GHETTO
James B. Conant

The youth in the big city slums dwell in a mammoth social complex. The surrounding city extends for many blocks. The business and industrial areas hem in the impoverished youth. In the case of

Negro Youths in the Ghetto: From *Slums and Suburbs,* James B. Conant (New York: McGraw-Hill Book Company, 1961), pp. 36–39.

James B. Conant. Consultant on education; former president of Harvard University.

the Negro, added to all the negative influences of a slum is the absence of any evidence that there is a pathway out. In spite of the high mobility of the family unit, or perhaps because of it, a tone is set by constant talk and the prevailing attitude of the older people. The tone is not one to encourage education or stimulate ambition. One often finds a vicious circle of lack of jobs and lack of ambition; one leads to the other. It is my contention that the circle must be broken both by upgrading the educational and vocational aspirations of slum youth and, even more important, by finding employment opportunity for them, particularly for high school graduates. It does no good whatever to prepare boys and girls for nonexistent jobs.

The difference between the Negro slum of today and the slums of the Northern seaport cities of sixty years ago is a difference that deserves attention. The worries I have expressed about the continuation of present conditions may appear to be neutralized by contemplating the record of the past. Big cities have always had slums. In the United States in the past it was possible for people to raise themselves by their own bootstraps in the course of a generation. Why be alarmed about the present situation? Such a complacent projection of the past into the obscure future is fallacious for several reasons. First and foremost is the fact that in the past most of the inhabitants of slums were recently arrived white foreign immigrants. They knew that their predecessors for generations had worked their way out of poverty in the cities. They were convinced that they could do likewise. The almost complete lack of such conviction—a consequence of the tragic story of the Negro in the United States—is the outstanding characteristic of youth in the Negro slum. Secondly, a foreign immigrant came from an impoverished but stable society, for the most part a peasant society with its own ancient mores. The pride of family and often strong church connections were social cement that kept the slums from being complete social jungles in spite of the fact that the dwelling conditions were often as bad as they are today. Lastly, for most of the period of our history labor shortages rather than labor surpluses were characteristic of our economy. Particularly, unskilled laborers were in demand. When this was not so, namely, in the depression years, organized society had to step in on a large scale to bolster the tottering social structure. Today automation has affected the employment scene; there is much less demand for unskilled labor.

Racial discrimination makes unemployment chronic for the Negro male, North and South. In short, neither in terms of the kinds of people involved nor in terms of the economic and social setting is there much resemblance between the poor city districts of 1900 and those which are the sore spots of our modern cities.

What was especially disturbing to me in my visits to the largest cities was the discovery that the employment of youth is literally nobody's affair. To be sure, there are groups concerned with various aspects of the problem, but no single agency in any of the cities has the data as to the unemployment picture in that city. There is little up-to-date information about youth unemployment even citywide and only the estimate of school people about the slum neighborhoods. Seldom are figures available to distinguish between the unemployed who are high school graduates and those who have dropped out of school before completing the twelfth grade. Most important, it is not possible to say with any accuracy how the unemployed youth are distributed among various neighborhoods. . . . Special studies [have been] undertaken to ascertain the extent of unemployment among out-of-school youth in slum neighborhoods. These studies corroborated my guess that the situation was bad. There is a great need for reliable information of this sort. Until public opinion demands that the employment of youth be looked at with a microscope, so to speak, neighborhood by neighborhood, we are unlikely to rectify what may be a great hidden danger.

One gets just so far with a discussion of the urban problem and unemployment and then runs into a set of roadblocks set up by the leaders of the Negro communities and their friends. I refer to the fact that it is considered illiberal, if not reactionary, to use the phrase I have been using, "Negro slum." Indeed, it is difficult if not impossible to get statistics about school enrollment and employment in terms of the categories white and Negro. I understand the reasons for the erection of this roadblock, but I suggest that in the interest of the Negroes themselves it is time to remove it. The urban problem is in part a Negro problem. We do not facilitate its solution by trying to find phrases to hide this fact. And it is largely a Negro problem in the North because of the discrimination practiced quietly but extensively by employers and by labor unions. In an effort to overcome this unjust and nationally dangerous discrimination, Negro leaders and their friends have placed a taboo on the use of the word "Negro." I think this has proved to be a great mistake. How can we improve a situation if we are deprived by terminology from knowing what the situation really is?

Whereas the problems of Negro education are no different from those of all underprivileged socio-economic groups, the problems of Negro employment are distinctly different. The enforcement of antidiscrimination laws has proved a most difficult undertaking. It is generally agreed that only the projects which are supported by public funds can really be operated on a truly nondiscriminatory basis. Therefore because of the urgency of the situation, I think it is necessary for Congress to appropriate funds for public work programs to alleviate unemployment among youth of sixteen to twenty-one in the large cities.

WHO FAILS SELECTIVE SERVICE TESTS?

Robert S. McNamara

Mr. PERKINS.[1] Mr. Secretary, I first wish to compliment you on your statement. I feel that the Congress has not done nearly enough in helping the young people of this country acquire education, training, and jobs. What type of youngster will this Job Corps, in your judgment, take care of as differentiated from the Manpower Development and Training Act and the vocational education legislation that the Congress has passed?

Secretary McNAMARA. It will take care of the youngster who, as I say, perhaps through inheritance, has failed to develop the physi-

[1 Representative Carl D. Perkins, Democrat from Kentucky.]

Who Fails Selective Service Tests?: From Testimony of Robert S. Mc-Namara, *Hearings on the Employment Opportunity Act of 1964,* Subcommittee on the War on Poverty Program, Committee on Education and Labor, House of Representatives, 88th Congress, 2nd Session, March 18, 1964, pp. 110–11 and 119.

Robert S. McNamara. U.S. Secretary of Defense.

Results of preinduction examinations of draftees, by Army area, State, and territory, 1962

Area and State	Percent found acceptable	Percent disqualified, by disqualifying cause				
		Total	Administrative reasons	Failed mental tests only	Failed mental tests and medically disqualified	Medically disqualified only
Total United States	50.2	49.8	2.6	21.5	3.0	22.7
Z1	51.3	48.7	2.7	19.9	2.6	23.5
1st Army area	44.2	55.8	3.3	27.1	2.6	22.8
Connecticut	51.1	48.9	2.0	21.9	1.3	23.7
Maine	48.5	51.5	3.4	10.2	4.5	33.4
Massachusetts	47.5	52.5	5.9	11.4	2.7	32.5
New Hampshire	59.9	40.1	5.3	8.9	2.7	23.2
New Jersey	47.9	52.1	4.1	29.5	2.7	15.8
New York	40.5	59.5	2.8	31.6	2.6	22.5
Rhode Island	54.1	45.9	0.2	11.7	2.6	31.4
Vermont	63.2	36.8	2.3	6.4		28.1
2d Army area	56.2	43.8	3.0	14.6	2.8	23.4
Delaware	45.5	54.5	3.6	20.4	4.5	26.0
District of Columbia	46.4	53.6	9.1	22.6	1.8	20.1
Kentucky	51.2	48.8	3.4	25.9	3.4	16.1
Maryland	49.2	50.8	8.0	18.6	3.4	20.8
Ohio	57.4	42.6	1.4	10.1	1.8	29.3
Pennsylvania	61.4	38.6	2.3	10.7	2.6	23.0
Virginia	47.4	52.6	3.4	25.2	4.7	19.3
West Virginia	51.5	48.5	3.2	18.3	4.9	22.1
3d Army area	42.0	58.0	2.0	34.0	4.6	17.4
Alabama	38.1	61.9	2.9	33.9	6.3	18.8
Florida	43.3	56.7	3.4	33.9	3.2	20.4
Georgia	42.9	57.1	3.5	31.4	3.7	18.5
Mississippi	36.6	63.4	.3	44.6	6.6	11.9
North Carolina	46.3	53.7	1.2	30.2	3.9	18.4
South Carolina	33.8	66.2	.2	46.8	5.0	14.2
Tennessee	50.6	49.4	1.4	27.1	4.1	16.8
4th Army area	52.3	47.7	1.9	22.6	2.8	20.4
Arkansas	52.6	47.4		27.7	4.0	15.7

Area and State	Percent found acceptable	Percent disqualified, by disqualifying cause				
		Total	Administrative reasons	Failed mental tests only	Failed mental tests and medically disqualified	Medically disqualified only
Louisiana	43.2	56.8	2.0	40.1	2.9	11.8
New Mexico	64.9	35.1	1.9	13.5	1.8	17.9
Oklahoma	65.2	34.8	.1	7.8	1.3	25.6
Texas	51.8	48.2	2.5	18.0	2.8	24.9
5th Army area	60.5	39.5	1.5	11.2	1.4	25.4
Colorado	66.9	33.1	3.9	6.2	1.1	21.9
Illinois	56.6	43.4	.5	21.1	1.5	20.3
Indiana	53.1	46.9	5.1	8.1	1.1	32.6
Iowa	67.1	32.9	1.3	3.5	1.5	26.6
Kansas	69.7	30.3	.2	4.3	.9	24.9
Michigan	57.8	42.2	.2	12.5	1.6	27.9
Minnesota	63.7	36.3	3.3	2.0	.7	30.3
Missouri	62.3	37.7	2.1	11.4	2.0	22.2
Nebraska	71.9	28.1	.2	3.9	.5	23.5
North Dakota	69.4	30.6	1.5	5.1	1.3	22.7
South Dakota	60.8	39.2	4.1	2.8	1.3	31.0
Wisconsin	57.9	42.1	3.4	6.6	1.5	30.6
Wyoming	65.9	34.1	4.6	4.4	1.0	24.1
6th Army area	52.5	47.5	4.3	11.5	1.5	30.2
Arizona	48.5	51.5	6.4	12.8	2.4	29.9
California	50.8	49.2	4.1	14.1	1.6	29.4
Idaho	61.9	38.1	1.2	4.9	1.4	30.6
Montana	64.6	35.4	.3	2.9	1.0	31.2
Nevada	49.7	50.3	4.7	12.6	2.9	30.1
Oregon	60.9	39.1	.4	3.7	1.3	33.7
Utah	66.6	33.4	.9	3.1	.7	28.7
Washington	54.5	45.5	7.9	2.6	1.0	34.0
Outside Z1	33.8	66.2	.5	43.7	9.1	12.9
Alaska	74.5	25.5	1.4	3.2	3.2	17.7
Hawaii	50.8	49.2	1.3	13.8	4.7	29.4
Guam	70.7	29.3		28.0		1.3
Puerto Rico	30.5	69.5	0.4	48.3	9.9	10.9

cal and mental skills which qualify him for even the levels of training provided by those other facilities that you referred to. Perhaps I can add to that statement by referring to some of the characteristics of the men who failed to pass the selective service tests, the 600,000 men per year who are stated to be unqualified for either mental or physical reasons for service in the Army.

These men, for example, we find have these characteristics: I will run down a list of them to give you a profile of the kind of person who might well enlist voluntarily in the Job Corps.

Three out of ten of the men who failed to pass the selective service test for mental reasons are not working, are unemployed at the time they take the test. Two out of five of the men who are disqualified for mental reasons have dropped out of school to support their families or themselves. They lack the economic base on which to continue schooling.

More than four out of five of the men rejected for mental reasons have stated voluntarily that they wished they could be exposed to further education. Of those who have stated that they wished to be exposed to further education, that is to say 80 percent of those who have been rejected for mental reasons, two-thirds have stated that they are willing to leave home to receive that additional training.

Almost half of the men rejected for mental reasons come from families with six or more children, again indicating this inheritance of poverty.

About one-fifth of the mental rejectees' fathers are not working and one-fourth of the employed parents—in addition to the one-fifth not working, one-fourth of the employed parents hold unskilled jobs.

About one-fifth of the mental rejectees' families have received public assistance in the past 5 years. More than one-half of the fathers of the mental rejectees never completed grade school, another indication of this inheritance of poverty as a trait.

So it is men with profiles such as these who we believe will volunteer in large numbers for the Job Corps.

INCOME AND COLLEGE ATTENDANCE

Willard Wirtz

The most important source of data on the relationship between family income and college attendance, among high school students with various levels of academic aptitude, is "Project Talent," a cooperative research study carried out by the University of Pittsburgh and the American Institute for Research, and financed primarily by the U.S. Office of Education. In the overall project, about 440,000 students in grades 9 to 12 were tested with a battery of tests measuring general intelligence, various specific aptitudes, personality and social maturity, etc. Information was also obtained on scholastic performance, economic and social characteristics of the student's family, and characteristics of the schools attended.

In one special study undertaken by Project Talent, high school graduates who were in the project's sample of 12th grade pupils were contacted by mail questionnaire to determine which of them had entered college within 1 year after completing the 12th grade. For the approximately 60,000 graduates who responded (about 67 percent of the sample) it was then possible to relate the data on college attendance to other information, including the income of the student's family and the individual's relative rating on academic aptitude. Academic aptitude was measured by a composite of four Project Talent tests, and respondents were ranked in percentiles based on a representative sample of pupils in grade 12. Those in the 90th to 100th percentile, for example, represent high school graduates whose academic aptitude falls in the top 10 percent of all 12th grade students.

.   .   .

Income and College Attendance: From Testimony of Willard Wirtz, *Hearings on the Employment Opportunity Act of 1964,* Subcommittee on the War on Poverty Program, Committee on Education and Labor, House of Representatives, 88th Congress, 2nd Session, March 19, 1964, pp. 205–07. Willard Wirtz. U.S. Secretary of Labor.

Table 1 shows the percentage of male high school graduates, classified by family income and by percentile ranking on academic aptitude, who had not entered college within 1 year after completing high school. Among those with an extremely high level of general college aptitude (the upper 2 percent) nearly all male high school graduates entered college, regardless of family income. In every income class, more than 95 percent entered college, and because of the small numbers in the sample for some income classes, the differences between income levels are not significant.

At every other level of aptitude, however, there is a marked relationship between reported family income and college entry. Of the boys in the second quartile for general college aptitude (50th to 74th percentile) about 52 percent of those from families with incomes below $3,000 per year failed to enter college, while only 20 percent of those from families with incomes above $12,000 failed to enter college. In fact, boys with below-average college aptitude who came from families in the highest income group were actually more likely to enter college than boys in the second quarter of the aptitude ranking who came from families with incomes of less than $3,000.

TABLE 1 Percentages of male high school graduates who responded to mail questionnaire and who did not enter college within 1 year after completing grade 12, by aptitude percentile and family income

Aptitude level percentile	Less than $3,000	$3,000 to $5,999	$6,000 to $8,999	$9,000 to $11,999	$12,000 and up
98 to 100	0	3.9	4.8	4.1	1.5
90 to 97.9	12.1	13.3	11.4	7.5	3.3
75 to 89.9	24.6	26.7	19.4	16.1	9.9
50 to 74.9	51.8	47.5	40.3	33.2	20.3
0 to 49.9	80.4	72.7	68.1	59.8	50.3

NOTE.—Data are taken from Project Talent in U.S. Office of Education cooperative research program, project 2333.

Table 2 presents similar data for female high school graduates. Since more of the girls than the boys were unable to estimate their family income, the trends for girls are a little less consistent than for boys. At every level of aptitude, however, the proportion of girl high school graduates who failed to enter college was much higher for those who came from the lowest income families than for those who came from high-income families. Among girls in the second quartile of the aptitude range, for example, 70 percent of those from the highest income families went to college, while only 25 percent of those from the lowest income families did so.

TABLE 2 Percentages of female high school graduates who responded to mail questionnaire and who did not enter college within 1 year after completing grade 12, by aptitude percentile and family income

Aptitude level percentile	Less than $3,000	$3,000 to $5,999	$6,000 to $8,999	$9,000 to $11,999	$12,000 and up
98 to 100.0	10.5	2.5	6.7	6.0	3.2
90 to 97.9	36.7	19.2	16.1	14.9	4.8
75 to 89.9	38.9	43.2	30.2	28.2	10.1
50 to 74.9	74.8	64.2	57.4	40.8	29.2
0 to 49.9	82.6	81.8	77.2	69.6	52.1

NOTE.—Data are taken from Project Talent in U.S. Office of Education cooperative research program, project 2333.

The following additional comments on the findings of Project Talent are from a memorandum prepared by the program director, Dr. John T. Dailey:

Project Talent . . . found that 30 percent of the 1960 high school seniors in the 80 to 90 academic percentile of their class and 43 percent of those in the 70 to 80 percentile range failed to enter college. This represents a very serious loss of many of our most capable young men and women with high aptitudes and interest in college. While it is difficult to determine exactly how many of our qualified young people fail to enter college because of financial inability to do so, much of this talent loss is clearly associated with low family income.

The accompanying exhibits show that boys and girls from low-income families, except those in the upper 2 percent of ability, have a much poorer chance of going to college than do those from high-income families. . . .

Nearly all students in the upper 2 percent in ability enter college, regardless of level of family income. This is a most remarkable exception to the general association of low family income and talent loss and perhaps indicates that the availability of student aid today is adequate—for 2 percent of our youth. For the other 98 percent, and even for the 8 percent just below the top 2 percent, family income is an important determiner of who will enter college and rise to positions of leadership and personal fulfillment.

Our success with the top 2 percent should give us hope and determination to extend the adequacy of student aid downward to meet the needs of our highly talented youth—not just the top 2 percent.

However, the problem is not just one of student aid and family resources. The opportunities for attending college vary greatly from one part of the country to another. Large regional differences were found in the proportion of high school graduates at the same level of academic aptitude who went to college. Among pupils at about the 75th percentile in academic aptitude, 70 percent of the high school graduates in the Southwest and Far West entered college, while only 50 percent of those in the Northeastern and Midwestern States did so. Significant regional differences in the rate of college entry were found at every aptitude level, although they were less pronounced among very bright graduates. Rated according to the proportion of high school graduates who went to college, four large regions are in this order: (1) Southwest, Far West; (2) Southeast; (3) Great Lakes, Plains, Rocky Mountain; (4) New England, Mideast.

Low-cost junior colleges and State colleges that offer programs suited to the needs of students whose interests and aptitudes vary widely are more widely available in regions where college attendance is high.

Providing adequate college programs of this sort in all areas of the country could help eliminate much of the talent loss of our youth.

Young Persons Reaching 18 Annually, 1950 to 1970.

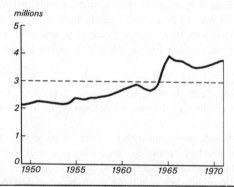

Arthur Mauch, *Education and Training* (Ames, Iowa: Center for Agricultural and Economic Development, Iowa State University), p. 3.

Education of People Employed in Different Occupations.

	Percent With	
	Less Than High School	Some College Training
Professional and technical workers	6	75
Clerical or sales workers	25	22
Unskilled workers	80	3

Arthur Mauch, *Education and Training* (Ames, Iowa: Center for Agricultural and Economic Development, Iowa State University), p. 3.

DROPOUTS, DELINQUENCY, AND LOWER-CLASS CHILDREN

Erdman Palmore

In [my] analysis of 384 lower-class children born in 1942–44, dropout rates were found to be significantly higher among those from the lower-class neighborhoods, those moving frequently, the males, and those with below-average intelligence. Dropout rates were not found to be significantly related to receipt of assistance. In fact, the students receiving assistance did as well as or better in terms of school deportment and grades.

Delinquency was found to be significantly associated with several individual characteristics (nonwhite, male, low intelligence, and leaving school) that were considered as indicators of barriers to legitimate opportunity that produce anomie and delinquency. Delinquency was also significantly related to characteristics of deviant

Dropouts, Delinquency, and Lower-Class Children: From "Factors Associated With School Dropouts and Juvenile Delinquency Among Lower-Class Children," Erdman Palmore, *Social Security Bulletin*, Vol. 26, No. 10 (October, 1963), p. 9.

Erdman Palmore. Division of Research and Statistics, Social Security Administration.

School Grades of Youth Leaving Before High School Graduation

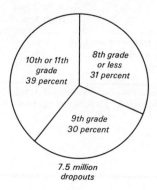

7.5 million
dropouts

L. T. Wallace, *Policy Alternatives for Increasing Employment Opportunities* (Ames, Iowa: Center for Agricultural and Economic Development, Iowa State University), p. 5.

families (illegitimacy, absent parents, and delinquent siblings) and to characteristics of deviant neighborhoods (public housing and high neighborhood delinquency rates). These characteristics were considered to be indicators of access to illegitimate opportunities that increases delinquency rates.

Although the children receiving aid to families with dependent children had twice the rate of delinquency for those not receiving aid, the evidence indicates that this is a spurious association resulting from other factors. The background characteristics of the assistance recipients are those that tend to produce higher delinquency rates, and when some of these characteristics (class, age, race, and sex) were controlled there was little or no association left between receipt of assistance and delinquency.

Since this sample was limited to 384 lower-class children in one metropolitan area, most of whom were recipients of aid to families with dependent children, generalizations should be made with caution. The study indicates, however, that dropouts and delinquency found among the lower-class children result from a complex of factors that fit into recent theory on legitimate opportunity, illegitimate opportunity, and deviance.

"Want to Transfer to My School, Kid?"

Courtesy *The Washington Post*

The Unemployed and the Underpaid

Alfred Michel, Unemployed Steelworker

Alfred Michel, 54, of West Mifflin, Pa., is a gap-toothed, broken-nosed steelworker who hasn't worked in three years and who will probably never work again. Like a third of the long-term unemployed, he is too old. ("When jobs are tight," says [Secretary of Labor] Wirtz, "the day a man over 45 loses his job is the day he becomes 'old'.") Despite his 37 years in the mills, Michel was furloughed when United States Steel closed its outmoded and inefficient open-hearth plant at Clairton, near Pittsburgh, and he was placed in U.S. Steel's huge "labor pool" to await reassignment. He is still waiting.

Nor is he alone in his predicament. There are currently 100,000 steelworkers drawing supplemental unemployment benefits (up to 65 per cent of base pay); there are many more, like Michel, who have long since exhausted such benefits. His sole subsistence is a relief check for $78.10 every two weeks, out of which he must pay $54 a month on the house into which he has sunk his life's savings. At the moment, he is a year behind in his payments.

Were there only Michel and his wife, he wouldn't complain. But though he has raised five children on his laborer's pay, he still has two daughters to go, one 14 years old and the other 16.

Alfred Michel, Unemployed Steelworker: From *Newsweek,* April 1, 1963, pp. 59–60.

"I don't mind so much," Michel says, his voice choked with emotion, "but it's the girls. They're growing up. They want to go to dances and parties and things. They need pretty dresses and things so they don't feel ashamed, so they don't feel different from other people. But I can't give it to them. I can't give them nothing."

Does he feel bitter? "No," he says, yet he adds quietly, like a child: "But they did away with my plant. They ought to get me a new plant."

PROFILE OF THE UNEMPLOYED

Robert L. Stein

In April 1962, a detailed survey of the characteristics of the unemployed was conducted. For the first time, factual evidence was provided on many of the controversial issues that relate to the nature of unemployment in the United States. Although there is still room for wide differences of interpretation, the new facts gathered and presented in this article make it more difficult to cling to extreme positions. The unemployed were found to be a very diverse group of workers with significant variations in financial resources, need for work, attachment to the labor force, and qualifications and prospects for steady employment in the future. In general, they cannot be regarded as personally responsible for their own difficulties, unwilling to accept suitable jobs, more or less voluntarily unemployed, and only casually interested in an occasional job. The basis for these generalizations is a Bureau of Labor Statistics survey of an estimated 9.6 million workers 18 years old or older who experienced at least 5 full weeks of unemployment in 1961 (counting all spells). This nationwide study, conducted to

Profile of the Unemployed: From *Work History, Attitudes, and Income of the Unemployed,* Robert L. Stein (Washington, D.C.: U.S. Department of Labor, Special Labor Force Report No. 37, 1964), reprinted from *Monthly Labor Review,* December, 1963, pp. 1405–13.

Robert L. Stein. Division of Employment and Unemployment Analysis; Bureau of Labor Statistics, U.S. Department of Labor.

obtain information not readily available from the regular monthly surveys of the labor force, also included a 5-year labor force history of these unemployed workers for the period 1957–61.

Of the 9.6 million unemployed, nearly 70 percent were men—the vast majority in the prime working years of 20 to 64. Family heads accounted for three-fifths of the unemployed, and nonwhite workers for one-fifth. A fourth of the group suffered more than 6 months of unemployment in 1961. Only a third of the unemployed, compared with over half the civilian labor force, were high school graduates.

LABOR FORCE ATTACHMENT

In April 1962, 67 percent of the 9.6 million workers who were unemployed 5 weeks or more in 1961 were back at work, while another 26 percent were looking for work. Only 7 percent had left the labor force. . . . the proportion of women who were no longer working, or seeking work was larger than that of men—15 percent compared with 3 percent.

Government statistics on unemployment measure the extent of unutilized labor immediately available in the economy; they have never been intended as a measure of financial need or hardship. There is considerable diversity in the extent to which unemployment affects the total economic situation of workers and their families, depending on such factors as the position of the unemployed person in the family, the duration of his unemployment, and his eligibility for unemployment insurance. In any case, unemployment necessarily has some effect on the welfare of each person and family involved. In the April 1962 survey of the work history of the unemployed, an attempt was made to measure the seriousness of unemployment in terms of its effect on income and living standards. Respondents were asked questions relating to individual and family income, dependency, and methods used to meet living expenses while unemployed.

PERSONAL INCOME

The average income from all sources for the 9.6 million persons unemployed a month or longer in 1961 was $2,300. This was nearly 40 percent below the $3,700 average for all other persons with income who had some work experience during the year.[1] Moreover, the $3,700 average would have been higher and the difference greater if it had been possible to exclude all students, persons under 18, and those currently unable to work, all of whom were omitted from the survey of the unemployed.

As expected, the duration of unemployment had a strong effect on individual income. The median income of the long-term unemployed was only about $1,400, or a little over half that of those unemployed from 1 to 6 months.

Persons employed all year primarily at full-time jobs averaged $5,000; but only 1 out of every 8 unemployed persons had an income of that size or greater. However, only part of this difference can be ascribed directly to the loss of income resulting from unemployment; another substantial part reflects the fact that even when the jobless were employed, their average weekly earnings were considerably lower than those of year-round full-time workers. On their current or last job, the 9.6 million unemployed earned about $70 a week; the comparable weekly wage or salary for year-round full-time workers during 1961 was roughly $95. This gap arises from the lower educational levels of the unemployed, their greater concentration in the less skilled and lower paying occupations, and their more frequent part-time workweeks. In addition, their average yearly income was lowered even further when slightly over a fifth of the 9.6 million left the labor force entirely part of the year.

Despite the effects of unemployment, about 80 percent of the income received by unemployed persons in 1961 came from their own wages and salaries. Another significant but much smaller proportion—12 percent—was derived from unemployment insurance. The remaining 8 percent was obtained from all other sources combined, principally from welfare and pension programs established by legislation or collective bargaining agreements.

WAGE AND SALARY INCOME

During 1961, wage and salary income of the 9.6 million unemployed averaged about $1,900, compared with nearly $5,000 for year-round full-time workers. Nevertheless, even for persons with unemployment, wages and salaries were the most important source

[1] Averages in this discussion are medians based on distributions of persons with income.

of income; 95 percent received at least some wage income during 1961, whereas only 69 percent received income from other sources.[2] The average wage income was 3½ times larger than the average income from other sources.

Conversely, although nearly 90 percent of the long-term unemployed had at least some wage income during the year, the amount received was actually smaller than the $950 median income received from other sources by the 75 percent who had some non-wage income. In the aggregate, a little over half the total income of the long-term unemployed came from wages and salaries.

UNEMPLOYMENT INSURANCE

Unemployment insurance was an important, although only partial, offset to the loss of wage income during 1961. Slightly more than half (5.3 million) of the unemployed reported that they received unemployment insurance benefit payments. Of those who did not receive these payments, most had not applied for them, presumably because they were not eligible. The median weekly benefit was about $36. The median period for those receiving compensation was about 14 weeks, half of the maximum duration allowable in most States (not counting temporary extensions, such as those provided in 1958 and 1961). Most of the unemployed apparently found jobs before the expiration of their right to regular and extended benefits; however, one-fifth did exhaust their benefits during 1961.

Among those jobless 27 weeks or more in 1961, unemployment insurance benefits were of great significance, averaging almost 10 percent more than their 1961 earnings from wages and salaries. In fact, 1 out of 9 of the long-term jobless had no wage or salary income in 1961, compared with only 1 out of 40 of those unemployed 5 to 26 weeks.

INCOME FROM OTHER SOURCES

The combination of all other types of nonwage income contributed less to the aggregate income of the unemployed than did unemployment insurance alone. The proportion of unemployed

[2] The proportion of the unemployed who received other types of income was considerably larger than for the population as a whole (49 percent), but smaller than the proportion receiving wage income.

persons receiving such income ranged from the 8 percent who obtained supplementary unemployment benefits to the 1½ percent who received private pensions. About 4½ percent of the 9.6 million with unemployment received income from social security which averaged close to $700 annually—the largest amount from any single source other than wages. In fact, income from all sources other than wages and salaries averaged only a little over $500 during 1961. Moreover, not only were these average income amounts relatively small, but they were calculated on the base of those who received $1 or more of such income. Thirty percent had no such income at all.

Even for the long-term unemployed, wages and unemployment insurance were by far the most important sources of income. For this group, however, social security benefits and public assistance were relatively more significant than for those unemployed for shorter periods of time.

DEPENDENCY STATUS

Although concern for the well-being of the family unit is raised whenever a member become unemployed, the situation is most serious if the unemployed person has others dependent on him. The majority (55 percent) of the jobless were family heads, financially responsible for other persons. Another 25 percent were unrelated individuals or family members who took care of their own living expenses. The remainder were mostly wives of family heads (17 percent); a very small proportion (only about 3 percent) were family members who did not provide for their own living expenses. About three-fifths of the 1.6 million married women who were unemployed had children under 18; in the estimation of the number of unemployed with dependents, these women were not included, although the children obviously benefited from their mothers' earnings.

The effect of unemployment of the family head on the family situation was mitigated somewhat in those families in which other members had jobs. In one-third of the 4.8 million families which included a wife or other relative 18 years old or over, someone else in the family was employed at the time the family head suffered his first stretch of unemployment in 1961; in most instances his wife was the other worker. Only to a small extent did the unemployment of the family head induce other family members to enter the labor force. In 12 percent of the families, another member 18 years old or older (usually the wife) looked for or took a job as a direct result of the unemployment status of the head.

FAMILY INCOME AND LIVING STANDARDS

In 1961, the average family income of the 8.8 million unemployed persons in families was $4,400. In addition, there were 800,000 unrelated individuals with unemployment whose incomes averaged about $1,800. The 8.8 million in families included 5.3 million family heads—almost 90 percent of them married men, wife present. Most of the following discussion deals with families in which the unemployed person was the head.

The average income of these families was $4,100, compared with $5,700 for all families and $6,900 for families in which the head was a year-round full-time worker. While these figures provide a measure of the differences in the level of living of families with unemployment and of families where the head worked steadily, the differences cannot be taken as an indication of the effect of the head's unemployment alone. As noted earlier, the weekly earnings of all persons with unemployment (when employed during 1961) were $25 lower than those of year-round workers; if a similar gap is assumed for family heads, it would imply an annual difference of $1,300, apart from the effects of unemployment. Assuming further that the weekly earnings of unemployed family heads ($75–$80 a week) were somewhat higher than for the unemployed as a whole, their average loss of potential earnings through unemployment could be estimated at about $1,100 to $1,300, since their average duration of unemployment was about 15 to 16 weeks. Roughly two-fifths of this loss was offset by unemployment compensation for the 3.4 million heads who received these benefits.

Despite his loss of earnings through unemployment, the family head's wage income was a major component of his family's income. During 1961, the head's wage income ($2,700) accounted for nearly three-fifths of aggregate family income for these 5.3 million families. At the same time, however, the nonwage income of the head, principally from unemployment insurance benefits, and the earnings of other family members were important contributions to family income—accounting for two-fifths of the aggregate income.

Since the earning ability of the head tends to exceed that of other family members, his unemployment strikes a much greater blow at the family's financial solvency than does the joblessness of other members. Among the 3.5 million families in which the unemployed person was the wife or other relative, family income averaged $800 more than for the 5.3 million families in which the head was unemployed. No doubt in many families, the head continued to work and to receive his regular earnings while family members were seeking work, as indicated by the fact that the personal incomes of wives and relatives with unemployment averaged less than one-third of their total family income. This low ratio, however, was partly the result of unemployment itself.

On the other hand, in about one-fourth of the 3.5 million families in which the unemployed person was the wife or other relative, these family members provided more than half the family's wage or salary income in spite of their unemployment. Of course, their loss of income while unemployed had a serious effect upon the financial structure of their families.

NUMBER OF DEPENDENTS

Sharing the total income of families with an unemployed head were an estimated 19 million persons (over 10 percent of the country's total population in April, 1962). These included 5.3 million family heads, 4.7 million wives, 8.5 million children under 18 years old, and 600,000 dependent relatives and other persons. Families with an unemployed head not only had incomes about one-fourth lower than for all families and two-fifths lower than for families whose heads had steady full-time employment, but they were also faced with the need to distribute their lower income among relatively more consumers. For example, among the families affected by the head's unemployment, some 26 percent had 3 children or more under 18 (including 14 percent with 4 or more), whereas among other families, 22 percent had 3 children or more (including 11 percent with 4 or more). Conversely, while 36 percent of the families hit by unemployment had no young children, 41 percent of the other families were in this position.

Among the families with an unemployed head, the total income available rose as family size increased, up to five persons. This reflects the contribution of additional earners plus the fact that the head's earning power reaches a peak in his late thirties and early forties. However, in families with more than five persons the increases in income were slight and per capita income dropped sharply.

HOW LIVING EXPENSES WERE MET

In a high proportion of families, total income apparently was insufficient to maintain living standards without resorting to other means, such as using savings, borrowing money, or turning to friends and relatives for help. Use of most of these methods was much more likely if the unemployed person was the family head or was jobless over half the year.

The most usual method of replacing some of the missing income was by the use of savings. Almost half the families withdrew from their savings, averaging $400. Nearly one-quarter of the families borrowed money, with half of the borrowers obtaining $300 or more. Other means of meeting living expenses in times of unemployment included cash assistance and surplus food from public and private welfare agencies and moving to cheaper housing. Each of these methods was resorted to in proportionately more families where the jobless person was unemployed more than 26 weeks.

CONCEALED UNEMPLOYMENT

Ad Hoc Committee on the Triple Revolution

The increased efficiency of machine systems is shown in the more rapid increase in productivity per man hour since 1960, a year that marks the first visible upsurge of the cybernation revolution. In 1961, 1962, and 1963, productivity per man-hour rose at an

Concealed Unemployment: From *The Triple Revolution: An Appraisal of the Major U.S. Crises and Proposals for Action* (New York: Ad Hoc Committee on the Triple Revolution, March 22, 1964), pp. 10–13.

average pace above 3.5%—a rate well above both the historical average and the post-war rate.

Companies are finding cybernation more and more attractive. Even at the present early stage of cybernation, costs have already been lowered to a point where the price of a durable machine may be as little as one-third of the current annual wage-cost of the worker it replaces. A more rapid rise in the rate of productivity increase per man-hour can be expected from now on.

In recent years it has proved impossible to increase demand fast enough to bring about the full use of either men or plant capacities. The task of developing sufficient additional demand promises to become more difficult each year. A $30 billion annual increase in Gross National Product is now required to prevent unemployment rates from rising. An additional $40–60 billion increase would be required to bring unemployment rates down to an acceptable level.

The official rate of unemployment has remained at or above 5.5% during the sixties. The unemployment rate for teenagers has been rising steadily and now stands around 15%. The unemployment rate for Negro teenagers stands about 30%. The unemployment rate for teenagers in minority ghettoes sometimes exceeds 50%. Unemployment rates for Negroes are regularly more than twice those for whites, whatever their occupation, educational level, age or sex. The unemployment position for other racial minorities is similarly unfavorable. Unemployment rates in depressed areas often exceed 50%.

These official figures seriously underestimate the true extent of unemployment. The statistics take no notice of underemployment or featherbedding. Besides the 5.5% of the labor force who are officially designated as unemployed, nearly 4% of the labor force sought full-time work in 1962 but could find only part-time jobs. In addition, methods of calculating unemployment rates—a person is counted as unemployed only if he has actively sought a job recently—ignore the fact that many men and women who would like to find jobs have not looked for them because they know there are no employment opportunities. Underestimates for this reason are pervasive among groups whose unemployment rates are high —the young, the old, and racial minorities. Many people in the depressed agricultural, mining, and industrial areas, who by official definition hold jobs but who are actually grossly underemployed, would move if there were prospects of finding work elsewhere. It is reasonable to estimate that over 8 million people are not working who would like to have jobs today as compared with the 4 million shown in the official statistics.

Even more serious is the fact that the number of people who have voluntarily removed themselves from the labor force is not constant but increases continuously. These people have decided to stop looking for employment and seem to have accepted the fact that they will never hold jobs again. This decision is largely irreversible, in economic and also in social and psychological terms. The older worker calls himself "retired"; he cannot accept work without affecting his social security status. The worker in his prime years is forced onto relief: in most states the requirements for becoming a relief recipient bring about such fundamental alterations in an individual's situation that a reversal of the process is always difficult and often totally infeasible. Teenagers, especially "dropouts" and Negroes, are coming to realize that there is no place for them in the labor force but at the same time they are given no realistic alternative. These people and their dependents make up a large part of the "poverty" sector of the American population.

Statistical evidence of these trends appears in the decline in the proportion of people claiming to be in the labor force—the so-called labor force participation rate. The recent apparent stabilization of the unemployment rate around 5.5% is therefore misleading: it is a reflection of the discouragement and defeat of a people who cannot find employment and have withdrawn from the market rather than a measure of the economy's success in creating jobs for those who want to work.

THE UNDERPAID

Walter Reuther

A major factor in the poverty of many families is the miserable pittance which millions of American wage earners still receive for a week's work. Almost half the heads of poor families are employed, and 70 percent of poor families have at least one wage earner in the family; nearly a quarter have two or more wage earners. Obviously, substandard wages are a major cause of poverty.

The prevalence of inadequate wages is also indicated by Department of Labor data. In those industries for which BLS [Bureau of Labor Statistics] earnings data are available, 1.7 million workers, or 5½ percent of the total, are employed in industries in which the average hourly earnings are less than $1.50 per hour. If these workers are employed steadily the year around, they cannot earn enough to maintain a family above the poverty line of $3,000 suggested by the CEA [Council of Economic Advisers]. And if the average is $1.50, it must follow that approximately half the workers are getting even less than the average.

The BLS earnings data show that another 6 million workers, almost 20 percent of the total, are in industries where the average earnings are from $1.50 to $2 per hour. Thus there are altogether 7¾ million workers, 25 percent of all those covered by BLS earnings data, who work in industries where average hourly earnings are insufficient to maintain an annual income of $4,000, an income equal to only two-thirds of the amount which the Department of Labor, on the basis of largely obsolete standards, has found necessary for a "modest but adequate" budget for city workers' families.

Even these figures are not all inclusive. They do not include, for

The Underpaid: From statement of Walter Reuther, *Hearings on the Economic Opportunity Act of 1964,* Subcommittee on the War on Poverty, Committee on Education and Labor, House of Representatives, 88th Congress, 2nd Session, April 9, 1964, pp. 435–36.

"I'm sorry, but I believe in strengthening the over-all economy instead."

Drawing by Alan Dunn; © 1964 The New Yorker Magazine, Inc.

example, the large number of workers who are individually low paid even though they are employed in industries where average earnings of all workers are above $2. They do not include white-collar workers in several broad industry categories, including manufacturing, many of whom are also low paid. They do not include workers in the industries not covered by the BLS earnings data, such as agriculture. According to the Census Bureau there are more than a million migrant farmworkers who get for their back-breaking work annual average earnings of $1,263 for men and $328, presumably for part-time work, for women. Federal minimum wage laws do not cover these workers, practically none of them have unemployment insurance protection, and, lacking social security coverage, they must work until they die.

The incidence of poverty among those who are able to work,

and do work, but are still poor, underlines the inadequacy of the present minimum wage law. For those who are covered, the present minimum of $1.25 will provide an annual income of only $2,500—at least $500 less than is needed to keep a family above the poverty line.

In consequence, many families whose heads are earning only the $1.25 an hour minimum now have to be given income supplementation through public assistance in order to maintain even a bare subsistence level of living. Taxpayers' money, in short, is being used to subsidize sweatshop employers.

Yet even the inadequate protection of the present minimum wage is denied to the more than 16 million workers not covered by the minimum wage law at all, workers in agriculture, in laundries, in hotels, in hospitals, in all the noisome corners of industry from which the foul odor of the sweatshop still rises unchecked.

The Minority Poor

Family on Relief: Puerto Ricans in New York

Antonia Matos is a tall, overweight, 26-year-old with a pretty face, large warm brown eyes, three small children and no husband. She is also a special sort of poverty statistic—an entry on the relief rolls.

Her family is one of the 389,000 defined by Welfare Commissioner James R. Dumpson as "having only the necessities for subsistence." Without the Department of Welfare she would be in subpoverty.

As it is, the $2,280.82 a year the family receives in welfare payments is $1,000 less than the "minimal budget requirement" called for by the Mayor's Council on Poverty in a report last week.

The only money that comes into the family's three-room apartment, which is badly in need of paint and floor covering, is a $94 check from the city every 15 days. Life depends on this check, on the monthly free Federal surplus foods and free medical care.

The very existence of Miss Matos and her family, a 7-year-old son, and two daughters, rests with her welfare investigator and his

---

Family on Relief: Puerto Ricans in New York: From "Family on Relief: Study in Poverty," Philip Dougherty, New York *Times,* April 5, 1964, p. 117. © 1964 by The New York Times Company. Reprinted by permission.

Philip Dougherty. Reporter, the New York *Times.*

little black book—the omnipresent Manual of Policies and Procedures. The book tells the agent in minute detail what an individual's "entitlement" is, depending on age, sex, employment and physical condition.

Exclusive of rent, utilities and a few other recurring items, the official daily budget, which is required by state law, comes to $1 for the mother, 90 cents for the son, 74 cents for the 4-year-old daughter and 66 cents for the baby. These allowances must provide food, clothing, personal care and household supplies.

The big days each month for Miss Matos in her rat-infested, fifth-floor walkup on East Fourth Street, are the 1st and the 16th. Those are the check days. Where she goes and what she does with the check depend a lot on the thyroid condition that keeps her seriously overweight, the five flights that leave her breathless, and the children.

She goes just across cobblestoned, pushcart filled Avenue C to the bodega, which she and other Puerto Ricans simply call "the Spanish store."

"The kids like Spanish food," she said. "Me, I eat half English and half Spanish." She likes the rice she gets there and the cans of Spanish beans, which she and the two oldest children have every day. She spends $25 for food every two weeks, which means she'll have meat five of the 15 days.

"I don't count welfare meat," she said, stroking Jean's curly head. Welfare meat and its kindred welfare beans and welfare rice are the names used for the Federal surplus items.

Each month she gets about 19 packages of food with a retail value of $17.50—eight pounds of meat, two pounds of peanut butter, 10 pounds of flour, five pounds of cheese, four pounds of butter and two pounds of lard. There is also rice, cereal, cornmeal and powdered milk. Next month a pound of powdered eggs will be added.

The investigator arranges for the check-like voucher for these staples. He also arranges for grants for such items as suits, overcoats and overshoes.

When the investigator visits he always checks on the receipts for rent and utilities. Many persons on relief fall behind on gas and electricity payments because the bills come bimonthly and they have failed to save for them.

"I don't owe nobody," Miss Matos said with pride.

The budgets worked out by the Welfare Department do not include such items as the 15 cents every couple of weeks for her son's milk and cookies at school, or the television set that takes the place of movies.

When the investigator works out the family budget he is guided by tables compiled by state home economists down to the last hairpin and bar of soap. Each family must be given a budget, although they do not have to follow it.

A welfare client must scrimp on the necessities for any luxuries. With Miss Matos, the luxury item is extra makeup.

"My face is something I don't fool around with," she said.

There is going to be an average 5 per cent increase to public assistance recipients on July 1. The other day, in the sudden darkness before a thundershower when her flat was looking its worst, Miss Matos was asked what she would do with $10 more in every check.

She surveyed the peeling paint, dirty wood floor, cheaply colored statues, pastel-print drapes, second-hand furniture—unrelieved drabness with the smell of poverty.

"Just look around," she said.

THE MINORITY POOR

Sargent Shriver

There is a substantial segment of the poor in this country who need not puzzle over the complicated economics of poverty. They are the minority group poor. For them the equations are simpler. They are hired last, paid less, and fired first. They work mainly in the low-pay occupations, and in those, get lower pay then their white counterparts. The Negro college graduate can expect to earn only as much income as the white worker who never went beyond the eighth grade; in comparable occupations, the white man can expect to earn almost 50 percent more in his lifetime than the Negro and the Puerto Rican, almost one-third more than the Spanish-speaking American.

Eight million Negroes—nearly half the total Negro population in the United States—are poor. A third of the Negro population lives in southern cities, one-fourth on southern farms, and the balance largely in the northern cities. In both the North and the

The Minority Poor: From The War on Poverty. A Compilation of Materials Prepared for the Select Subcommittee on Poverty of the Committee on Labor and Public Welfare, United States Senate, Sargent Shriver, 88th Congress, 2nd Session, March 1964, p. 38.

Sargent Shriver. Director of the Office of Economic Opportunity.

South the Negro faces the same problem: in relation to his white counterpart, he is falling further and further behind. During the fifties the average income of the Negro male improved substantially. For every dollar he earned in 1949, he earned $1.75 in 1959. But the white man running ahead of him ran a little faster. While the Negro was earning $1 in 1949, his white counterpart earned $1.90; in 1959, every time the Negro earned $1.75 the white man earned $3.20.

In 24 of the 26 States with large Negro populations, the Negro's share of per capita income fell; and in some of these States the gap between white and Negro income widened dramatically. In Michigan in 1949, when the equalizing effect of World War II was still being felt, the Negro earned 87 percent as much as the white. Ten years later he earned only 75 percent as much. In North Carolina his comparative earnings fell from 54 percent of his white counterpart's to 43 percent; in Tennessee, from 68 to 56 percent; in Arkansas, from 53 to 39 percent.

Nearly a million Puerto Ricans live in the United States today, primarily in Metropolitan New York City. Fifty-three percent of New York's Puerto Ricans earned less than $4,000 in 1959, only 8 percent earned more than $8,000. Three-quarters of them never entered high school. Moreover, the primary and junior high schools in Puerto Rican neighborhoods tend to be more crowded and less equipped than the average city school.

In the Southwestern United States live 3½ million Spanish-speaking Americans. Not only does the Spanish-American face the burdens of prejudice and inadequate education; like the Puerto Rican, he also faces a language barrier, and moreover a peculiar structure of laws, both Federal and local, which tend to isolate him even more from the opportunities of the community.

FAYETTE COUNTY: NEGRO FARMERS' EXPERIENCE WITH RURAL DEVELOPMENT

National Sharecroppers Fund

Fayette and Haywood Counties achieved national prominence in 1960 when 700 sharecroppers and tenant farmer families received eviction notices as the result of a voter-registration drive. Such economic reprisals have been widespread in the South and lend greater significance to Fayette County's experience.

Dr. C. G. Gomillion, Chairman of the Social Science Division at Tuskegee Institute, Alabama, chaired the panel. It included Fay Bennett, Executive Secretary of the National Sharecroppers Fund, Allen Yancey, Jr., President of the West Tennessee Development Company of Fayette County, Tennessee, and John H. Myhre, Operations Specialist of the Rural Electrification Administration.

The role of the Sharecroppers Fund, as a non-governmental private agency, in helping local development groups benefit from federal rural development programs, was explained by Miss Bennett.

The NSF was organized more than twenty-five years ago by such outstanding leaders as Mrs. Franklin D. Roosevelt and Dr. Frank P. Graham, when Southern sharecroppers were fighting to receive their fair share of New Deal benefits. Then, too, the "boss-man" —plantation owner or large farmer—was receiving his federal subsidy, or "plow-up money" that Dr. Jones mentioned, and the NSF worked to assure that low-income farmers were not left out. Our current program, in addition to our concern for migratory farm workers, many of whom are former sharecroppers, is to help those farm families that need help most, to share in federal pro-

Fayette County: Negro Farmers' Experience with Rural Development: From National Sharecroppers Fund Southern Rural Conference, *A Better Life for Farm Families* (New York: National Sharecroppers Fund, 1962), pp. 20–24.

grams designed to aid them. We are working to make these domestic "Point Four" programs a reality.

The work that Allen Yancey has done in Fayette County is an example of what can be done by working quietly and consistently, according to Miss Bennett. After national attention was focused on the sharecropper evictions there, NSF went to work on a long-range project to provide economic security as a basis for future social progress.

Mr. Yancey then described the situation that led to the evictions. "There were no Negro lawyers or doctors in Fayette County. There were 28 one-teacher schools. The white leadership sought to keep the county's 20,000 Negroes (of a total population of 30,000) living in poverty and without political power, and economic pressure was forcing many residents to seek work in the cities. We younger people felt that a voter registration drive was the only way in which we could make progress toward a better life." "But," Mr. Yancey explained, "our efforts met strong resistance from white county officials, and the slowness of the Justice Department to act in upholding our rights led to the mass evictions of January, 1961. [Eventually the Justice Department won a court case proving that the evictions resulted from the voter registration drive and were not simply caused by mechanization of the farms.] With hundreds of people living in surplus army tents, many unions and church groups responded with material emergency aid, and finally a federal injunction halted further evictions."

The NSF program in Fayette County began in June, 1961, when a meeting was arranged with John A. Baker in the Department of Agriculture to discuss how existing federal programs such as FHA [Farmers Home Administration] loans, and new ones such as the recently enacted ARA [Area Redevelopment Act] could benefit poor farm families in areas like Fayette County, Mr. Yancey reported.

"Following this meeting, I became NSF's Tennessee representative to work on a pilot project in my area. Our plan was to determine whether the programs could be made to work in the area, and, if so, to broaden NSF assistance to other needy counties of the rural South."

Mr. Yancey then listed the steps taken in the Fayette County project, stressing that they suggest a plan that other local groups can follow if they adapt it to their own circumstances.

1. The first and immediate problem faced was the county welfare officials' withdrawal of federal surplus food distribution from needy families. After several fruitless meetings with these officials, Mr. Yancey became convinced that the food distribution had been halted because of the voter registration drive. He protested directly to Secretary of Agriculture Freeman, and NSF and other groups backed his demand that the federal government distribute the food on an emergency basis. The protest was heeded, and federal officials were sent to Fayette and Haywood counties to handle distribution. More than 4,000 needy families have received this food to date. Further protests to the government on its hiring practices resulted in employment of Negroes in both clerical and manual jobs associated with the food distribution.

2. Mr. Yancey spoke to many church, civic, and student groups in the area, informing them about government loans for farming and education and welfare aid. He then helped residents to prepare applications for student loans, Aid to Dependent Children programs, and the various FHA programs. He followed up applications that had been denied, kept records, and was instrumental in having many applications approved.

3. Evidence was gathered showing that applications from Negroes were not receiving equal consideration by the local FHA office. This information was sent to Washington and resulted in an investigation of the local office. A special registrar was sent to Haywood County. In one week he accepted more than 100 FHA loan applications from Negro farmers who previously had been discouraged from going to the local FHA office.

4. In July, 1961, NSF asked the ARA [Area Redevelopment Administration] to declare both Fayette and Haywood counties eligible for ARA assistance as depressed rural areas. Fayette County was one of the first counties so designated under the new rural development program and became eligible to apply for industrial loans, retraining projects, and public works grants.

5. Mr. Yancey immediately approached white leaders in Fayette County to urge that they work together to take advantage of this new program for the benefit of all the county's residents. Mr. Yancey related that he told the county judge:

> I want to be a good citizen of Fayette County. Instead of fighting we should sit down and work together to develop new jobs and make the

area prosperous. We want to establish a bi-racial committee to administer this new program, but if the white leadership won't cooperate, we shall go ahead on our own.

6. After several more meetings (held outside the county), the white leaders agreed to establish a nine-man ARA committee composed of four Negroes, four whites, and a chairman, who would be voteless, to be elected from either race. There was then a three-month wait, but still no meeting of this proposed ARA committee was held.

7. When it became clear that the white leadership was not willing to work with Mr. Yancey and his group, NSF asked for a meeting between members of the Yancey group and ARA officials in Washington. A bi-racial group from the county met with federal officials in Washington in early November, 1961. They asked that they be recognized as a "can do" local ARA committee since the white leadership, which included all county and town officials, didn't seem interested in rural development. As a first step, they asked for technical assistance in surveying their assets and needs and in determining which industries would be most suitable to establish in Fayette County with ARA financial assistance.

As a result of the meeting, RAD [Rural Area Development] agencies were instructed to cooperate with the group, and the Rural Electrification Administration was delegated responsibility for giving the group technical aid.

8. "A few days after we returned to Fayette, the county judge announced the appointment of an all-white ARA committee. He had been granted authority to do this, according to routine practice, by the governor of Tennessee. Naturally we felt very discouraged, but nevertheless we put in a formal request for technical aid."

9. The first representatives of REA were sent to Fayette in February, 1962, for preliminary meetings with the local REA borrowers and the "official" white ARA Committee.

10. "In April, REA sent its Operations Specialist, John Myhre, to meet with us. We discussed the economic situation of our area and all the problems facing us. After returning to Washington and giving the problems full study, Mr. Myhre recommended that a metal-plating plant would be ideally suited for the area and contacted a plating company in Memphis which was planning an

expansion of its operations. He also recommended that we incorporate our local committee."

Thus when one local committee (the all-white one, appointed by the county judge) failed to take any action, federal agencies were able to cooperate with a locally constituted committee which was acting.

11. In May, the West Tennessee Development Company was incorporated and began work with Mr. Myhre on the loan application for the plating plant. At the same time, ARA recognized the all-white local committee with the understanding that it would approve any loan applications which were prepared with federal technical assistance.

12. The loan application was completed in August and quickly approved by both local and state ARA committees. It arrived in Washington in September and has received preliminary approval. The proposal asks for a $350,000 ARA industrial loan to construct and equip a metal-plating plant that will provide jobs for 200 full-time workers within its first year of operation. The West Tennessee Development Company is now raising the $55,000 of local financing (10 percent of the total investment) required by the ARA, and the remainder will be invested by the plating company. The local group is raising these funds by selling interest-bearing shares at $5.00 each. The plating company will eventually repay this $55,000, with interest, to the Development Company.

In conclusion, Mr. Yancey said that many federal programs appear very good on paper, but their local impact varies widely. "By showing the obstacles we have had to overcome in Fayette County, however, I hope I have demonstrated what can be done by local groups, the federal government, and private organizations working together."

THE AMERICAN INDIAN, DISPOSSESSED AND ABANDONED

Editorial, The Christian Century

His average annual income is one-half the amount which has been determined to be the general poverty level for the poor in the United States. He can expect to live to age 42. His segregation from the rest of society makes the Negro's degree of acceptance look good. The level of unemployment among his people is seven or eight times that of his nation's average unemployment. He suffers more from poor health, malnutrition and ignorance than does any other ethnic group in his country. Who is he? Any American school child should know that the American Indian and only the American Indian answers to that description. Conquered, dispossessed, exploited, abandoned, the American Indian confronts the nation as its primary challenge. When President Johnson first addressed himself to the problem of poverty in the United States he promised that the Indian's poverty would have the nation's first attention. Speaking to 400 Indian delegates to the American Indian capital conference on poverty at the Washington Cathedral (Episcopal), Senator Hubert H. Humphrey (D., Minn.) said that President Johnson would keep his promise and would use the 400,000 Indians of the nation in a pilot test to demonstrate "how the war on poverty can be won." Here the war on poverty should begin— among the group in American life most victimized by poverty. The nation can never pay its full debt to the Indians. It can for their sake and for its sake redress some of the injustices the white man has heaped upon the first American.

The American Indian, Dispossessed and Abandoned: From editorial, "Help the Neediest First," *The Christian Century*, May 27, 1964, p. 693.

The Ill and the Elderly

Edmund MacIntosh: How to Be 74 on $50 a Month

Edmund MacIntosh had been depending on the theory that hard-boiled eggs and opened cans of meat need no refrigeration. And he was sick.

He had also depended on the theory that if you work hard, live frugally and mind your own business you will get by without help. And now he was 74 years old and needed help.

MacIntosh, to use a descriptive but not a real name, depended on hard-boiled eggs because his Los Angeles hotel room has no refrigerator, and he cannot afford to eat out. He is trying to live on his $50-a-month Social Security check. Room rent is $38.50 a month, which provides a room with clean linen every two weeks and clean towels every day. The remainder goes for food and chewing tobacco. Every week friends on the same floor do his shopping for him: two dozen eggs, seven small cans of V-8 juice, two cans of meat, a carton of dry cereal and his tobacco. He boils the eggs at once and eats them morning and evening. He stretches a can of meat for three days or so. He has just discovered that hard-boiled eggs and canned meat need refrigeration in warm weather.

MacIntosh has a solid, dignified manner, even as he lies on his bed, propped on an elbow, his square-jawed face ashen. He looks vital, but he has dizzy spells, and so fears to walk outside. "I'm afraid I'll fall down, and the cops will think I'm a wino. That happened to a friend of mine, and when I couldn't find twenty-one dollars bail money for him he got thirty days."

His response to the present problem is one of hurt rather than anger. He was always able to earn money. He finished high school in North Carolina and two years in a military institute. He was in the Navy in World War I, married a Georgia girl, had a daughter and after the war bought a newsstand on Times Square in New York and made $2,500 a year. When the depression ended that, he worked in a Baltimore hospital, then in the late 1930's got back to newspaper distribution in Washington at $3,000 a year. He joined the Navy the day after Pearl Harbor and was on a troop transport

Edmund MacIntosh: "How to Be 74 on $50 a Month": From "The Invisible Americans," Ben Bagdikian, *Saturday Evening Post,* December 21–28, 1963, p. 37.

Ben Bagdikian. Staff writer, *Saturday Evening Post;* author of *Poverty in the Midst of Plenty.*

at Midway when he got the letter saying his wife was getting a divorce.

After the war he became a watchman at a California air base for $38 a week with free room; then a railroad guard at $80 a week, until 1954, when the railroad began laying off men.

Then he came to Los Angeles—"because it's warmer here, and that helps"—and began doing a variety of odd jobs. He had a regular clientele for lawn cutting until automation reached him in its own way. "People began getting those power mowers. That was the end of me."

He had known he was eligible for Social Security but let it pile up. When the power mowers took over, he collected an accumulated $1,250 and began his $50 a month. He bought a suit of clothes and prepared for the rest of his days. But it became apparent $50 a month would not care for the rest of his days. He sold his TV set when he was economizing. But this only brought $15.50. He is down to $250 of his nest egg and needs medical care for his stomach, his dizziness, his failing eyesight. And he needs something to help through his loneliness. "I got a letter a year ago. It was from the bank telling me how much I had left."

Edmund MacIntosh is one of eight million Americans who form the aged poor. He lives, or tries to, on $600 a year. There are 1.5 million lone individuals who live on less, tucked away in the cheapest rooming houses. Millions of others live in poverty as couples. These are the lonely old people known mostly to welfare workers, to postmen delivering the Social Security checks on the first of the month, and to the firemen who carry the elderly outdoors when an alarm flushes them out of the geriatric warrens.

When Edmund MacIntosh was a boy, there were fewer than four million Americans over 65. Today there are more than 16 million. In 1920 more than 30 percent of the aged were working, today only 20 percent work. Science is keeping them alive longer but it is taking away their jobs, making them obsolete.

MacIntosh did nothing wrong in planning for his old age, but his plans were not good enough. And now he needs help.

"What I need most is medical attention. I need a suit of clothes. I'd like to go to church. I'd love to go to a picture show. And if I had some good company, I guess that would be pretty good."

PSYCHIATRISTS AND THE POOR

Robert Coles

Psychiatrists have to know a lot about what their patients are thinking and about what they themselves are thinking. In the United States they are called in consultation on so many problems that one would suppose they know a good deal more than they sometimes do. The demands upon them are enormous, and some of them inappropriate. Unlike the work of their friends in many other fields, their work is still to be satisfactorily defined, and information badly needed by others from them is sometimes simply not to be had at all.

Psychiatrists should not be particularly blamed for their predominantly middle-class clientele or for their increasing concern with the certification of their position in medical centers and wealthy suburbs. Although some people think of them as gods, there is ample proof to the contrary. Psychiatrists are all clearly human, and in America clearly doctors. Whatever general criticism can be made of them is also applicable to others in American professional life. Lawyers are now beginning to see how hard it is for the poor to obtain "equal protection under the law," and for the first time our highest courts are prodding them in this regard. Educators are troubled by their failure to reach millions of potentially educable, even gifted children. The fact that money purchases the best medical care and that the want of it frequently consigns one to the worst is a fact of life throughout the nation. When psychiatric goods and services follow similar patterns of distribution, they are simply conforming to the way our society is set up.

Psychiatrists and the Poor: From "Psychiatrists and the Poor," Robert Coles, *Atlantic,* Vol. 214, No. 1 (July, 1964), pp. 103–06.

Robert Coles, M.D. Child psychiatrist; consultant, Southern Regional Council; research psychiatrist, Harvard University Health Services.

There have been important advances in what is now called social psychiatry. Before the term came into popular professional use, Anna Freud had done her moving and courageous work with English children under the Nazi blitz, establishing the practical value of psychoanalytic advice in a serious social crisis. In America a few bold spirits were intent on finding out how our isolated and rejected Indians survived individually, with their separate culture. In the thirties, Sol Ginsberg, a compassionate New York psychiatrist, studied the reactions of the unemployed to their grim and unnerving lot; and years before the 1954 Supreme Court decision, Erik Erikson had described the effects of segregation on the Negroes in America.

These pioneering efforts were followed by three major studies which stand out as landmarks: the Yale study by A. Hollingshead and F. C. Redlich of the relationship between social class and mental illness, and the two studies which have come from the social psychiatry unit of the Cornell Medical School—the Stirling County Study of Psychiatric Disorder and Sociocultural Environment and the Midtown Manhattan Study, whose findings were published in book form under the title *Mental Health in the Metropolis*. These carefully documented researches have all been concerned with the relationship of class—social and economic background—to mental illness, and with the incidence of mental illness in cities and towns. What we learn from these reports is revealing about psychiatrists, their patients, and our society. There is, in fact, a self-scrutiny, an honest self-appraisal in these investigations which represents the very best tradition of scholarly research.

The Yale study, published under the title *Social Class and Mental Illness,* concerns itself with the relationship between social class and both psychiatric symptoms and care, and is a sociological and psychiatric study of New Haven. It was done with scrupulous concern for statistical validity. The class structure of the city was analyzed and described. The patterns of mental illness and its treatment are shown. The book reveals that poor people tend to have a higher incidence of diagnosed psychoses, the most serious form of mental disease, and also receive radically different forms of medical and psychiatric care for their difficulties. Whereas the wealthy and the well-to-do are more likely to be treated with individual psychotherapy, purchased privately or secured at clinics which largely provide for the middle classes, the poor are usually sent to hospitals and, once there, receive the less humane treatment of electric shock or drugs.

The authors of the Yale study are not content merely to emphasize these cold-blooded facts and the influence of money on psychiatric diagnoses and treatment. They examine the interesting relationship of the psychiatrist, as a middle-class citizen, to the large number of poor patients he may be called to see and subsequently—persuaded by forces in his own life—reject or diagnose in ways reflecting more about his life than their illness. These two social scientists, Dr. Hollingshead and Dr. Redlich, have the courage and honesty to face directly the serious differences between psychiatry and the rest of medicine. An infection is an infection, and rich or poor respond to the same dosage of penicillin. Mental illness is not so easy to treat, and the psychiatrist cannot depend upon pills, vaccines, or intravenous solutions, all nicely free of biases of personality and prejudices of class.

In a sense, most of the findings of the Yale study confirm the difficult problems of psychiatry as a profession under heavy demands in American life. The calls for it are everywhere; the respect for its capabilities is sometimes even too generous. The hopes for its future ability to cure mental illness and even change future generations through its understanding of child behavior and growth are certainly high. Yet, as Redlich and Hollingshead point out at the end of their book, there are too few good therapists, meeting all too many patients; the poor, the culturally or socially exiled, are frequently hard for many psychiatrists to understand, hence suitably treat; large numbers of patients therefore find their way to those sad and sometimes outrageous back wards of state institutions. Or they may run the risk of inadequate evaluation and hasty, basically faulty treatment. Such are the troubles with which the poor and their society, including its psychiatrists, must cope.

The apathy of the poor needs no psychiatric study for its proof, nor do their widespread dependency, their common lack of tidiness, thrift, and respect for the legal and moral codes embraced by their "betters." What is needed, the Yale investigators emphasize, is careful studies of incidence, of prevalence of disease in communities, of attempted correlation of such occurrence with as large a number of environmental facts as possible. The more we know of the external forces involved in mental illness, the more we understand the obviously complex connection between individual and social pathology.

The Cornell unit in social psychiatry has taken up where its brother group in New Haven suggested the need was greatest. Its work is both extensive and impressive. Its intention, exemplified by such studies as the Yorkville one in Manhattan and the Stirling County one in Nova Scotia, has been to find out how many people actually are mentally ill in a large city, or a small town, or a village, and who those people are, by race, religion, occupation, education, marital status, and a host of significant social and economic variables.

One of their crucial findings ties in all too neatly with the Yale study: social disorganization is associated with a significantly higher incidence of mental illness. And, in any case, the incidence of mental illness may well be higher than the statistics indicate. Among the poor it frequently goes unrecorded or unrecognized. Indeed, the gist of the Cornell studies is that psychiatric symptoms bear substantial relationship to various social, cultural, and economic conditions. Worse, among large numbers of poor these symptoms abound and tend to be handed down to children as a kind of grim social inheritance, making it harder and harder for each generation to escape the bondage rising out of the hopelessness and shallowness of life in the rural or city slum.

What these statistics and research studies with their abstractions tell us, all too many testify to in their daily lives—lives hobbled with joblessness, with uselessness, with arbitrary unkindness or contempt at the hands of others. Millions in such straits know constant mental hurt, emotional suffering, despair of the soul without any possibility of help. Their troubles are both real and imaginary—hunger breeds suspicion, hate breeds fear and retaliatory hate—and relief for both kinds of troubles is often inadequate. It is an ironic sorrow for many well-intentioned people in the social sciences that they know these facts and are unable to do much to correct them.

The irony revealed by both the Yale and Cornell studies is that psychiatrists are frequently out of touch with the conditions which help create their potentially sickest patients. The incidence of paranoid schizophrenia among Negroes is high, probably an example of social reality kindling medical ruin. How many Negroes in the South can go to strictly segregated psychiatric facilities and feel secure and wanted enough to discuss their innermost thoughts and fears? We talk about segregation, by custom, law, or fact; we easily denounce it. A state of affairs which renders a mentally disturbed

Negro, wherever he lives, unable to seek or secure competent medical and psychiatric care is a personal tragedy, not an abstract injustice, for millions of individuals—and not the least for the doctors concerned.

I have seen some segregated Negro "state hospitals" in the South, and all too many seriously disturbed Negro children, youths, and adults in Northern cities. The mother of one of the Negro children who is pioneering desegregation in his state had received the care of that state's mental hospital system. Curious, I went there for a visit. She had called the place "that hell." I found her description a bit subdued. The real hell for anyone, especially when troubled, is loneliness. It is hellish to be mentally ill, additionally so to be confined and largely ignored, particularly at the hands of white officials who have little respect for one's basic human dignity. "Maybe I could talk with *some* white doctors; I'm not saying I can't," the mother said, "but I sometimes wonder—and anyway, even if I could, they never have wanted to talk with me." She suffered from periodic depressions, crippling while they lasted. She could be reached, be helped, at least in theory. Her name is indeed legion, just as the Cornell social scientists suggested when they gave one of their books the title *My Name Is Legion*.

Those pockets of poverty whose existence is increasingly acknowledged are also pockets of many kinds of psychopathology, mostly untreated. In some instances—with migratory farm workers, Indians, and many of the Appalachian whites—the people are not merely poor, not only beyond the reach or even ken of medical or psychiatric attention, but are really striking examples of what social scientists call "subcultures." They mean by such a term groups of people living significantly apart from the rest of us in habits, customs, and beliefs, so that even though we speak a common language, even though we share a national history and citizenship with them and need the same goods and services, they see a different world or have different assumptions about our world.

Such people may confuse, then alarm, and finally anger us, doctors included. Their experience has not been ours. We are provoked by their laziness or various forms of easy living. They, in turn, are at a loss to understand, given what is possible for them, what we would have them do. "I tried," a white hillbilly told me, and he repeated the words, "I tried to get a job for a long time here, and then I even went up to Chicago, but there wasn't anything to do, and so we figured we'd rather die here where our kin come from."

There was no question in my mind that two of his children needed the help of a child psychiatrist. One was irritable, still wet the bed at ten, was much too mean to herself (picking at her scalp) and to her all too many brothers and sisters as well. Another child, a boy of twelve, was deeply, deadly silent and had been so for a long time. Regional sentimentality aside, it is a hard life the poor live anywhere, and one filled with high risks for diseases of the body and mind. This is so in Appalachia, in spite of those lovely pictures of quaint rural pathways along fetching hills whose inhabitants, always smiling, sing their specially pure ballads and appear to be our last nostalgic contact with our pioneer ancestors.

What do they do, these millions of our poor? What happens to their neuroses and psychoses? They live with them and die with them or of them. In cities, violence, vagrancy, alcoholism, addiction, apathy, high suicide rates, high murder rates, high delinquency rates bespeak the hopelessness which becomes depression, the doubts which become paranoia, the confusions which become addiction, the frantic attempt to make sense of a senseless world which becomes drunkenness or sudden irrational ferocity. In rural areas, on farms or reservations, the same human scene can be found: retarded children, epileptic children kept, and their limitations accepted, not as possible challenges to be overcome, but as the grim reminders of an all-too-familiar fate; disgruntled, liquored parents venting their frustrations and discouragement in angry feuds and spells of silence or inaction which in many of us would warrant immediate hospitalization.

The solutions to some of these problems will come in part with the recognition of them, followed by laws which authorize more money and more trained personnel to deal with them. As for the problem of the limited relationship between psychiatrists and some of the neediest of our mentally ill, the Yale and Cornell studies emphasize the necessity to look closely at the training of psychiatrists and those in associated professions. They suggest changes in training programs, a fresh look at how to get more suitably trained and better motivated recruits.

• • •

Yet, even with more planning and some new professional flexibility from social scientists, there will remain serious problems for both the poor and our American psychiatrists. Psychiatrists cannot solve many difficulties really created by unfair social and economic conditions, and they had better know that. . . .

The public must become more informed about just what psychiatrists can and what they cannot do. The flashy, the glib, the dogmatic, and sometimes even the absurd and commercial have plagued and tarnished some areas of American psychiatry, as they have touched American life generally, fulfilling Freud's premonition of just such a possibility. For the most part, American psychiatrists are dedicated, serious, and socially concerned citizens. If, like others, they have not freed themselves of all of the contaminants supplied by their culture, they have at least been willing to examine their own limitations while learning facts that are hard to live with, or, for that matter, live by.

The poor neither know about us nor can they afford our expensive care. And often we do not know about the poor and seem little concerned about getting to know them. These are the facts, plain to see but not so easy to change. Nevertheless, the medical profession and its several specialties will have to serve the large numbers who neeed them most and can afford them least. To do this will require effort in changing curricula and effort in living up to the old but sometimes forgotten ideals of what a doctor should be. The Yale study is even more explicit: doctors largely come with middle-class views when they approach the poor and usually have little interest in going beyond those views, many of them unsympathetic or outright antagonistic to lower-class people and their kind of living. I have seen many bright young men and women who will never get to college, let alone medical school, because of who they are and their environmental handicaps.

Some of them might become doctors and psychiatrists if they could get financial assistance and continue their education. And then they might help their own people and their profession to achieve an urgently needed mutual understanding.

PHYSICAL AND MENTAL ILLNESS
AND THE MEDICAL CARE
OF THE POOR

Dwight Macdonald

The poor are . . . different in a physical sense: they are much less healthy. According to "Poverty and Deprivation," the proportion of those "disabled or limited in their major activity by chronic ill health" rises sharply as income sinks. In reasonably well-off families ($7,000 and up), 4.3 percent are so disabled; in reasonably poor families ($2,000 to $3,999), the proportion doubles, to 8 percent; and in unreasonably poor families (under $2000), it doubles again, to 16.5 percent. An obvious cause, among others, for the very poor being four times as much disabled by "chronic ill health" as the well-to-do is that they have much less money to spend for medical care—in fact, almost nothing. This weighs with special heaviness on the aged poor. During the fifties, Mr. Harrington notes, "all costs on the Consumer Price Index went up by 12 percent. But medical costs, that terrible staple of the aged, went up by 36 percent, hospitalization rose by 65 percent, and group hospitalization costs (Blue Cross premiums) were up by 83 percent."

This last figure is particularly interesting, since Blue Cross and such plans are the A.M.A.'s alternative to socialized medicine, or, rather, to the timid fumblings toward it that even our most liberal politicians have dared to propose. Such figures throw an unpleasant light on the Senate's rejection of Medicare. The defeat was all the more bitter because, in the usual effort to appease the conservatives (with the usual lack of success—only five Republicans and only

Physical and Mental Illness and the Medical Care of the Poor: From *Our Invisible Poor*, Dwight Macdonald (New York: Sidney Hillman Foundation, 1963), pp. 11–18.

Dwight Macdonald. Essayist and staff writer, *The New Yorker*.

four Southern Democrats voted pro), the bill was watered down in advance. Not until he had spent $90 of his own money—which is 10 percent of the annual income of some 3,000,000 aged poor—would a patient have been eligible. And the original program included only people already covered by Social Security or Railroad Retirement pensions and excluded the neediest of all—the 2,500,000 aged poor who are left out of both these systems.

Mental as well as physical illneess is much greater among the poor, even though our complacent cliché is that nervous breakdowns are a prerogative of the rich because the poor "can't afford them." (They can't, but they have them anyway.) This bit of middle-class folklore should be laid to rest by a study made in New Haven: "Social Class and Mental Illness," by August B. Hollingshead and Frederick C. Redlich (Wiley). They found that the rate of "treated psychiatric illness" is about the same from the rich down through decently paid workers—an average of 573 per 100,000. But in the bottom fifth it shoots up to 1,659 per 100,000. There is an even more striking difference in the *kind* of mental illness. Of those in the four top income groups who had undergone psychiatric treatment, 65 percent had been treated for neurotic problems and 35 percent for psychotic disturbances. In the bottom fifth, the treated illnesses were almost all psychotic (90 percent). This shows there is something to the notion that the poor "can't afford" nervous breakdowns—the milder kind, that is—since the reason the proportion of *treated* neuroses among the poor is only 10 percent is that a neurotic can keep going, after a fashion. But the argument cuts deeper the other way. The poor go to a psychiatrist (or, more commonly, are committed to a mental institution) only when they are completely unable to function because of psychotic symptoms. Therefore, even that nearly threefold increase in mental disorders among the poor is probably an underestimate.

·   ·   ·

And this is not the end of tribulation. The poor, who can least afford to lose pay because of ill health, lose the most. A National Health Survey, made a few years ago, found that workers earning under $2,000 a year had twice as many "restricted-activity days" as those earning over $4,000.

Although they are the most in need of hospital insurance, the poor have the least, since they can't afford the premiums; only 40 percent of poor families have it, as against 63 percent of all families. (It should be noted, however, that the poor who are war veterans can get free treatment, at government expense, in Veterans Administration Hospitals.)

HEALTH CARE PROBLEMS
OF OLDER AMERICANS

President's Council on Aging

Millions of older Americans enjoy relatively good health and many of them can be almost as active as they were when they were years younger. Many of those with disabilities have learned to live with them and accept their limitations.

But, most have become the prey of at least one disease that will stick with them as long as they live. It is part of the toll the years have taken. It is grim evidence that the causes and cures are still to be found for the diseases that come with age.

And it is dramatic proof of the health-care problem faced by older Americans who are caught between rising medical and hospital costs and their low, relatively fixed incomes.

Statistically, here is the health report of today's older Americans:

More than 12 million have at least one chronic condition such as high blood pressure, arthritis, diabetes, heart disease, or mental disorder.

More than half of those with a chronic ailment have some limitation on their activities.

More than 800,000 older people are in institutions.

About 1,250,000 elderly people are invalids who, though not in institutions, are unable to get along without help from others.

Tragically, many of those with serious conditions would be in

---

Health Care Problems of Older Americans: From *The Older American* (Washington, D.C.: President's Council on Aging, first annual report, May, 1963), pp. 12–19.

better health if known preventive and restorative services had been promptly used. Until more is known about the causes and cures of chronic diseases, the most potent weapon against them is early detection and prompt treatment.

Part of the problem lies with the older people themselves. They delay going to a physician until it is too late. This is obvious from one of the studies of the National Health Survey which showed one out of four people 65 or over had not been to a physician for 2 years or more.

Sole responsibility, however, cannot be placed on the older people for this. They have not been made fully aware of the need for regular medical checkups, the dangers of self-doctoring, or the methods of accident prevention.

Many older Americans do not get the care they need because they are too proud to accept charity or other outside financial help. And they do not want to be a burden on their families.

Many make the mistake of treating themselves when they really need to see a doctor. Others use medications which have worked on similar symptoms in neighbors or friends. They want to avoid the cost, or they may be afraid of treatment and hospitals.

Others are the victims of poor nutrition because they are caught by food fads, poor food habits, or lack of interest in eating, primarily because they have to eat alone.

Accidents—many of them preventable—also take a high toll among older people. They have nearly twice as many home accidents as the average adult and three times as many fatal accidents.

Part of the fault for the poor health of many of the aged also must be borne by physicians, communities, States, and the Federal Government, which have been slow in starting health programs for them.

·   ·   ·

But, many of the nearly 18 million older Americans find it difficult, if not impossible, to pay the price for the care that is available. As shown by the picture drawn earlier of the income status of the aged, they cannot afford to be ill for very long.

Added to this, they are much more likely to need care than the younger generations:

The average older person is incapacitated 5 weeks of the year by illness or injury, with 2 of these weeks spent in bed.

One out of every 6 older Americans will go into a hospital during a year.

The average hospital stay for an older person is 2 weeks, twice as long as for the average younger person.

And his hospital bill will be twice as large.

Thus, the Older American—because he is more likely to need medical care—will have to spend more to stay healthy. In 1961, for example, the average medical care expenses for an older person was $226, compared with $103 for a younger person.

• • •

How do older Americans now pay their medical bills when they are ill?

Many are able to manage on their own, especially if they have insurance against some costs. Some seek help from others—relatives if there are any and public assistance if relatives cannot help. Some get free care under other public programs and through private charity. Some borrow money.

And there are many who do not get the care they need. The extent to which they go without care is unknown. But a strong hint of it is found in these facts: Nearly half the older Americans with arthritis, rheumatism, hernias, or who have trouble seeing or hearing are not now under care. And one out of seven with a heart condition is going without medical attention.

Most of the aged when they do go into hospitals pay at least some of their bills out of income or savings. But a high percentage are unable to pay them all either with their own resources or through health insurance.

For example: A 1957 survey of aged people drawing social security showed that, of those who went into a general hospital during that year, two out of five of the couples and three out of five of the nonmarried people did not meet all their medical bills from their own income, assets, and health insurance.

Thus, we have a serious gap between the care most older people need and their ability to pay for the care—either through health insurance or from income or savings.

One deceptive feature of the health-care picture is the degree to which private health plans cover costs. While more than half of the aged have such coverage, much of this insurance is very limited.

A study of the health problems of the Older American made recently estimated their health insurance does not meet more than one-sixth of total medical costs of the insured or one-fourteenth of the total for all the aged.

Another study of older people discharged after a short stay in hospitals from July 1958 through June 1960 showed that health insurance covered:

No part of the bill in over half the cases.

Seventy-five percent or more of the bill in only 3 out of 10 cases.

The main reason coverage is not more complete relates directly to the income of most older Americans. The plain fact is they cannot afford the premiums for comprehensive private health plans.

For broad health insurance coverage for a couple, the premiums even on a nonprofit basis are about $400 a year—one-sixth of the total income of an average couple.

THE AGED

Sargent Shriver

Living in the United States are 6.8 million heads of families who are over 65. Half of them have incomes of less than $3,000 a year, and half of these support their families on less than $1,000 a year.

Many of the aged are ending in poverty because they began in poverty. Their income throughout their working lives was never sufficient to provide that margin of savings which affords independence and dignity after retirement.

The majority of all the aged are covered by social security. But nearly two-thirds of the poorest aged—those living alone and earning less than $1,000 a year—are not covered by social security.

The great medical advances which continually discover new

The Aged: From *The War on Poverty, A Compilation of Materials Prepared for the Select Subcommittee on Poverty of the Committee on Labor and Public Welfare, United States Senate,* by Sargent Shriver, 88th Congress, 2nd Session, March 1964, pp. 39–40.

ways to prolong life have assured a steady growth in the number of aged persons in our society, and accordingly a growth in the problems of the aged. During the last 15 years the number of aged heads of families increased 37 percent. It is estimated that by 1980 there will be 9 million persons over 75 in this country and if the present pattern is allowed to continue, many millions of them will be living in stark poverty.

INCOME OF THE AGED

Lenore Epstein

Among the richest persons in the United States, a few aged men and women are, of course, included. Yet families headed by a person aged 65 or over make up one-third of all families counted as poor in the 1964 *Annual Report of the Council of Economic Advisers*—a proportion much higher than the 1-in-7 frequency of aged families in the population. And the aged account for an even larger proportion of the adults living alone who are considered poor.

The incidence of poverty among the aged would be immeasurably higher and its severity much greater were it not for old-age, survivors, and disability insurance (OASDI). Under this program, payments were made to 70 percent of the 17½ million persons aged 65 and over at the end of 1962—four-fifths of the aged couples and more than three-fifths of all other persons aged 65 or older.

Despite the large number of aged persons who now can count on OASDI benefits, many still live on very low incomes. The non-married—the widowed, the divorced, the separated, and the never married—together make up about half the population aged 65 and over. Their median income was $1,130 for the year 1962. For the

Income of the Aged: From "Income of the Aged in 1962: First Findings of the 1963 Survey of Aged," Lenore Epstein, *Social Security Bulletin,* Vol. 27, No. 3, (March, 1964), pp. 3–23.

married, who tend to be younger, the median income was $2,875. Almost 3 in every 10 couples had less than $2,000.

Aged persons who work are, of course, likely to have more income than those who do not. Hence, among the nonmarried aged, who only rarely are in the labor force, those drawing OASDI benefits had the higher income. By contrast, among the married couples, who often had substantial earnings if they were not on the beneficiary rolls, it was the nonbeneficiaries who had higher median income.

Benefits under OASDI were practically the sole source of cash income for almost one-fifth of the couples and for more than one-third of the nonmarried beneficiaries who had been entitled to benefits for a year or more.

Public assistance was important as a supplementary source of cash for 1 in 12 of the married couples and 1 in 6 of the nonmarried aged. The proportion receiving cash assistance payments was almost three times as large for nonbeneficiaries as for those on the OASDI rolls.

Nonbeneficiaries past age 65 are a particularly diverse group. At one extreme are persons with full-time employment throughout the year—37 percent of the married men and 13 percent of the nonmarried men—many of whom earn as much as or more than they had when they were younger. At the other extreme are persons totally dependent on relatives, public assistance, or care in a public institution. They tend to be older than beneficiaries, whereas those with full-time employment tend to be younger.

Although the great majority of the aged are at least partially retired, earnings still account for a sizable share of the income of the total aged population. In 1962, earnings accounted for 32 percent of the aggregate money income of all persons aged 65 and over and their spouses. Benefits under OASDI ran a close second to earnings as a proportion of their aggregate money income. Benefits from public and private retirement programs combined represented two-fifths of aggregate income. The aged received 15 percent of their income from interest, dividends, and rents. Public assistance and veterans' compensation accounted for the smallest proportion (5 percent and 4 percent, respectively).

* * *

Today's problems are clear: Even with four-fifths of the aged now eligible for an OASDI benefit, a considerable number have income insufficient for their needs. But many concerned with programs to lighten the financial burden of old age will seek out the implications of these new data for the aged in the years ahead.

• • •

It is known that a growing proportion of the aged will be eligible for OASDI benefits. As the proportion of all those aged 65 and over who are eligible for benefits approaches 90 percent—as it will by 1975—there will be fewer with cash incomes as pitifully small as those reported in 1962 by most nonbeneficiaries aged 73 and over. And fewer should need public assistance—unless it is to meet medical needs.

If, on the other hand, the labor-force participation rate for aged men continues downward, there may be relatively fewer past age 65 who do as well as the nonbeneficiary couples and nonmarried men aged 65–72 did in 1962. Although some of them received retirement benefits under other programs, the great majority were at work. Today OASDI benefits represent only about 30 percent of average factory earnings—less for the higher-paid worker and more for the worker in a lower-paid job.

Coverage of private pension plans has grown sharply during the past 10–15 years. Aged persons with private pensions in addition to OASDI benefits make out comparatively well. Their numbers are still small, however, in relation to the size of the aged population. Even 10 or 15 years from now it is expected that no more than 25–30 percent of the aged will be drawing income from a private pension.

Average OASDI benefits will continue to increase—slowly under present legislation—because of rising earnings levels. In addition, as a progressively larger proportion of women become eligible for benefits on their own work record, married couples and nonmarried women alike should enjoy some improvement in income position.

In considering adequacy of benefits, thought must be given to the reduced amounts for which many beneficiaries will settle. One may well wonder whether a provision intended to ease the way for workers forced out of the labor force prematurely may not be creating a new group of poor—people who will have many years with little income but a benefit, and that a small one.

There seems little doubt that OASDI will remain the major source of retirement income. The level of protection afforded by the program becomes a measure of what our society intends for its aged members.

The Multi-Problem Family

Homer Burleigh: How Many Problems Can a Man Have?

"You mean you want to take a look at a hillbilly?"

Homer Burleigh, 33, out of Anniston, Ala.—hefty, freckle-faced and sandy-haired—stood in the doorway of his flat, dressed in T-shirt and slacks, immobile with resentment. Like 20,000 other southern whites now living in the 2½ square miles of Chicago's Uptown, he has his troubles, his pride, and an innate suspicion of the city slicker.

But he is too good-natured to stay sullen. Inside, four of his five children, ranging from two to seven years old, ran about in underpants. His wife, a wan, tired woman, was pregnant. The five-year-old chanted at the visitor, "You got on a necktie. You got on a necktie."

Once Homer Burleigh decides he likes you, he is an engaging man. His mother had died when he was three. As he tells it, he had fought with his stepmother, gone with an uncle to Detroit; and, by persistent trial and a winning honesty about his lack of experience but his desire to learn, was soon earning $100 a week. Two years later, with a 1940 Chevrolet and $3,000 in savings he went back to Anniston. "Between me and the car and a few good-looking women, that $3,000 didn't last ten months."

Like many southern white men, he shifted from the North, when plants shut down or work slackened, to the $40-a-week jobs back home in Alabama. Then he met his wife, a waitress with a child by a previous marriage. They decided to get married and try Chicago. Four days after his arrival he was earning $100 a week on a punch press.

In the next seven years there were four more children, more rent, more food, more medical bills. They learned to make his pay stretch fairly well until work began to slacken. He couldn't support his family on less than 40 hours' work, so when his plant went on short time he went out and found another job working full time. But this meant he built up no seniority, and when the new

Homer Burleigh: How Many Problems Can a Man Have?: From "The Invisible Americans," Ben Bagdikian, *Saturday Evening Post,* December 21–28, 1963, p. 37.

plant had to lay off men, he, being the last hired, would be the first fired.

A familiar set of walls moved in on him. Machine-shop work in the city went on shorter time. He had the almost universal desire for a car and the $60 a month on his 1954 Pontiac became harder than ever to squeeze out of his $300 take-home pay. He developed running sores under his arms that interfered with his work. The finance company attached his pay. So Homer Burleigh committed folly. He got a new Social Security number and drew his pay under another name, to balk the finance company.

A doctor gave him a letter saying he should not work. He applied for welfare aid, which would take about two weeks to be processed and during those weeks he kept on working.

When I saw Homer Burleigh, his welfare had been cut off because of fraud. He did not know what would happen about the Social Security number. He said the finance company had seized the car. Because he was out of work and without welfare aid for a month, he had fallen behind in his rent, and he was going to be evicted in four days. Already the furnishings of normal life were beginning to fall away. One room of the flat was bare except for a sewing machine in the middle of the room, one chair and a caged parakeet in the corner. The living room had two pieces of furniture, a sofa and a TV set.

"If the arm continues this way and if they don't give me assistance," he said gloomily, "I'm going to have to put the kids in a home."

Homer Burleigh is a likable man who reacted foolishly to a crisis. Whether society punishes him is yet to be seen. But there remain his wife, five children and a sixth expected, and whether they head down the road to perpetual dependence upon others will be governed by how far-sighted society is in dealing with the poor, the foolish and the unlucky.

THE CONVERGENCE OF POVERTY-LINKED CHARACTERISTICS

Oscar Ornati

The demographic characteristics [of low-income families] obviously overlap; being non-white may also mean being a farmer, or being aged, or being a female head of family. The poor do not usually have only one problem and many poor families are classified as "multi-problem" families. Available data point clearly to low education and shrinking occupational mobility as one of the major causes of poverty. Here the increased requirements in education for employment are one of the major causes of poverty. In addition, bad physical and mental health contribute to poverty to an undetermined but clearly significant degree.

Our rough estimate is that of the 20 million abject poor more than two-thirds, or somewhere between 12 and 14 million, are deficient in either health, mental or physical, or education, and a very large number of individuals are affected by more than one disadvantage. The proportions do not change significantly at the $3,500 or $4,500 level.

If we are to move against poverty, we must understand the dynamics of the process. Then we can move from the broad discussions of complex causality which determines an individual's risk of being poor to the isolation of characteristics which, in the aggregate, appear to contribute more, and of those that contribute less, to poverty.

Analysis of the 1960 census data allows, at least for that year, a precise count, at different levels of income, of population units

The Convergence of Poverty-Linked Characteristics: From *Poverty in America,* Oscar Ornati (Washington, D.C.: National Policy Committee on Pockets of Poverty, 1964), pp. 12–18.

Oscar Ornati. Member, National Policy'Committee on Pockets of Poverty; Professor of Economics, Graduate Faculty, New School for Social Research.

which had one or more of four key poverty-linked characteristics. It also provides a set of major preliminary clues as to how to move against poverty along the lines suggested above. Fifteen different poverty-linked family populations were constructed, ranging from units possessing one characteristic to those with all four. Here the problem of overlapping characteristics is eliminated. A non-white family is only non-white. There is no aged family head, no female family head, and no rural-farm resident. The same for the other characteristics. The cumulative total of all families with one characteristic holds no duplication—each family is counted only once. Nor is there duplication when families with two or more characteristics are examined.

As expected, by correcting for overlap, we note that: (1) there are more families with only one poverty characteristic than with two, with three or four, (2) the risk of poverty increases with the number of characteristics. The data in Table 1 indicate that while the relationship is not perfect, the possession of two characteristics means a greater chance of very low income than the possession of one, three a greater chance than two, etc. The degree of poverty, measured by the proportion of families below the three budget levels varies considerably.

Families that have only one characteristic find between 30 and 40 percent of their membership at or below subsistence, between 55 and 60 percent below the minimum adequacy level and roughly 70 percent below minimum comfort.

Possessing two characteristics condemns a considerably larger portion of the population to subsistence living. For all but one of the six sub-populations with two attributes the proportion below $2,500 is better than half. For non-white families with the added characteristic of rural farm residence, the probability of abject poverty is three out of four. The chance of living at or below the minimum adequacy level is 75 percent or better for all but one of these twice-cursed families. Ninety percent of all non-white farm families, 80 percent of all the non-white aged and 82 percent of all the non-white families with female heads lived under this level. For all but one of these combinations the chance of escaping from the poverty band is less than 2 in 10. Conversely, families with two poverty-linked attributes rarely have incomes placing them above the poverty level. Extreme poverty is the fate of families

TABLE 1 The percentage of each poverty-linked population below three low income levels

(1960)

Characteristic(s) of Family Head	No. of Units	Per Cent	Per Cent Below		
			2,500	4,500	5,500
One Characteristic					
Aged	4,276,016	100	39.6	60.2	70.5
Female	2,387,443	100	38.0	60.4	73.3
Rural-farm	2,434,041	100	34.5	57.5	71.0
Non-white	2,786,211	100	28.6	54.7	70.9
Two Characteristics					
Non-white, Female	743,115	100	64.6	82.2	88.4
Aged, Female	787,975	100	37.2	56.1	68.4
Aged, Rural-farm	489,732	100	54.9	74.7	83.2
Aged, Non-white	331,316	100	62.6	80.1	87.5
Non-white, Rural-farm	208,047	100	78.3	90.8	94.8
Rural-farm, Female	73,842	100	54.8	73.9	83.1
Three Characteristics					
Non-white, Aged, Female	115,444	100	67.5	83.5	89.8
Non-white, Rural-farm, Aged	40,901	100	81.1	91.9	95.4
Rural-farm, Aged, Female	55,444	100	52.5	70.8	80.3
Rural-farm, Non-white, Female	22,784	100	86.6	94.9	97.8
Four Characteristics					
Non-white, Rural-farm, Aged, Female	7,698	100	84.0	93.9	97.0

with 3 or 4 poverty attributes. For three groups the figure is 8 in 10, for one, 7 in 10, and for one 5 in 10.

The policy implications of the data and the analysis presented so far should be clear. On the one hand, families with one poverty characteristic make up the largest part of the low income population; on the other hand, families with more than one attribute, although less numerous, suffer the heavier burdens. Noting that they are less numerous in no way means they are insignificant. Families with two characteristics involve roughly ten million men, women and children. Half of these live below the contemporary subsistence level. Another quarter of a million families are marked by the even more extreme poverty associated with three or four characteristics. They contribute another million human exceptions to American affluence.

Examination of the differential impact of particular characteristics sharpens the focus of policy. Not only does this provide guidelines for the future, it also gives insight into the effect of past policies.

Table 2 measures the income effect of removing one poverty-linked characteristic from the population of families with three such characteristics. The table shows how, in every case, the removal of the characteristic non-white reduces the percentage of families below subsistence to a greater degree than removing the characteristic rural-farm. The effect is least marked in terms of removing any third characteristic from families with rural-farm as one of their three poverty-linked characteristics.

TABLE 2 The effect of removing a poverty-linked characteristic from a family possessing three characteristics (changes in percentages of families below the subsistence level)

Characteristic	Percent	Characteristic	Percent
Non-white, Rural-farm, Female	86.6	Non-white, Rural-farm, Aged	81.1
Minus:		Minus:	
Non-white	54.8	Non-white	54.9
Rural-farm	64.6	Rural-farm	62.6
Female	78.3	Aged	78.3
Non-white, Aged, Female	67.5	Aged, Rural-farm, Female	52.5
Minus:		Minus:	
Non-white	37.2	Rural-farm	37.2
Aged	64.6	Aged	54.8
Female	62.6	Female	54.9

Table 3 shows—in a manner similar to Table 2—the effect of removing one poverty-linked characteristic from families with two. The pattern that emerges throws some light on the success of a past policy, Social Security. In the first set of percentages and the fifth set we find that subtracting the aged has a modifying rather than a depressing effect on the percentage of extremely low income units. Rural-farm families headed by aged females were slightly better off than rural-farm families headed by non-aged females.

Age is the one area where, adequate or not, there does exist a national policy and program of insurance. Removing the non-white characteristic helps here, too, but less so.

TABLE 3 The effect of removing a poverty-linked characteristic from a family possessing two characteristics (changes in percentages of families below the subsistence level)

Characteristic	Percent	Characteristic	Percent
Non-white, Rural-farm	78.3	Non-white, Female	64.6
Minus:		Minus:	
Rural-farm	28.6	Female	28.6
Non-white	34.5	Non-white	38.0
Non-white, Aged	62.6	Rural-farm, Aged	54.9
Minus:		Minus:	
Aged	28.6	Aged	34.5
Non-white	39.6	Rural-farm	39.6
Rural-farm, Female	54.8	Aged, Female	37.2
Minus:		Minus:	
Female	34.5	Aged	38.0
Rural-farm	38.0	Female	39.6

Defining poverty through poverty-linked characteristics leads to the following major conclusions: First, the poverty population in 1960 is characterized by identifying specific socio-demographic attributes. Families that are aged, rural-farm, non-white, headed by females, or combinations of these, account for 70 percent of the abject poor. Second, in absolute terms, the largest groups are those families possessing only one characteristic. Third, the most severe poverty exists among families with more than one attribute and, fourth, among the multi-characteristic families, non-whiteness is most damaging.

In the strictest sense of the word, the poor of today are less endowed. "Underprivileged" has long been a fashionable word. It seemed less offensive than "poor." On the whole, until recent years, it was an inappropriate euphemism. Now it fits. It means those who are less endowed and less able to participate in the Affluent Society. It means those who are out of the mainstream of American life.

The underprivileged are not of, even though they are in, the market society. Their poverty is a poverty of structure. They sit outside as marginal sellers and weak buyers. They are economic as well as physical invalids and are discriminated against socially and economically. *Their poverty is the result of special circumstances,* rather than of the rate of economic activity. They do not directly reflect an inadequate growth rate as they are not part of the economic structure. Our economy takes care of those who are within its embrace, but it does not take care of the underprivileged.

The policy implications are clear. The redefinition presented here casts poverty in a context in which action is possible. Poverty is a structural problem and thus policies to deal with it must be structurally-oriented. This presents many problems. Many policy-makers and economists contend that poverty will be done away with by policies aimed at bringing about full employment. Such policies are necessary prerequisites and have a social and economic value and priority of their own. But, the elimination or drastic reduction of poverty in America demands additional measures pinpointed to those structural characteristics of the affluent society that have permitted a large pool of underprivileged in the midst of a relatively efficient economy.

7 / Other Cultural Dimensions of Poverty

If success breeds success and to those who have shall be given, then the aphorism may also be turned around: those who have not shall be deprived. The latter appears all too socially valid, as the following selections suggest. Here we deal somewhat eclectically with three poverty-reinforcing dimensions of our culture. The first is lack of education. It is well established that educational deprivation, when associated with poverty and poverty-linked features, becomes converted into functional illiteracy in a generation or two. This is the time-span aspect of self-reinforcing poverty. The educationally barren home—insofar as it may qualify as a home—transmits its intellectual bankruptcy into succeeding generations. The transmission occurs not only because of the complete lack of books, reading, good music, drama, art and other such components of our cultural heritage, but also through the positive indoctrination in fatalism, caste consciousness, and limited achievement horizons. Hence, being born into the educationally deprived home and community, be it city slum, marginal farm, or deserted Appalachian mining town, entails a grim inheritance that even a Horatio Alger hero could not overcome. Furthermore, the technical training of even the well-paid worker is becoming increasingly complex and costly. These interacting social and economic barriers may be nearly insurmountable obstacles to the vertical mobility of the poor, and especially so when environmentally generated levels of aspiration are low or lacking.

Earlier selections have shown that the poverty subculture induces and reinforces certain characteristic behavior patterns. High unplanned legitimate and illegitimate birth rates among the low income population is another such behavior pattern. Neither the right to have many children nor the wisdom of the poor in having them is questioned here. Presumably the long-run solution lies in the elimination of poverty. All that is here advanced is the hypothesis that poverty is accentuated by high birth rates and high birth rates are stimulated by poverty and its connected characteristics. This reciprocal relationship may tend to perpetuate poverty in the United States, and thus represents a form of "vicious circle" that, given our resources, can much more readily be broken through in this country than it can in the less developed nations of the world.

The political apathy, alienation, and inarticulateness of the poverty-stricken have now a firmly established empirical grounding in the social sciences. It seems clear that the poor make most inadequate use of the available political channels through which their interests could be expressed. This is a third poverty-reinforcing feature of our culture. A possible exception to this generalization is forcefully presented by S. M. Miller.

A fourth poverty-reinforcing cultural influence should also be noted. Poverty is associated with legal discrimination, and legal discrimination tends to keep the indigent in their allotted status. In an address approaching greatness before the New York University School of Law, in February 1964, Associate Justice Arthur J. Goldberg pointed to the shocking and costly injustices visited upon even the nonminority poor simply because of their low economic and educational level. Although the Bar Association has acknowledged its unique responsibility in this regard, chiefly through its advocacy of the public defender system, it is nonetheless a responsibility of every American to rectify the present *de facto* inequality that confronts the poor before both the judicial and the enforcement authorities. We add only a reminder here of the very special injustices visited upon the Negro and other minorities, whose life-long travail before the bar of justice has been made known to most Americans through the civil rights struggle.

The Self-Reinforcing Nature of Poverty

POVERTY BREEDS POVERTY

Council of Economic Advisers

Poverty breeds poverty. A poor individual or family has a high probability of staying poor. Low incomes carry with them high risks of illness; limitations on mobility; limited access to education, information, and training. Poor parents cannot give their children the opportunities for better health and education needed to improve their lot. Lack of motivation, hope, and incentive is a more subtle but no less powerful barrier than lack of financial means. Thus the cruel legacy of poverty is passed from parents to children.

Escape from poverty is not easy for American children raised in

Poverty Breeds Poverty: From *Economic Report of the President, 1964,* Council of Economic Advisers (Washington, D.C.: U.S. Government Printing Office, 1964), pp. 69–70.

families accustomed to living on relief. A recent sample study of AFDC recipients found that more than 40 percent of the parents were themselves raised in homes where public assistance had been received. It is difficult for children to find and follow avenues leading out of poverty in environments where education is deprecated and hope is smothered. This is particularly true when discrimination appears as an insurmountable barrier. Education may be seen as a waste of time if even the well-trained are forced to accept menial labor because of their color or nationality.

The Michigan study shows how inadequate education is perpetuated from generation to generation. Of the families identified as poor in that study, 64 percent were headed by a person who had had less than an eighth grade education. Of these, in turn, 67 percent had fathers who had also gone no further than eighth grade in school. Among the children of these poor families who had finished school, 34 percent had not gone beyond the eighth grade; this figure compares with 14 percent for all families. Fewer than 1 in 2 children of poor families had graduated from high school, compared to almost 2 out of 3 for all families.

LEGACY OF POVERTY

Mollie Orshansky

A considerable body of data is being accumulated on the subject of transmission of poverty. Some of the results of current study are conflicting and difficult to interpret, and much research is still needed. There seems sufficient basis, however, for adopting as a working hypothesis that perhaps the single medium most conducive to the growth of poverty and dependency is poverty itself. The corollary might be that, although adequate family income alone is

Legacy of Poverty: From "Children of the Poor," Mollie Orshansky, *Social Security Bulletin,* Vol. 26, No. 7 (July, 1963), pp. 12–13.

Mollie Orshansky. Staff member, Division of Research and Statistics, Social Security Administration.

not a sufficient condition to guarantee that children will escape low-income status as adults, it is usually a necessary one. There are people whose only legacy to their children is the same one of poverty and deprivation that they received from their own parents.

A recently released study of cases assisted by aid to families with dependent children shows that, for a nationwide sample of such families whose cases were closed early in 1961, "more than 40 percent of the mothers and/or fathers were raised in homes where some form of assistance had been received at some time." Nearly half these cases had received aid to families with dependent children. This estimated proportion that received some type of aid is more than four times the almost 10 percent estimated for the total United States population. With education so important these days for any chance at a well-paying job, the educational attainment of children formerly receiving aid to families with dependent children fell well below that of the same age group in the general population. Thirteen percent of the total population aged 18–24 had not gone beyond the eighth grade, but in the sample of families receiving aid the corresponding proportion was twice as high.

Similarly, the University of Michigan study reported that among all families with children no longer in school the children had gone through high school or beyond in 65 percent, but that in only 45 percent of the families defined as poor was this true.

Poor families have been found in various studies not only to have less resources but much less often to have aspirations toward providing a college education for their children, despite the fact that education today is the key not only to a better job but to any job at all. A recent study of young people aged 16–24 in the labor force and no longer in school reported the relationship of unemployment to educational attainment, as shown below.

Educational attainment	Percent unemployed
Not high school graduate	14
High school graduate, no college	7
Some college, not graduate	6
College graduate	3

Despite recent advances, it is still expected that almost 3 out of every 10 youths entering the labor force during the years ahead will not have completed high school and that a third of these—about

250,000 a year—will not even have gone through elementary school. Almost surely, they will have to live out their lives and support their own children on only a minimum wage.

Children from the broken families who represent so large a proportion of the poor undoubtedly will often fall in the same unskilled category. The mothers with no education or cultural expectation for themselves, with little money to provide a home environment conducive to study, and needing the help of their older children's earnings to satisfy the bread-and-butter needs of the younger ones, often are in no position to encourage even gifted children to stay in school, though scholarships are available. The fact that schools in poor neighborhoods are likely to be short on counselors, books, and other tools needed by the student will serve to compound rather than mitigate the home deficiency.

The deleterious effects of poverty on health, nutrition, and other living conditions have also been noted. There is, to be sure, no unanimity on the question of inherited deprivation. Some feel that it is lack of motivation or an innate lack of ability that is transmitted rather than lack of opportunity. For some children an overlay of discrimination combines with low-income status to perpetuate the deprivation. In his Civil Rights Message of February 1963, President Kennedy said:

> The Negro baby born in America today—regardless of the section or State in which he is born—has about one-half as much chance of completing high school as a white baby born in the same place on the same day, one-third as much chance of becoming a professional man, twice as much chance of becoming unemployed, about one-seventh as much chance of earning $10,000 per year, a life expectancy which is 7 years less, and the prospects of earning only half as much.

There is need for considerable refinement of the definition or standards by which poverty is to be measured, if we are to trace its course with assurance. Nevertheless, compelling evidence already suggests a lingering reservoir of self-perpetuating low-income status among particular population groups—toils the individual often is powerless to escape and a deprivation that falls in large part outside the scope of existing remedial programs. Along with the basic research into the cause and long-range cure for chronic low income, there is need for more thoroughgoing inquiry into the characteristics of those currently affected and a means of counteracting some of the more dire social consequences, at least for children.

If it be true that the children of the poor today are themselves destined to be the impoverished parents of tomorrow, then some social intervention is needed to break the cycle, to interrupt the circuits of hunger and hopelessness that link generation to generation. For the common benefit of all we must assure the security and well-being of all our children—at the same time the Nation's most precious and most perishable resource.

Population and Poverty

THE HIGH PRICE OF HIGH FERTILITY
Philip M. Hauser

Our post-war boom in babies is exacting a high price from the American people—as measured in human as well as financial costs. The baby boom will from now on worsen the U.S. unemployment problem, greatly increase the magnitude of juvenile delinquency, exacerbate already dangerous race tensions, inundate the secondary schools and colleges, greatly increase traffic accidents and fatalities, augment urban congestion and further subvert the traditional American governmental system.

Needless to say high fertility is by no means the only factor accounting for these difficult problems. But it is a major factor in

The High Price of High Fertility: From an address given by Philip M. Hauser at the Symposium on Cost of U.S. Population Growth, at the Annual Meeting of Planned Parenthood—World Population, New York City, October 16, 1963, pp. 1–3.

Philip M. Hauser. Chairman, Department of Sociology, University of Chicago.

making them worse. This is well illustrated by the way in which the baby boom is now contributing to high unemployment. Our post-war babies who reached flood stage after demobilization in 1946, are reaching labor force age in the sixties. The number of new workers under 25 years of age entering the labor force, averaging 600,000 per year during the sixties, is three times the number of new workers who entered the labor force between 1955 and 1960. The bulge in new entrant workers, coming at a time when we are experiencing a high level of chronic unemployment and increasing automation, may constitute the gravest challenge our economy has ever faced in peace time. If the volume of unemployment mounts as our post-war offspring begin to reach age 18 in 1964, it may be anticipated that unemployment compensation and relief costs will mount; and that the government will be obliged to experiment with various types of programs to effect decreases in unemployment. Under such circumstances it may also be anticipated that consumer demand will slough off in many areas—the teen age market, the marriage market and other markets oriented to the marriage market including consumer durables; and that general consumer demand may decline as the public interprets mounting unemployment as indicating an uncertain economic outlook. *We have yet to demonstrate that we can generate new jobs as fast as we did babies after the war.*

Similarly although the high birth rate is not responsible for juvenile delinquency it will greatly increase the volume of juvenile delinquency during the sixties. Persons 15 to 19 years of age, who account for most juvenile delinquency, will increase by 44 percent during the decade. This means that even if juvenile delinquency rates remain the same the number of delinquents of this age will increase by 44 percent at a time when the social order is already sorely troubled by its present magnitude.

High fertility does not directly produce internal migration but it does accelerate imbalance between population and resources in the relatively underdeveloped areas of the country and, therefore, stimulates increases in migratory streams. There can be no doubt that high fertility has increased the volume of internal migration from the South to the North and West and from rural to urban areas.

The tremendous range of problems we face in our central cities, furthermore, is being increasingly compounded by the persistence of fertility differentials based primarily on income and educational status. Low income and minority families continue to have more children than they say they want, in large part because of the discriminatory medical services we make available to them so that they are virtually denied access to modern fertility control. The children, in turn, receive inferior and discriminatory educations, and the combination of high fertility and inadequate training is a major deterrent to the economic and social advance of families in the culture of poverty. The price we are paying for these discriminatory practices is already high—and will soon become staggering.

High fertility in the forties and early fifties inundated the elementary schools of the U.S. during the later fifties. It will swamp secondary schools which can expect a 48 percent increase in enrollment during the sixties and colleges which will almost double in enrollment between 1960 and 1970. The anticipated deleterious effect upon the quality of education will be among the prices we will pay for our baby boom.

In similar manner the baby boom will exact many other high costs in human and financial terms. The great increase in persons under 25, especially males, will increase the number of dangerous drivers and, therefore, traffic accidents, injuries and fatalities. The great increase in population concentrated in our already overcrowded metropolitan areas will worsen congestion and make the "commuter's crisis" among other things even more acute.

Finally, it may be noted that high fertility has not been an unimportant factor in subverting the traditional patterns of government in the U.S. To the extent that rapid population increase has augmented urban and metropolitan concentration and produced chronic and acute economic, social and political problems, it has had a major influence in altering our traditional division of responsibilities between the Federal, State and local governments. For one thing the record shows that the functions of American government on all levels have tremendously expanded and multiplied in the course of our history. There can be no doubt that the reason for this continued expansion of government, despite our ideological traditions to the contrary, is a direct result of increased population and especially increased population concentration which has produced our mass society and metropolitanism as a way of life. Examples are given by the acute form of urban problems requiring Federal government participation in public housing, urban renewal, and public highway and expressway programs. The worsening education and transport problems mentioned above may well bring further Federal programs during this decade.

Finally, the rapidly increasing urban and metropolitan populations have drastically altered the form of local government envisioned by the Constitutional fathers. Local government today is by no means that envisaged by the founding fathers in that it is supplemented by governmental structures such as the school district, the port authority, the sanitary district, the water district, the drainage district, the park district, the metropolitan area planning commission, and, also, by such instrumentalities as the interstate compact and the Tennessee Valley Authority.

Rapid urban and metropolitan growth which has already outmoded local government structure is further accelerating its obsolescence. Twentieth century agglomerations of population and economic activities approximated by the Federal government's delineation of metropolitan areas, have long ago outgrown their inherited 18th and 19th century forms of local government. The crazy-quilt patch work of separate governmental agencies which has emerged over the years is becoming increasingly inefficient and ineffective. In 1950, the 168 metropolitan areas in the United States had amongst them something in excess of 16,000 local governmental units—that is, agencies with powers to tax or to spend. These to be sure included school districts, but the number is a good quantitative index of the anachronistic character of our inherited local governmental structure.

That there is growing public awareness of this situation is evident in the increased attention being given to metropolitan area government problems, and by the multiplicity of devices emerging to deal with them. The consolidation of city and county government, the creation of metropolitan area-wide agencies to perform specific functions, the creation of metropolitan area planning agencies, and the Toronto metropolitan governmental structure are among the important developments. The basic deficiencies of present metropolitan governmental organization, are becoming ever more apparent and proposals for changes in local governmental structure may be expected to increase.

The Political Inarticulateness
of the Poor

THE POLITICAL INVISIBILITY
OF THE POOR

Michael Harrington

The poor are politically invisible. It is one of the cruelest ironies of social life in advanced countries that the dispossessed at the bottom of society are unable to speak for themselves. The people of the other America do not, by far and large, belong to unions, to fraternal organizations, or to political parties. They are without lobbies of their own; they put forward no legislative program. As a group, they are atomized. They have no face; they have no voice.

Thus, there is not even a cynical political motive for caring about the poor, as in the old days. Because the slums are no longer centers of powerful political organizations, the politicians need not really care about their inhabitants. The slums are no longer visible to the middle class, so much of the idealistic urge to fight for those who need help is gone. Only the social agencies have a really direct involvement with the other America, and they are without any great political power.

To the extent that the poor have a spokesman in American life, that role is played by the labor movement. The unions have their

---

The Political Invisibility of the Poor: From *The Other America: Poverty in the United States,* Michael Harrington (New York: Macmillan, 1962), pp. 6–9 and 172–74.

Michael Harrington. Journalist specializing in the problems of poverty.

own particular idealism, an ideology of concern. More than that, they realize that the existence of a reservoir of cheap, unorganized labor is a menace to wages and working conditions throughout the entire economy. Thus, many union legislative proposals—to extend the coverage of minimum wage and social security, to organize migrant farm laborers—articulate the needs of the poor.

That the poor are invisible is one of the most important things about them. They are not simply neglected and forgotten as in the old rhetoric of reform; what is much worse, they are not seen.

• • •

Forty to 50,000,000 people are becoming increasingly invisible. That is a shocking fact. But there is a second basic irony of poverty that is equally important: if one is to make the mistake of being born poor, he should choose a time when the majority of the people are miserable too.

J. K. Galbraith develops this idea in *The Affluent Society,* and in doing so defines the "newness" of the kind of poverty in contemporary America. The old poverty, Galbraith notes, was general. It was the condition of life of an entire society, or at least of that huge majority who were without special skills or the luck of birth. When the entire economy advanced, a good many of these people gained higher standards of living. Unlike the poor today, the majority poor of a generation ago were an immediate (if cynical) concern of political leaders. The old slums of the immigrants had the votes; they provided the basis for labor organizations; their very numbers could be a powerful force in political conflict. At the same time the new technology required higher skills, more education, and stimulated an upward movement for millions.

Perhaps the most dramatic case of the power of the majority poor took place in the 1930's. The Congress of Industrial Organizations literally organized millions in a matter of years. A labor movement that had been declining and confined to a thin stratum of the highly skilled suddenly embraced masses of men and women in basic industry. At the same time this acted as a pressure upon the Government, and the New Deal codified some of the social gains in laws like the Wagner Act. The result was not a basic transformation of the American system, but it did transform the lives of an entire section of the population.

In the thirties one of the reasons for these advances was that misery was general. There was no need then to write books about unemployment and poverty. That was the decisive social experience of the entire society, and the apple sellers even invaded Wall Street. There was political sympathy from middle-class reformers; there were an élan and spirit that grew out of a deep crisis.

Some of those who advanced in the thirties did so because they had unique and individual personal talents. But for the great mass, it was a question of being at the right point in the economy at the right time in history, and utilizing that position for common struggle. Some of those who failed did so because they did not have the will to take advantage of new opportunities. But for the most part the poor who were left behind had been at the wrong place in the economy at the wrong moment in history.

These were the people in the unorganizable jobs, in the South, in the minority groups, in the fly-by-night factories that were low on capital and high on labor. When some of them did break into the economic mainstream—when, for instance, the CIO opened up the way for some Negroes to find good industrial jobs—they proved to be as resourceful as anyone else. As a group, the other Americans who stayed behind were not originally composed primarily of individual failures. Rather, they were victims of an impersonal process that selected some for progress and discriminated against others.

Out of the thirties came the welfare state. Its creation had been stimulated by mass impoverishment and misery, yet it helped the poor least of all. Laws like unemployment compensation, the Wagner Act, the various farm programs, all these were designed for the middle third in the cities, for the organized workers, and for the upper third in the country, for the big market farmers. If a man works in an extremely low-paying job, he may not even be covered by social security or other welfare programs. If he receives unemployment compensation, the payment is scaled down according to his low earnings.

One of the major laws that was designed to cover everyone, rich and poor, was social security. But even here the other Americans suffered discrimination. Over the years social security payments have not even provided a subsistence level of life. The middle third have been able to supplement the Federal pension through private plans negotiated by unions, through joining medical insurance schemes like Blue Cross, and so on. The poor have not been able to do so. They lead a bitter life, and then have to pay for that fact in old age.

Indeed, the paradox that the welfare state benefits those least who need help most is but a single instance of a persistent irony in the other America. Even when the money finally trickles down, even when a school is built in a poor neighborhood, for instance, the poor are still deprived. Their entire environment, their life, their values, do not prepare them to take advantage of the new opportunity. The parents are anxious for the children to go to work; the pupils are pent up, waiting for the moment when their education has complied with the law.

Today's poor, in short, missed the political and social gains of the thirties. They are, as Galbraith rightly points out, the first minority poor in history, the first poor not to be seen, the first poor whom the politicians could leave alone.

•   •   •

In times of slow change or of stalemate, it is always the poor who are expendable in the halls of Congress. In 1961, for instance, the laundry workers were dropped out of the minimum wage as part of a deal with the conservatives. Precisely because they are so poor and cruelly exploited, no one had to fear their political wrath.

•   •   •

All the forces of conservatism in this society are ranged against the needs of the other America. The ideologues are opposed to helping the poor because this can be accomplished only through an expansion of the welfare state. The small businessmen have an immediate self-interest in maintaining the economic underworld. The powerful agencies of the corporate farms want a continuation of an agricultural program that aids the rich and does nothing for the poor.

And now the South is becoming increasingly against the poor. In the days of the New Deal, the Southern Democrats tended to vote for various kinds of social legislation. One of the most outspoken champions of public housing, Burnet Maybank, was a senator from South Carolina. For one thing, there is a Southern tradition of being against Wall Street and big business; it is part of the farmers' hostility to the railroads and the Babylons of the big city. For another, the New Deal legislation did not constitute a challenge to the system of racial segregation in the South.

But in the postwar period, this situation began to change. As industrialization came to the South, there was a growing political opposition to laws like minimum wage, to unions, and to other aspects of social change. The leaders of this area saw their depressed condition as an advantage. They could lure business with the promise of cheap, unorganized labor. They were interested in exploiting their backwardness.

The result was the strengthening of the coalition of Southern Democrats and conservative Northern Republicans. The Northern conservatives went along with opposition to Civil Rights legislation. The Southerners threw their votes into the struggle against social advance. It was this powerful coalition that exacted such a price in the first period of the Kennedy Administration. Many of the proposals that would have benefited the poor were omitted from bills in the first place, and other concessions were made in the course of the legislative battle. Thus poverty in the United States is supported by forces with great political and economic power.

On the other side, the friends of the poor are to be found in the American labor movement and among the middle-class liberals. The unions in the postwar period lost much of the élan that had characterized them in the thirties. Yet on questions of social legislation they remained the most powerful mass force committed to change in general, and to bettering the lot of the poor in particular. On issues like housing, medical care, minimum wage, and social security, the labor movement provided the strongest voice stating the cause of the poor.

Yet labor and the liberals were caught in the irrationalities of the American party system, and this was an enormous disadvantage to the other America. The unionists and their liberal allies are united in the Democratic party with the Southern conservatives. A Democratic victory was usually achieved by appealing to those who were concerned for social change. But at the same time it brought the forces of conservatism powerful positions on the standing committees of the Congress.

Indeed, part of the invisibility of poverty in American life is a result of this party structure. Since each major party contained differences within itself greater than the differences between it and the other party, politics in the fifties and early sixties tended to have an issueless character. And where issues were not discussed, the poor did not have a chance. They could benefit only if elections were designed to bring new information to the people, to wake up the nation, to challenge, and to call to action.

In all probability there will not be a real attack on the culture of poverty so long as this situation persists. For the other America cannot be abolished through concessions and compromises that are almost inevitably made at the expense of the poor. The spirit, the vision that are required if the nation is to penetrate the wall of pessimism and despair that surrounds the impoverished millions cannot be produced under such circumstances.

What is needed if poverty is to be abolished is a return of political debate, a restructuring of the party system so that there can be clear choices, a new mood of social idealism.

THE POLITICAL POTENTIAL
OF CLASS AND RACE
S. M. Miller

The urban poor is composed of many strata: refugees from the land and older settlers of the urban slums, Southern mountaineer whites and Southern Negroes, Puerto Ricans and Mexican-Americans. Despite their diversity, the poor in the largest urban centers are rapidly evolving into a "colored" poor of Negroes and Spanish-name persons. These are the groups that seem most likely to be politicized. *It is the confluence of class and race issues which gives the poor a much greater political potential than is usually true of low income, depressed populations.*

This group might be described as a "new" working class. The "old" working class, who still comprise the bulk of skilled and semi-skilled union members as well as the majority of blue collar workers, is made up of "old-settler" Protestant recruits largely from farm and rural areas and the second and third generation of

The Political Potential of Class and Race: From "The Politics of Poverty,"
S. M. Miller, *Dissent,* Vol. 11, No. 2 (Spring, 1964), pp. 212–18.

the predominantly Catholic Eastern and Southern European nations. The "new" working class is more likely to be "colored," unskilled, in low-wage service and nonunionized industries, e.g., hospitals.

• • •

The concept of the "new" working class is more a fishing net than a hard container. Nevertheless, it emphasizes some common economic issues which many low-income people face in affluent America and raises the possibility that they might act politically to do something about it. The term "new" working class implies that low-income people are trying to get a foothold into urban industrial life.

Harrington has pictured the poor as passive, inert and apathetic, lacking generally the capacity for action. I find this portrait misleading. The aged have been active in political movements—from the Townsend Plan to the fight for Medicare. Mexican-Americans have recently won political control in Crystal City, a small Texas town. In many cities, the young and adult poor have organized to protest their conditions, as recently in Chicago where women on welfare strongly demonstrated against the cessation of allowances. And what the Negro has done in recent years constitutes a virtual revolution in American life.

World War I was the breakthrough for the Southern Negro. During and immediately after the war, great numbers of them left for the North, and in the following years there was a steady if not spectacular movement of Negroes out of the South. Again, a war led to a rapid change; during and after World War II, there was a rapid movement of Negroes into urban centers, both North and South. The Negro is no longer primarily a rural resident; soon, a majority of Negroes will be living in Northern cities.

The importance and power of Negroes in the large Northern cities was demonstrated in the 1960 election in which an almost solid Democratic vote in many Negro districts swung the populous industrial states into Kennedy's column. The increase in the number of Southern Negro voters accentuates the national role of Negroes. Legislative reapportionment, which will increase the importance of the urban vote, though not as much as it will the suburban vote, should make the Negro vote more effective in state elections. With the rapid concentration of Negroes in central cities, they will increasingly become a power group there; in New York City, it now seems a Democratic Party practice that the Borough President of Manhattan be Negro. A Negro Mayor in one of our large cities is a distinct possibility in the next years. The interest of Presidents Johnson and Kennedy in poverty results from the potential importance of the votes of the poor.

Negroes then are beginning to develop a political "clout" which will give them the ability to demand and get services and rights at both the federal and local levels. Formally, these rights have almost always been available to all; in practice, only to whites and more slowly to working-class whites. As the whites—first the Irish, later the Jews and still more recently the Italians—strengthened their organizations, they were able to obtain a more equitable share of political and economic rewards. This same process is beginning with Negroes and at a slower rate with many other members of the new working class. *It promises to be the decisive political condition of the sixties in this country.*

The political awareness of the Negroes already has been realized, and it is a distinct possibility for others of the poor as well. The intermeshing of a variety of economic and class factors will lead to political mobilization. Usually, the long-term economically depressed are unlikely candidates for a dynamic political movement, but the racial as well as economic factors are propelling the poor toward politics, whether they be Negro, Mexican-American or Puerto Rican.

Nor should we ignore the possibilities of political organization of the poor whites. Bayard Rustin's suggestion that white students might best work in poor white areas rather than Negro areas is important. But in the next months the political pressures will come from the "colored" poor.

Many of the leaders of the "colored" poor will probably come from middle-class families providing qualities and abilities that may not emerge early among others of their group. E. Franklin Frazier's notion of a "black bourgeoisie" that in rising cuts itself off from the mass of Negroes, was probably overstated when he expressed it a few years ago; it undoubtedly is today. Less and less does "going up" mean "going out" of the Negro community: even those who can and do move out of the Negro ghetto frequently maintain ties with it and are deeply and actively concerned about the Negro poor. While older successful Negroes are less likely to be identified with poorer Negroes and are more likely to emphasize "progress," they frequently are pushed along by the dynamism and pressure of the younger generation of Negroes.

The cohesion which comes from racial issues might serve to separate each of the poor ethnic groupings from one another, leading each to be concerned only with issues peculiar to it. This self-centering pressure and inter-ethnic hostility may, however, be overcome by the large number of issues which are common to all of the poor.

The high rate of unemployment among the new working class, their low wages, their inadequate housing as they suffer the ravages (and reap little of the benefits) of urban redevelopment, the poor schooling offered their children, the neglect of public services in their neighborhoods, the frequent callousness of the police and welfare departments, the bilking by merchants—in short, their second-class economic and political status—provide the issues which may mold the new working class into a potent political force.

.   .   .

In the immediate future, the poor are the most likely to provide leverage for significant change. The common need for decent employment and social services, which binds together the various groups of the poor, can be satisfied only through political action; for today economic issues are political issues.

Political action for the poor implies action at the grass roots—in the community. Saul Alinsky in Chicago, Jesse Gray in Harlem rent strikes and others elsewhere have demonstrated the possibilities of social action and self-help programs; and in many communities, low-income Negroes have been drawn into civil rights actions.

While indigenous leadership in the poverty areas of the large city is an important consideration, the thing that can be done most effectively by outsiders—non-colored, non-poor—coming into the impoverished areas is to try to develop the kinds of issues which encourage the growth of indigenous leadership. The situation is not, of course, an easy one. In many communities of the new working class the immediate prospect of concerted action toward political or any other kind of goals seems unlikely. These are communities which have very little internal dynamics of control and no real momentum. There are other communities of the poor which are controlled largely by the police; these are the areas in which a counter-movement seems likely. Finally, there are areas in which local control is imminent and even to a limited degree already present.

The "gripes" of low-income neighborhoods—whether about unemployment, the welfare department, the regulations of public housing, the behavior of the police—are political issues, and will emerge as such if the new working class acquires a political style. At first, the issues may very well have to be local and immediate, directly affecting the new working class. But many of the problems facing the new working class cannot be resolved at local levels: they need national action. Linking local issues to broader national concerns and building an orientation to the national political scene is one of the most difficult and important tasks facing local leaders.

8 / Policy

Probably the most important short-run result of the declaration of war on poverty is that the elimination of involuntary poverty as an explicit national goal has been reiterated for our times on the highest levels, and the means of achieving the goal have been made a matter of widespread public and private controversy. Certainly the significant aspect is not the very modest financial commitments under the Economic Opportunity Act.

This declaration, and the social, economic, and political issues it has raised, represent a vital new force in our national life. The direction and strength of this force may encourage a hitherto indifferent public to break through the affluence barrier and close the ideological chasm separating what Disraeli called the "two nations" of the rich and the poor.

Throughout this volume the editors have emphasized the need for the middle and upper classes to increase their understanding of the nature and causes of poverty and of the life of the poverty-stricken, a focal task to which we hope modestly to contribute. Achievement of this higher level of understanding, premised as it must be upon exposure to contemporaneously advanced theories and policy proposals, should also help to increase and maintain the momentum of public determination in the pursuit of the antipoverty goal.

There will be indifference, reluctance, diversion, and outright resistance to a war on poverty, however well conducted. The contours of such possible opposition may be discovered in some of the following selections. These contours may at times be somewhat obscured, but typically they take the form of disagreement over means. Such disagreement over the appropriateness of specific social policies deliberately disguises the underlying protest against the ends sought, and it often delays and obstructs the achievement of social goals.

It seems desirable to deal in this analytical headnote with value judgments rather than merely to review the largely concrete discussions that follow in "Governmental Programs and Their Critics." It is not part of our purpose to take explicit stands on these concrete proposals; we leave this task to the reader. All such stands involve value judgments, just as do the broader and more basic policy perspectives represented in the section entitled "Poverty in Perspective." We prefer to deal here with some of the underlying, and often more subtle, differences in values behind both the specific policy proposals and the broader policy perspectives. After all, only if the air is cleared by explicit revelation of variations in fundamental viewpoint can we move forward on the more obvious programatic aspects.

In the first place, then, we should note the dangers emanating from the well-wishers who adopt a panacea approach regarding some one line of attack. The panacea viewpoint is as vulnerable as it is unscientific. It is, of course, to be distinguished from a policy framework that has an *emphasis* on a single line of attack. An example of both the danger and the distinction might be found in the degree of reliance one places upon economic growth. We share the view that a high rate of economic growth is the single most important measure for the elimination of poverty, and we incline toward the position of those economists who urge a 4 per cent annual growth in our real gross national product, rather than toward the "three-percenters." A high rate of growth tends, by raising productivity, to lift many low-income activities to higher absolute levels per capita. It brings with it a movement of people out of low-wage occupations, industries, areas, and regions into higher wage employment and localities. Furthermore, it seems to increase the number and percentage of multiearner families.

However, we would hasten to point out that a nearly exclusive reliance upon an attempt to achieve the elimination of poverty through the economic growth objective would be fatal. We trust this has been made clear earlier: there would be too many hard core poor with poverty-linked mental, social, and related characteristics who would be left without treatment. Moreover, for many poverty exists in spite of employability. Also, as viewed by one school of thought, the existence of structural unemployment, due to the lack or the obsolescence of skills, would represent a type of poverty-inducing characteristic that would frustrate the attempt to achieve high growth at full employment. Those outside the labor force for retirement or other reasons would likewise be bypassed.

Another active candidate for the panacea approach is education. Since World War II our culture has thrown off much of its historic anti-intellectualism and come to embrace an educational explosion having dimensions never before dreamed of. This breakthrough has received invaluable theoretical buttressing by the discoveries of Theodore W. Schultz, Edward F. Denison, and others that investment in human beings has been the major single source of productivity growth in this country in the twentieth century. We may therefore by now be inordinately susceptible to the notion that overcoming the lack of education will more or less automatically dispel poverty, since they are almost universally correlated. We consider, for example, that despite a reference to "civil rights . . . slum abatement, the rest," John Kenneth Galbraith in essence falls victim to education as a panacea in his proposal to bring educational performance up to the nation's best standards in a selected group of the country's poorest counties (*Harper's,* March, 1964). We would put education next to a high rate of economic growth in order of policy importance. But we do not think education, even when broadly conceived as in Galbraith's proposal, can assure that in the lowest-income counties, incomes would ". . . rise above a specified level," even when supplemented with food and clothing gifts, medical and psychiatric care, and the provision of other social services. Does the New Haven program go much beyond this? Worthy as it certainly is, we are inclined to doubt it.

Then there is the viewpoint that we are already doing so much that there is no need to commit vast new additional resources to the antipoverty campaign. It seems plausible that in many cases the true conscious or unconscious objective of this approach is to minimize the resources devoted to the campaign, or at least to postpone a serious attack. After all (and this gives us a partial clue to the rationale behind the resistance currents to which we are referring), some people will have to sacrifice something to make the antipoverty campaign effective. Such sacrifice involves violation of the still widely held proposition of classical economics that personal rationality in a world guided by the invisible hand of self-interest requires shifting burdens to others. Good estimates have yet to be made of the required total costs of a domestic war on involuntary poverty. We suspect that for the next generation they will be substantial, although in the long run the net costs will probably be much less than is anticipated by our more reluctant contemporaries. In any case, the benefits are much like those traditionally claimed for private investment: some must sacrifice consumption now so that they and other also can escape low levels of living in the future. As Theodore W. Schultz so aptly put it,[1]

> The low earnings of particular people have long been a matter of public concern. Policy all too frequently concentrates only on the effects, ignoring the cause. No small part of the low earnings of

[1] "Investment in Human Capital," *American Economic Review,* Vol. LI, No. 1 (March, 1961), p. 14.

many Negroes, Puerto Ricans, Mexican nationals, indigenous migratory farm workers, poor farm people, and some of our older workers, reflects the failure to have invested in their health and education. Past mistakes are, of course, bygones, but for the sake of the next generation, we can ill afford to continue making the same mistakes over again.

In addition, there is the fact that we are dealing with divided authority. What level(s) of government must share primary responsibility for a campaign such as this? What should be the role of private organizational effort? True, the federal government has inaugurated the campaign, and Harrington emphasizes that its leadership role must be continued. Most seem to agree that all levels of government, together with private groups, should cooperate. But this still does not identify the *principal* actors. Our point is that the existence of several likely participating agencies provides conscious or unconscious resisters with the opportunity to weaken a program by perpetually calling for shifting the initiative or the major responsibility.

Then there are those who carry into the present the now generally rejected traditional notions, represented by several excerpts in Section 3 above, that poverty is basically the result of inherent, biological deficiencies in the individual. This view was historically identified with arguments designed to assure an elastic labor supply. Unless it be recognized that this view applies to only a miniscule and readily identifiable proportion of the poor, then a war on poverty can never be successful. The campaign must be waged by environmentalists.

A variant of the innate-deficiency philosophy is found in the view that high birth rates among the poor are the single, most important cause of poverty. Whatever may be said about this aspect of the poverty subculture, and it certainly possesses elements of empirical validity, we have already pointed out that in our view it is merely ancillary, reinforcing and symptomatic rather than basic, at least in the United States.

Finally, if the United States should participate in an extensive foreign aid program dedicated to the eventual elimination of world poverty, an effort that would take much longer than a domestic program, we may anticipate more than a reasonable and legitimate use of the scarcity argument. For example, we might well expect it to be said that we would be devoting so much to a domestic program that nothing would be left for foreigners, or, alternatively, all that we might do would be only a drop in the bucket.

So much for basic thought processes that could arrest the unfolding of an effective antipoverty program. What of the more positive elements of a larger philosophy of poverty? Here it is by no means certain that we can or should proceed simply and obviously to do more of what we are already doing, or to do these things in a more coordinated and imaginative manner. This approach is amply represented in the first subsection below. That we shall so proceed, in part at least, seems very likely.

However, some more wide-ranging intellects have suggested that a war on poverty is but a striking aspect of a larger revolution in social policy, a "permanent revolution" dictated by the emergence of abundant economies in a number of places throughout the world. These emerging surplus economies, of which the United States is only the outstanding example, are in a position to adopt domestic policies, should they so desire, that would substitute quite new principles of distribution of the social dividend. On the basis of these new principles, rising levels of living for all low-income strata would be publicly assured by severing the historic connections established by private property between effort and property control on the one hand and material rewards on the other hand. At least, the linkage between work and income would be severed to the extent that a minimum income per person or per family would be guaranteed.

Such assurance has of course long been more or less explicit in the expansion of the welfare state throughout the world in the twentieth century. Many of the institutional arrangements inaugurating these new principles of distribution are already firmly established, and indeed could be shown to reach as far back as the English Speenhamland system of guaranteed support for the poor, dating from 1795. Contemporary examples of the same principle are found in the personal exemption of the income tax, the principle of progression in the income tax, the old age benefit, the family allowance and other transfer payments.

Thus, in the form of the guarantee of a minimum independent income, a number of much older ideas of social theorists are today being refurbished, enormously buttressed by the permanent and accelerating technological revolution of the twentieth century. Discussions along this line, as well as peripheral to it, are developing as part of the new literature on poverty, and are illustrated in the subsection "Poverty in Perspective" below. We hope that these controversial discussions will stimulate broader and deeper examination of the implications of various antipoverty policy proposals.

Governmental Programs and Their Critics

SUMMARY OF THE ECONOMIC OPPORTUNITY ACT OF 1964

Fiscal 1965 Authorization: $947.5 Million

The Economic Opportunity Act of 1964 establishes an Office of Economic Opportunity in the Executive Office of the President. The OEO is headed by a Director who has a planning and coordinating staff responsible for coordinating the poverty-related programs of all Government agencies. Within the OEO, separate

Summary of the Economic Opportunity Act of 1964: The President's Task Force on the War Against Poverty, August 20, 1964.

staffs operate a Job Corps, a program for Volunteers In Service To America (VISTA), a Community Action Program, and special programs for migrant workers. In addition, the OEO distributes funds to existing agencies to operate other programs authorized under the bill: work-training programs administered through the Labor Department; work-study programs and adult basic education through HEW [Department of Health, Education, and Welfare]; special rural anti-poverty programs through Agriculture; small business loans through the Small Business Administration; and community work and training projects for welfare recipients through HEW.

Following is a summary of the programs authorized under the Economic Opportunity Act of 1964:

Title I—Youth Programs: $412.5 million.

Part A–establishes a *Job Corps* to provide education, work experience, and vocational training in conservation camps and residential training centers; would enroll 40,000 young men and women, aged 16–21, this year, 100,000 next year. Administered by Office of Economic Opportunity. Total cost, $190 million.

Part B–establishes a *Work-Training Program* under which the Director of OEO enters into agreements with State and local governments or nonprofit organizations to pay part of the cost of full- or part-time employment to enable 200,000 young men and women, 16–21, to continue or resume their education or to increase their employability. Administered by Labor Department. Total cost, $150 million.

Part C–establishes a *Work-Study Program* under which the Director of OEO enters into agreements with institutions of higher learning to pay part of the costs of part-time employment to permit 140,000 students from low-income families to enter upon or continue higher education. Administered by Department of Health, Education, and Welfare. Total cost, $72.5 million.

Title II—Community Action Programs: $340 million.

Part A–authorizes the Director of OEO to pay up to 90 percent of the costs of anti-poverty programs planned and carried out at the community level. Programs will be administered by the communities and will coordinate poverty-related programs of various Federal agencies. Total cost, $315 million.

Part B–authorizes the Director to make grants to States to provide basic education and literacy training to adults. Administered by the Department of Health, Education, and Welfare. Total cost, $25 million.

Part C–authorizes the Director to establish and operate a clearing house to facilitate arrangements between foster parents willing to provide financial support and needy children under the guidance of a local agency. Only administrative funds required.

Title III—Programs to Combat Poverty in Rural Areas: $35 million.

Part A–authorizes loans up to $2,500 to very low-income rural families for farm operations and nonagricultural, income-producing enterprises, and loans to low-income family cooperatives. Administered by Department of Agriculture.

Part B–authorizes assistance to establish and operate housing, sanitation, education, and child day-care programs for migrant farm workers and their families. Total cost, not more than $15 million, financed from other Titles.

Part C–authorizes the Secretary of Agriculture to indemnify farmers whose milk has been polluted by pesticides recommended by USDA. No specific funds authorized.

Title IV—Employment and Investment Incentives

Authorizes loans and guarantees to small businesses of up to $25,000 on more liberal terms than the regular loan provisions of the Small Business Administration. Administered by the Small Business Administration. Would use SBA's regular spending authority.

Title V—Work-Experience Programs: $150 million.

Authorizes the Director of OEO to transfer funds to HEW to pay costs of experimental, pilot, or demonstration projects designed to stimulate the adoption in the States of programs of providing constructive work experience or training for unemployed fathers and needy persons.

Title VI—Administration and Coordination: $10 million.

Establishes the Office of Economic Opportunity and specifies its functions. Authorizes the Director of OEO to recruit and train an estimated 5,000 VISTA volunteers to serve in specified mental health, migrant, Indian, and other Federal programs including the Job Corps, as well as in State and community anti-poverty programs.

Title VII—Treatment of Public Assistance

A policy declaration that an individual's opportunity to partici-

pate in programs under this Act shall neither jeopardize, nor be
jeopardized by, his receipt of public assistance.

THE POLITICAL ANALYST:
IT WILL BE A LONG WAR
Bernard D. Nossiter

In what the President has called an "unconditional war" on poverty, the administration is aiming at nothing less than the destruction of the cultural conditions that cause and perpetuate poverty
in the United States. Because this is a vast and largely unex-
plored territory and because so many different disciplines will be
called upon to penetrate it, an evaluation of the administration's
program on economic grounds alone is impossible. Precisely how
long it will last and what it will cost is anybody's guess. Nevertheless, some educated estimates about the program's future are worth
noting. For example, Robert Lampman of the University of Wisconsin thinks that thirty years is a feasible goal. Another economist,
one of the principal architects of the administration's strategy,
contends that at least two generations will be needed to eradicate
poverty in East Harlem alone. In sum, the most informed guesses
foresee a campaign lasting several decades.

Lampman's views are entitled to special respect on several
grounds. His paper in 1959 before the Joint Economic Committee
was the first of the recent attempts to define and describe the dimensions of contemporary poverty. Lampman's unique contribution
was to demonstrate that the percentage of the population defined
as poverty-stricken fell rapidly during the first postwar decade
of reasonably high employment and relatively healthy growth, but

---

The Political Analyst: It Will Be A Long War: From "It Will Be A Long
War," Bernard D. Nossiter, *The Reporter,* Vol. 30, No. 7 (March 26, 1964),
pp. 20–21.

Bernard D. Nossiter. Reporter, the *Washington Post and Times Herald;*
author of *The Myth-makers: An Essay on Power and Wealth.*

much more slowly in the next few years of a lackluster economy. This effectively rebutted the contention that modern poverty is unrelated to the economy's total health. Last spring, when Walter W. Heller, the President's chief economic adviser, first determined to spur an attack on poverty, he turned to Lampman—then on Heller's staff—for a broad design.

To gauge the progress of the campaign, Lampman has devised the concept of the withdrawal rate. This is a measure of the number who each year climb above a set level defined as the poverty line. The idea of a withdrawal rate is likely to become a fixture in the government's planning. Given the current definition of poverty as a family income under $3,000, Lampman concludes that a withdrawal rate of a million a year is within reach of the programs that a Johnson administration is likely to adopt. This rate assumes a high level of employment and some acceleration of economic growth. Since more than thirty million Americans are now below the poverty line, an annual withdrawal rate of one million implies at least a thirty-year program.

This may look like a modest pace, but it is well above the rate sustained even during the buoyant decade after the Second World War. Between 1947 and 1957, Lampman estimates, about 800,000 a year rose from the poverty level. In the next five years, the rate fell to about 500,000. This decline was the result of sluggish growth, high unemployment, and a slower gain in the payments made directly to the poor from Social Security and other channels of transferring income. The economy's recent torpor, then, has left the nation with a deficit of 1.5 million who might otherwise have escaped from poverty. Against this background, Lampman's suggested yearly target of a million withdrawals appears more ambitious; it is in fact approximately double the recent rate.

In a recent conversation with me, Lampman discussed other proposals to transfer income. If Social Security payments were doubled, five million aged persons could be removed at once from the poverty rolls at a yearly cost of $6 billion. Lampman pointed out that in other countries, Canada and Great Britain for example, for years government allowances have been paid to families with children. These payments have helped rescue some deserted, divorced, and widowed mothers and their children from poverty. Indeed, nothing short of such direct payments is likely to do much for the impoverished aged, the fully disabled, and the poverty-stricken female heads of families. If Johnson is elected in November, his next administration probably will press for higher Social Security benefits and perhaps other welfare payments. But under the constraints of the current budget, direct payments of any significant size are simply not on this administration's agenda. A more limited program directed largely to rescuing some of those who can make a productive contribution is the most that the government economists envision now.

The long-range arithmetic of the economists follows these lines: $3 to $4 billion a year is now spent—or, perhaps more accurately, misspent—on scattered programs affecting the poor. The new programs, which will add less than $1 billion to the total effort in fiscal 1965, will be augmented by $2 to $3 billion annually in the next few years. At the peak, the Federal government will spend more than $6 billion a year on the poor. In perhaps ten years, these officials suggest, the Federal share of the costs might decline and state and local governments could be expected to pick up more of the burden.

The administration's strategy for its drive against poverty draws on a wide variety of sources; indeed, nobody can assert with authority what will and won't work. Even so, a set of common assumptions and conclusions underlies the whole project. Here are four essential points that guided the administration:

Because of the current budget restraints and the commitment to hold down public spending, at present the government can employ only limited resources for the huge problem it has chosen to deal with. A memorandum that circulated among the Cabinet in early November made this point explicit.

There are already a host of ill-defined programs to help the poor at the Federal, state, and local levels. They are scattered, uncoordinated, and often duplicating. For example, in one small area of New York, ten agencies are tackling the problems of children on probation.

Poverty is found in two general settings, but only one is strongly resistant to advances in the economy as a whole. Poverty when found in the midst of plenty is relatively easy to deal with. For instance, the children of the impoverished Negroes clustered on a few streets in the comfortable Georgetown section of Washington are able to attend relatively good schools and live in an atmosphere that encourages them to look for a better life. Poverty in the midst of poverty, as in eastern Kentucky or Harlem, poses problems of a different order. Here the whole environment fosters a circular process that traps whole generations.

Some of the planners believe that the tax cut will provide job openings on a larger scale than has been officially forecast. This thesis is disputed both within and without the administration. In any event, it may never be fully tested. Next year, it is quite possible that the budget restraints will be lifted and welfare and public-works spending will be permitted to rise. This prospect will be enhanced if the administration's promise of reducing military expenditures is fulfilled.

From this blend of fact and forecast, the administration drew several conclusions. Programs must rehabilitate impoverished human beings and prepare them for more productive lives. Although direct relief is necessary for some, it won't be granted because of the budget curbs. Thus public works and those measures designed for relief alone should be minimized, and a greater effort made in education and programs that increase the ability of the poor to improve their condition.

Finally, it was agreed that direct attacks must be launched in the sectors where poverty is concentrated and institutionalized, such as the South Side slums of Chicago and the played-out mining communities of West Virginia. This attack must be launched on a broad front, against the whole environment. It cannot be limited to better housing or better schools or vocational training. The principal beneficiaries should be the young, and the principal stratagem on this sector must be to bring the present scattered programs together in some coherent fashion. Also, community leaders must be drawn into the planning. Because of the limit on resources, the campaign may be pushed in only seventy-five communities this year and twice that number the next. But such an approach will yield more dividends than thinly financed programs on a national scale.

THE FAR LEFT: AN OUT-AND-OUT
POLITICAL SWINDLE

Monthly Review

So the "unconditional war on poverty" finally boils down to spending a billion dollars over a period of several years, only half of which is additional to what has already been authorized. This is obviously not enough to get a decent welfare program started in one good-sized city, let alone in the nation as a whole. Only one conclusion is possible: the whole thing is an out-and-out political swindle.

But we cannot leave the matter there. The fact that poverty has now moved to the center of the political stage is an extremely important fact which needs to be both explained and evaluated.

It was not so long ago that the leading theorists and spokesmen of what C. Wright Mills so aptly called the American celebration—Galbraith, Riesman, the younger Schlesinger—were assuring us that poverty in the United States was rapidly vanishing and that it had already ceased to be a major national problem. Then, quite suddenly around the turn of the decade, a new literature of poverty began to appear. During the 1950's anyone who so much as raised the subject of poverty was likely to be contemptuously dismissed as hopelessly out of date; now it's the other way around: no subject is more fashionable. And Johnson's verbal declaration of war puts the highest official imprimatur on the new vogue. How are we to account for this 180-degree turn?

There are two halves to the explanation. In the first place, as Marx pointed out more than a hundred years ago, the process of capitalist development always and everywhere, in the most advanced metropolis as well as in the most backward colony, gen-

The Far Left: An Out-and-Out Political Swindle: From "War on Poverty?" *Monthly Review*, Vol. 15, No. 10 (February, 1964), pp. 533–36.

erates wealth at one pole and want at the other. This is a law which bourgeois economics has, of course, never recognized, propagating instead the apologetic idea that a levelling-up tendency is inherent in capitalist development.[1] This is where the second half of the explanation comes into play. At the root of capitalist poverty, one always finds unemployment and underemployment, directly depriving their victims of income and undermining the security and bargaining power of those with whom the unemployed compete for scarce jobs. Now, during the Second World War—to a greater extent than during the First World War—unemployment was really wiped out for a few years. While 12 million men in the most productive age groups were mobilized into the armed forces, total production was being expanded by more than two thirds. Under these circumstances, every physically able person, regardless of color, age, or sex, could get a job, and most worked long hours overtime to boot. With several members of each family employed, family incomes in the lower-income brackets increased as never before. Poverty was not eliminated overnight, of course, but the improvement in the real living standards of poor people all over the country was nothing short of dramatic. And these favorable conditions for the underprivileged and disadvantaged persisted, even if in less intense form, during the postwar "replenishment" boom and then during the Korean War. For something like a decade, poverty in the United States first receded and then was held at bay, while the economy as a whole expanded under the extraordinary demands of war and its aftermath.

Bourgeois ideologists, wearing the blinkers provided by orthodox economic theory, not unnaturally misinterpreted these events completely. Here at last, they exulted, was capitalism behaving as they expected it to. The past was forgotten, especially the recent past of the Great Depression; the warning lessons of more than a century were ignored; and the future was charted as an extrapolation of the fantastically abnormal years surrounding the greatest war in history. Hence the American celebration, with its cheerful message

---

[1] To avoid misunderstanding, it perhaps needs to be added that the issue here has to do with the distribution of wealth and income, not with the absolute level. That a demoralized unemployable in the United States today receives more in the way of relief than his counterpart of fifty years ago or than the wage of the average worker in many less developed countries, does not make him any less poverty-stricken and miserable by the standards of his own country, which for him are naturally the relevant standards.

that poverty in this the most affluent of countries would soon be no more than an unpleasant memory.

Alas for dreams! Temporarily thwarted, capitalism's laws of motion soon resumed their sway. Unemployment crept steadily up and, what is even more important from our present point of view, tended to be heavily concentrated among the unskilled and semi-skilled. This would have happened in any case, but the nature of the new technologies of the postwar period sharply intensified the disadvantages of the poorly qualified worker. Those at the bottom of the economic ladder who were, in relative terms, the chief beneficiaries of wartime full employment found themselves doubly hard hit by the return to "normalcy." The differential impact of postwar unemployment appears in its most dramatic form when we compare the experience of whites and nonwhites. . . . In 1940 the unemployment rates were 13 percent and 14.5 percent for whites and nonwhites respectively. By 1962, the corresponding figures were 4.9 percent for whites and 11 percent for nonwhites. Negro unemployment was only 11 percent above white in 1940; it was 125 percent greater in 1962. The gap had grown tenfold.

By the end of the 1950's the real state of affairs could no longer be concealed: it was impossible to continue to believe in the existence of a meliorative trend which, given time, would lead to the automatic liquidation of poverty. Not only was poverty still with us, as it always has been; it gave every sign of spreading and deepening. Affluence began to appear for what it is—not a cure for poverty but its Siamese twin. Under these circumstances, it was inevitable that poverty should be looked upon in an entirely different light. From being a transitory annoyance, it suddenly became once again, as it had been before the war, a problem. The first fruit of this changed attitude was the new literature of poverty, the second its reappearance on the political stage. Lyndon Johnson's "war" on poverty is in truth a variation on a theme familiar to all who reached maturity before the war. Franklin D. Roosevelt vowed to change the situation in which "one third of a nation" was "ill-housed, ill-clad, and ill-fed." And before him, as *U.S. News and World Report* reminds us (in its issue dated January 20th), Herbert Hoover, running in 1928 as Republican candidate for President, declared that "We shall soon with the help of God be within sight of the day when poverty will be banished from this nation."

As we know, neither God nor FDR managed to do the job, and

Johnson's paper war is no more likely to succeed. What, then, is the future prospect?

One thing is clear: as unemployment grows under the impact of the new technologies, the poverty at the bottom of the economic ladder is going to get worse and worse.

Beyond that, nothing is certain, but it seems at least likely that if the victims of capitalist "progress" accept their fate passively, little more than empty declarations will come from Washington. If, on the other hand, they begin to raise hell and especially if they begin seriously to organize independently—that is, outside the framework of the present two-party political straitjacket—they may also begin to get some action. In that case, the political managers of American capitalism, of whom Lyndon Johnson may be taken as an archetype, will doubtless see less virtue in budget-balancing and more in spending ten billion dollars or so on the kind of projects listed in the State of the Union Message. If and when that happens, but not before, it will make sense to start talking about a new New Deal.

RIGHT OF CENTER: A BATTLE PLAN OF QUESTIONABLE VALUE

Carl H. Madden and John R. Miles

The various Federal agencies that attempt to measure poverty have no common yardstick for doing so. Without going into detail, the Bureau of Labor Statistics, the Council of Economic Advisers, the Office of Business Economics, and the Census Bureau all produce statistics relating to poverty, but they are not commensurable.

Right of Center: A Battle Plan of Questionable Value: From statement of Carl H. Madden and John R. Miles, Chamber of Commerce of the United States, *Hearings on the Economic Opportunity Act of 1964,* Subcommittee on the War on Poverty, Committee on Education and Labor, House of Representatives, 88th Congress, 2nd Session, April 14, 1964, pp. 663–72.

More importantly for purposes of adequate evaluation and framing of public policy measures, we have no assurance that they correctly identify the poor.

In the four major Federal-State public assistance programs, Congress has left to each State legislature the determination of what plane of living should be considered the poverty line for families and individuals in need. Congress acted in recognition that any such line would vary among the States in an economy as large and varied as the United States, and that the State legislatures are best able to weigh the factors involved in determining the needy among their own citizens.

According to data for 1961, the income deemed necessary to provide for basic living requirements for a mother and three children was fixed at less than $2,400 in 26 States; between $2,400 and $2,700 in 15 other States; and only one State—Alaska, where living costs are very high—puts its subsistence line above the $3,000 cutoff used by the President's Council of Economic Advisers to estimate poverty.

The important question is thus raised as to whether any national measurement of poverty is not likely to have serious shortcomings and to be of questionable value as a policy basis for proposals involving multibillion-dollar outlays.

· · ·

The poverty line of $3,000 takes no account of the assets of families or the process by which families may move into and out of poverty. From one year to another families shift about in the income distribution, some rising above a given poverty line, some falling below it. Such families may move permanently or temporarily from one class to another. For example, unemployed older workers may move permanently into poverty while self-employed professionals may, through chance factors, experience an occasional year of low or even negative income.

Any measure of poverty such as an income level may not only not correctly identify the presently poor but also takes no account of the flow in and out of poverty of families at various stages of life. Asset holdings of families also condition judgments of poverty. In this connection, for families and individuals over 65, asset holdings of children might also be considered by society to be relevant to poverty judgments. Otherwise, when a person 65 or over "moves out" of a child's family to take up separate residence, his income may place him below the poverty line whatever the child's income.

Thus, Government welfare or subsidy payments may mean, in effect, in some cases that the Nation's taxpayers in a complex way are required to subsidize separate residence of oldsters when the resources of their family would be more than adequate to avoid the oldster's poverty.

. . .

In placing the problem of poverty in perspective, the Congress should consider the growing scope of government in American life.

Since 1940, Federal Government spending on goods and services has risen more than twice as fast, and State and local government spending has risen 50 percent faster than personal consumption spending. Moreover, per capita social welfare spending by the Federal Government has risen more than 400 percent since 1929. The question is raised whether extreme caution should not be exercised in an economy of rising incomes and declining poverty before the Government is justified in spending more tax dollars for welfare purposes.

It likewise is important for the Congress to examine the successes and failures of Government in delivering on its promises that programs undertaken would, in fact, eliminate poverty.

The record of agricultural, vocational education, and other such programs should be reviewed objectively to evaluate Government claims. The disparity between the success of the relatively modest agricultural extension program—and its ingenious design to promote Federal-State cooperation—and the lack of success of Government subsidy programs to control production, and the like, should be pointed out. Finally, the Congress should appraise the relation between Government subsidy and Government control.

. . .

A remarkable aspect of the election year "war on poverty" is the extent to which those who, in 1 month, developed the "battle plan" appear to have ignored existing laws and programs that would enable them to get at the problem of poverty more quickly and more effectively than would the programs contemplated under the Economic Opportunity Act of 1964.

According to the Social Security Bulletin for November 1963, we already are spending in excess of $44 billion a year on welfare and welfare-type programs. And Congress last year authorized substantial expansions of many of those programs—not to mention several new ones.

The scope and magnitude of these programs were also spelled out in last week's issue of a leading news magazine—under the appropriate heading: "There's Already a War on Poverty."

Secretary Celebrezze of the Health, Education, and Welfare Department admitted during his recent testimony that 42 current Government programs "have a direct application to poverty."

And now the Congress is asked to create still another agency; to authorize still more programs of highly questionable value; to leave all such programs under the direction of existing agencies, but to give the Economic Opportunity Administrator virtually unlimited powers to coordinate their activities.

· · ·

The national chamber has these additional recommendations that go beyond and therefore do not correspond to any of the provisions of H.R. 10440 as introduced.

Vocational training for adults.—Amend the Vocational Education Act of 1963 to require the Government to encourage, through the U.S. Office of Education, a greater degree of concentration on providing basic skills, including literacy training, for middle-aged people and adults generally.

Compulsory education age limit.—The States should be urged to consider raising the compulsory age limits for education to 18, or high school graduation, with a modification of curriculums in accordance with the aptitudes of the non-college-going youths. This would not necessarily be accomplished through existing school systems, but could be done through vocational and technical training schools.

Draft younger persons.—The President should be urged to issue an Executive order reversing the current order of draft calls to take younger men first, in lieu of the current practice of first drafting 23- and 24-year-olds.

Draft rejectees.—Draft-age youth who fail to meet minimum mental requirements for military service should be remanded to the appropriate State educational system for further training. The States should be urged to establish special training programs for such rejectees, preferably as a part of their vocational-technical training programs.

Guidance facilities.—The States should be encouraged to step up their guidance facilities and to give increased support to research aimed at providing for "more learning in less time," with recognition of different ability levels and cultural backgrounds.

Assistance to educable adults.—There should be established—perhaps by a foundation—a special loan program for educable adults, utilizing long-term loans at low interest, operating through a revolving, nonprofit, self-perpetuating fund, donated by businesses and individuals, with a citizens board to administer the program. Consideration should also be given to establishment of a similar fund for the purpose of increasing mobility through loans to persons desiring to move to new locations. The States should contribute for moves to their State areas, but on a voluntary basis. Changes in State unemployment compensation laws could allow temporary support for those unemployed seeking work in another State. This is now permissible under some State laws.

Expanded or improved statistical program.—A citizens group should be called upon for assistance in the design and supervision of an improved Federal statistical program for unemployment and poverty statistics so we will have available the full characteristics of the unemployed and of the poverty-stricken families.

". . I'M 4–F . . !"

—Conrad in the *Des Moines Register*

LEFT OF CENTER: EMPLOYMENT OPPORTUNITIES BASIC IN COMBATTING POVERTY

AFL-CIO Executive Council

We applaud President Johnson for his pledge to lead the nation in an "unconditional war, here and now, on poverty." With forthrightness and courage he has forced millions of more affluent Americans to face up to the fact that one-fifth of the families in the richest and most productive nation of the world still lives in poverty. Even more important, he has challenged us to end this ugly blight.

The AFL-CIO has long sought to focus public attention on the paradox of poverty in the midst of America's plenty. . . .

In now launching all-out war on poverty, adequate measures to immediately alleviate human suffering are imperative. The food-stamp plan and other measures to provide an adequate diet for all needy families should be improved and extended. But at the same time that such humanitarian efforts are being pursued, fundamental measures must deal with the basic causes of poverty at their roots. In planning these actions, four major areas of responsibility in which the federal government must lead—but in which state and local governments and private groups must cooperate—are evident.

First, it is clearly self-evident that the long and persistent trend of rising unemployment and underemployment must be reversed if any significant progress is to be made in eradicating poverty. Achievement of the national goal of jobs at decent pay for all Amer-

---

Left of Center: Employment Opportunities Basic in Combatting Poverty: From "Waging War on Poverty," AFL–CIO Executive Council, *The American Federationist,* April 1964, pp. 1–6.

icans who are able and willing to work must underlie any realistic anti-poverty program.

The stubborn persistence of poverty since the mid-1950's—during a period in which the majority of Americans have continued to improve their living standards—is substantially rooted in the rising trend of unemployment and part-time work. What is more, if this deplorable situation is allowed to continue—as a consequence of labor displacement at a time when new jobseekers are increasing faster than ever before—we will experience spreading poverty rather than its reduction. If national economic policy continues to enthrone greater productive efficiency and higher profits as the top-priority goals, rather than fulfillment of the promises of the Employment Act of 1946, a crusade against poverty—no matter how well intended—will show only scant results.

National policies to sharply increase employment for the jobless and underemployed, for the victims of discrimination, for the young flocking into the labor force and for those who will be displaced by automation are the essential foundation of an antipoverty program. Through the rest of this decade at least, the American economy must create over 4 million job opportunities a year—more than 80,000 a week—in order to keep Americans at work. To the extent that we fail, want will grow.

On the basis of the record, this objective will not be reached without bold, far-reaching leadership by the federal government.

One of the major needs at this time—in addition to other long-range job-expanding actions—is a vast increase in federal outlays for job-creating public works. This will quickly create jobs—including substantial employment opportunities for unskilled and semiskilled workers—and at the same time provide vitally-needed public improvements of permanent worth. Toward this end, the now expiring Public Works Acceleration program should be extended with a $2 billion appropriation and similar measures should be enacted which would create jobs, producing schools, hospitals, housing, urban redevelopment and other improvements that all communities urgently need.

Special programs should be enacted to provide young people with useful employment opportunities, including jobs in the conservation of natural resources as well as part-time job opportunities in schools and community services for high school and college students to encourage young people to continue their education. Such youth employment measures, however, should be civilian programs, with civilian management and supervision.

These and other job-creating measures can succeed in sustaining full employment only if they are accompanied by effective adjustment procedures to the labor-displacement and community disruption of automation, defense cutbacks and, frequently, foreign imports.

In addition, special measures to assist the jobless and the underemployed are essential parts of the campaign to eliminate poverty. These include improvement of the federal-state unemployment compensation system through the application of federal standards, implementation of the national manpower program in a manner that upgrades skills while safeguarding worker standards, a more effective nationwide public employment service, relocation allowances to aid the jobless to move to areas where work is available, enactment of effective fair employment practices legislation and strengthening the area redevelopment effort. Such measures are vitally important to aid jobless and underemployed workers to improve their incomes and opportunities.

Second, programs to lift the incomes of low-paid workers must be an integral part of the campaign to eradicate the sources of poverty.

Extension of minimum wage coverage and an increase in the minimum hourly rate are essential, as well as special aids for our tragically exploited farm workers, including termination of the bracero importation program. These actions are essential to raise the income standards of the millions of impoverished employed workers and their families.

The federal government also must vigorously support the right of all wage and salary earners to organize and sustain effective unions and engage in collective bargaining—in agriculture as well as in industry and commerce. It is no accident that poverty is usually most prevalent among groups in which union organization is weak or nonexistent and in areas where trade unionism is compelled to function against the handicap of hostile state legislation. The experience of the 1930's clearly indicates that effective labor organization and collective bargaining are vital parts of an effort to help low-paid workers improve their economic status.

Third, a meaningful attack on the causes of want must deal effectively with the need for adequate income maintenance when unavoidable hardships destroy a family's ability to be self-supporting. This is particularly true in the case of most of the aged, broken families generally headed by a woman with children in her care and families in which the breadwinner has died or is incapacitated.

No war against poverty can be meaningful unless adequate family income protection is provided for those who cannot be self-sustaining, even in a full employment economy, because of such hazards. To meet the problems of these families, a whole series of special aids are vitally necessary.

A hospital insurance program for the aged, under social security, should be immediately adopted. Social security benefits for retirees, survivors and the disabled should be substantially increased.

The benefit and coverage levels of all state social insurance and welfare programs must be brought up to date. Moreover, public assistance payments must be increased to meet the family needs of the 1960's and improvements of community welfare programs are required.

To provide decent safeguards for the families of those who are injured or killed at work, federal standards are needed to upgrade the archaic workmen's compensation systems of the states.

Income maintenance when ill and the means to meet the rising costs of adequate medical care are problems confronting most families, but particularly those with the lower incomes. Insurance for the families of breadwinners separated from payrolls by illness—now limited to four states and the railroads—must be improved and extended nationally.

Fourth, in the effort to conquer poverty a substantially increased effort must be launched to meet special problems of the poor in the areas of health, education, housing and personal adjustment. Particularly, increased and improved opportunities for education must be made available for the children of the poor if the cycle of poverty is to be broken.

The war on poverty requires a vast increase in the quantity and improvement in the quality of education, health care, low-cost public housing, consumer counseling and personal guidance services for the members of low-income families. Without such efforts, their avenues toward higher living standards will also be blocked.

Improvement in the educational opportunities available to the children of low-income families, including federal aid for school construction and extension of free public education to the college level, must be viewed as basic public investments in the nation's future. Through supplemental federal aid for school districts where the need is greatest, the spread of junior colleges, substantial increases in the availability and amount of college scholarships and revival of the National Youth Administration idea of the 1930's, greater educational opportunities for these children can be achieved, the cycle of poverty can be broken and the entire nation can be enriched.

Successful war against poverty will automatically do more for American Negroes than for the population as a whole because they are such a disproportionately large part of our families still in want. But more than that, by taking the measures necessary to end poverty, we will create the conditions and climate that will enable us to end more quickly the ugly fact of discrimination in American life.

Action to achieve employment opportunities at decent wages for all Americans able and willing to work must be viewed as the primary underpinning of the anti-poverty program. This is true not only because so many impoverished families have a member who is, or could be, employed and the possession of a decent job is the best way to raise their income status and personal dignity. In addition, the restoration of a full employment, maximum-production economy is also of paramount importance because, as we rapidly raise our national income by effectively utilizing now-wasted resources, America will be even more able to meet the social costs of its anti-poverty crusade on every front.

Moreover, achievement of sustained full employment depends on success in rapidly reducing the prevalence of poverty. The expansion of jobs requires raising the buying power of the millions of low-income families since they are a vast potential market for the goods and services the economy can produce.

President Johnson's pledge to lead the nation in unconditional war on poverty lays down a long overdue challenge to the conscience of the American people. Already substantial public interest has been aroused but, if we really mean to wage this war, victory will not come easily. Offensives must be mounted on many fronts. Long-entrenched attitudes must change. A vast amount of effort and money will have to be expended.

AN ECONOMIC ANALYSIS:
THE NEGATIVE INCOME
TAX AND OTHER POLICIES
ROBERT J. LAMPMAN

Economists can assist in reaching a national consensus on the specific nature of the goal, of ways to measure the distance from and rate of movement toward the goal [of poverty-reduction and elimination]. Hopefully, out of current controversy there will emerge a refined and only infrequently changed measurement of poverty-reduction which will take its place along with the unemployment rate and the growth rate and the consumer price index as guides to appraisal of the performance of the economy.

. . .

It helps to think of the goal in two parts: the reduction of the poverty-rate [i.e., the percentage of all persons or families who are poverty-stricken] and the reduction of the poverty-income-gap [i.e., the aggregate amount by which the present poor population's income falls short of $3,000 per family or $1,500 per unrelated individual]. The aim of policy should be to do each type of reduction without slowing the other and to do both with the least possible sacrifice of and the greatest possible contribution to other important goals.

. . .

Approaches to the reduction of poverty can be seen as parallel to the causes [of poverty]. The first approach . . . is to prevent or counter the events or happenings which select some persons for poverty status. The poverty rate could be lessened by any reduction in early death, disability, family desertion, what Galbraith referred

From "Approaches to the Reduction of Poverty," a paper prepared for delivery at the 77th Annual Meeting of the American Economic Association, Chicago, December 30, 1964, pp. 3–12.

to as excessive procreation by the poor, or by containment of inflation and other hazards to financial security. Among the important events in this context the one most relevant to public policy consideration at this time is excessive unemployment. It would appear that if the recent level of over 5 per cent unemployment could be reduced to 4 per cent the poverty rate would drop by about one percentage point. Further fall in the poverty rate would follow if—by retraining and relocation of some workers—long-term unemployment could be cut or if unemployment could be more widely shared with the non-poor.

To the extent that events are beyond prevention, some, e.g., disability, can be countered by remedial measures. Where neither the preventive nor the remedial approach is suitable, only the alleviative measures of social insurance and public assistance remain. And the sufficiency of these measures will help determine the poverty rate and the size of the poverty-income-gap. It is interesting to note that our system of public income maintenance, which now pays out $35 billion in benefits per year, is aimed more at the problem of income insecurity of the middle class and at blocking returns to poverty than in facilitating exits from poverty for those who have never been out of poverty. The non-poor have the major claim to social insurance benefits, the levels of which in most cases are not adequate in themselves to keep a family out of poverty. Assistance payments of $4 billion now go to 8 million persons all of whom are in the ranks of the poor, but about half of the 35 million poor receive neither assistance nor social insurance payments. One important step in the campaign against poverty would be to re-examine our insurance and assistance programs to discover ways in which they could be more effective in helping people to get out of poverty. Among the ideas to be considered along this line are easier eligibility for benefits, higher minimum benefits, incentives to earn while receiving benefits, ways to combine work-relief, retraining, rehabilitation, and relocation with receipt of benefits.

Among the several events that select people for poverty the ones about which we have done the least by social policy are family break up by other than death and the event of being born poor. Both of these could be alleviated by a family allowance system, which the U.S., almost alone among western nations, lacks. We do, of course, have arrangements in the federal individual income tax for personal deductions and exemptions whereby families of different size and composition are ranked for the imposition of progressive rates. However, it is a major irony of this system that it does not extend the full force of its allowances for children to the really poor. In order to do so, the tax system could be converted to have negative as well as positive rates, paying out grants as well as forgiving taxes on the basis of already adopted exemptions and rates. At present there are almost $20 billion of unused exemptions and deductions, most of which relate to families with children. Restricting the plan to such families and applying a negative tax rate of, say 20 per cent, to this amount would "yield" an allowance total of almost $4 billion. This would not, in itself take many people out of poverty but it would go a considerable distance toward closing the poverty-income-gap, which now aggregates about $12 billion.

It would, of course, be possible to go considerably further by this device without significantly impairing incentive to work and save. First, however, let me reject as unworkable any simple plan to assure a minimum income of $3000. To make such an assurance would induce many now earning less than and even some earning slightly more than $3000 to forego earnings opportunities and to accept the grant. Hence the poverty-income-gap of $12 billion would far understate the cost of such a minimum income plan. However, it would be practicable to enact a system of progressive rates articulated with the present income tax schedule. The per cent rates fall from 70 per cent at the top to 14 per cent at income just above $3700 for a family of five, to zero per cent for income below $3700. The average negative tax rates could move, then, from zero per cent to minus 14 per cent for, say, the unused exemptions that total $500, to 20 per cent for those that total $1000 and 40 per cent for those that total $3700. This would amount to a minimum income of $1400 for a family of five; it would retain positive incentives through a set of grants that would gradually diminish as earned income rose.

The total amount to be paid out (interestingly this would be shown in the Federal budget as a net reduction in tax collections) under such a program would obviously depend upon the particular rates selected, the definition of income used, the types of income-receiving units declared eligible, and the offsets made in public assistance payments. But it clearly could be more than the $4 billion mentioned in connection with the more limited plan of a standard 20 per cent negative tax rate. At the outset it might involve half the poverty-income-gap and total about $6 billion. This amount is approximately equal to the total federal, state, and local taxes now paid by the poor. Hence it would amount to a remission of taxes paid. As the number in poverty fell the amount paid out under this plan would in turn diminish.

The approaches discussed thus far are consistent with the view that poverty is the result of events which happen to people. But there are other approaches including those aimed at removing barriers which keep people in poverty. Legislation and private, volunteer efforts to assure equal educational and employment opportunities can make a contribution in this direction. Efforts to randomize unemployment by area redevelopment and relocation can in some cases work to break down "islands of poverty." Public policy can prevent or modify the forming of a poverty subculture by city-zoning laws, by public housing and by regulation of private housing, by school re-districting, by recreational, cultural, and public health programs. It is curious that medieval cities built walls to keep poverty outside. Present arrangements often work to bottle it up inside cities or parts of cities and thereby encourage poverty to function as its own cause.

The third broad approach to accelerated reduction of poverty relates to . . . limited ability or motivation. The process of economic growth works the poverty line progressively deeper into the ranks of people who are below average in ability or motivation, but meantime it should be possible to raise the ability and motivation levels of the lowest. It is interesting that few children, even those of below average ability, who are not born and raised in poverty, actually end up in poverty. This suggests that poverty is to some extent an inherited disease. But it also suggests that if poor children had the same opportunities, including pre-school training and remedial health care, as the non-poor, . . . the rate of escape from poverty would be higher. Even more fundamentally, we know that mental retardation as well as infant mortality and morbidity have an important causal connection with inadequate pre-natal care, which in turn relates to low income of parents.

A belief in the economic responsiveness of poor youngsters to improved educational opportunities underlies policies advocated by many educational theorists from Bentham to Conant. And this widely shared belief no doubt explains the emphasis which the Economic Opportunity Act places upon education and training. The appropriation under that Act, while it seems small relative to the poverty-income-gap, is large relative to present outlays for education of the poor. I would estimate that the half-billion dollars or so thereby added increases the national expenditure for this purpose by about one-seventh. To raise the level of educational expenditure for poor children—who are one-fifth of the nation's children but who consume about a tenth of educational outlay—to equal that of the average would cost in the neighborhood of $3 billion. Such an emphasis upon education and training is justified by the fact that families headed by young adults will tend, in a few years, to be the most rapidly increasing group of poor families.

THE DISENGAGEMENT OF SOCIAL WORKERS FROM THE POOR

S. M. Miller

Richard Cloward writes of social work's increasing disengagement from the poor. Other professions have never engaged themselves or have insufficiently engaged themselves with the plight of the poor. Each profession and social service has to confront the issue of how much existing practice is aimed at dealing with the problems of the poor as they presently exist in the United States.

The "welfare state" is a slogan rather than a reality. As Harrington has pointed out for the United States and Richard Titmuss for Great Britain, the extension of welfare services in the "semi-affluent society" has not primarily benefited those at the bottom of the economic ladder. Mainly the upper working class and especially the middle classes have gained from the extension of social services.

The varied character of the poor suggests that differential poli-

The Disengagement of Social Workers From the Poor: From "Poverty and Inequality in America: Implications for the Social Services," S. M. Miller, *Child Welfare,* Vol. XLII, No. 9 (November, 1963), pp. 444–45.

cies must be carried out to deal effectively with particular segments of the poor—no one measure will be effective with all. For example, "heating up the economy" so that more jobs will be generated will not benefit those of the poor who are unable to work, whether for physical or familial reasons (for example, female heads of households). On the other hand, improvement in social services will not basically solve the problems of unemployment in distressed areas, even though it might alleviate them.

Consequently, it becomes especially important today to clarify the goals of professionals and of the social services. If many of the poor are likely to be a permanent poor, there must be a search for the kind of programs that will be most effective in ameliorating their conditions. On the other hand, those of the poor who can be helped to improve their conditions—who have some economic potential—need a kind of help that is aimed at this potential.

We do not have a coordinated and well-aimed set of policies to deal with the extent and character of poverty today. We are not dealing with the poverty of the 1930's nor with the poverty of the turn of the century when all immigrant groups were to be helped to "Americanize," with the facile idea that they would then rapidly work their way up the occupational ladder.

The goals of various social services have to be redirected to meet the changed conditions of the sixties. Many of the poor will be permanently poor, and so will their children; others may escape into the main economy. Are the strategies and tactics of the social services differentiated enough and suitable to deal with the varied kinds of poor with their different prospects and conditions?

Services aimed at individual treatment are not enough. Professionals and their organizations must support and encourage action that will deal with the larger American scene in which poverty is being produced and maintained. The professional role cannot end with the limited services that the profession provides; it must extend itself to pressure for social changes that will make individualized professional services more meaningful and effective. Concentrating on individualized services, without concern for the forces outside the profession that are molding and limiting possibilities, is tantamount to adopting professional blinders. These blinders may promote confidence in one's expertise and effectiveness, but they force the professional to ignore the barriers to deep and continuing change among the clientele.

Casework services have to be flexible, adaptive, and able to range over a variety of activities. Are services predicated on the likelihood that, in the near future, the number of female-based families will not decrease and that most of them are permanently without a male figure? Have we developed unmechanical "functional equivalents" to provide the kinds of experiences and feelings that a father might give to his children? And are we even certain what these "experiences and feelings" are? In the effort to deal with such questions, casework services must be remolded to handle more effectively the pressing and continuing problems of today.

There is inadequate understanding of the styles of life of low-income groups. Programs of professional action are frequently not based on and oriented to these styles of life—sometimes the professional strategies and tactics are extensions of what is believed to be important for middle-class individuals.

Education is the escape route from poverty. Therefore, many services to families should be more directly oriented to improving the educational chances and performances of the youth and, perhaps, also the adults in low-income families. In this connection, it is important to recognize that many low-income families, especially Negro families, have a very high regard for education. Nonetheless, many children of these families are early school-leavers. Among other reasons, this is because of the parents' inability to translate their general strong interest in education into effective support of the children in school, and the inability (and frequent indifference) of schools to capitalize on the particular emphasis on education in many low-income families.

Public and private agencies dealing with low-income groups might seek to orient and concentrate their services on enhancing the educational prospects of low-income youth rather than having a less specific and less efficient emphasis on a "general improvement" in family and individual functioning.

The example of education underlines the importance of stressing the positive elements in low-income life. In contrast to Harrington's pessimistic portrait of a "culture of poverty," of apathy, indifference, and of withdrawal, the professional must seek out the signs of strength and accentuate them. Recent political events in Negro and Spanish-speaking communities point up the lack of attention to and understanding of these strengths.

ONLY THE FEDERAL GOVERNMENT CAN ABOLISH POVERTY

Michael Harrington

There is only one institution in the society capable of acting to abolish poverty. That is the Federal Government. In saying this, I do not rejoice, for centralization can lead to an impersonal and bureaucratic program, one that will be lacking in the very human quality so essential in an approach to the poor. In saying this, I am only recording the facts of political and social life in the United States.

The cities are not now capable of dealing with poverty, and each day they become even less capable. As the middle class flees the central urban area, as various industries decentralize, the tax base of the American metropolis shrinks. At the same time, the social and economic problems with which the city must deal are on the rise. Thus, there is not a major city in the United States that is today capable of attacking poverty on its own. On the contrary, the high cost of poverty is dragging the cities down.

The state governments in this country have a political peculiarity that renders them incapable of dealing with the problem of poverty. They are, for the most part, dominated by conservative rural elements. In every state with a big industrial population, the gerrymander has given the forces of rural conservatism two or three votes per person. So it is that the state legislatures usually take more money out of the problem areas than they put back into them. So it is that state governments are notoriously weighted in the direction of caution, pinchpenny economics, and indifference to the plight of the urban millions.

Only the Federal Government Can Abolish Poverty: From *The Other America: Poverty in the United States,* Michael Harrington (New York: Macmillan, 1962), pp. 170–71.

The various private agencies of the society simply do not have the funds to deal with the other America. And even the "fringe benefits" negotiated by unions do not really get to the heart of the problem. In the first place, they extend to organized workers in a strong bargaining position, not to the poor. And second, they are inadequate even to the needs of those who are covered.

It is a noble sentiment to argue that private moral responsibility expressing itself through charitable contributions should be the main instrument of attacking poverty. The only problem is that such an approach does not work.

So, by process of elimination, there is no place to look except toward the Federal Government. And indeed, even if there were alternate choices, Washington would have to play an important role, if only because of the need for a comprehensive program and for national planning. But in any case there is no argument, for there is only one realistic possibility: only the Federal Government has the power to abolish poverty.

In saying this, it is not necessary to advocate complete central control of such a campaign. Far from it. Washington is essential in a double sense: as a source of the considerable funds needed to mount a campaign against the other America, and as a place for coordination, for planning, and the establishment of national standards. The actual implementation of a program to abolish poverty can be carried out through myriad institutions, and the closer they are to the specific local area, the better the results. There are, as has been pointed out already, housing administrators, welfare workers, and city planners with dedication and vision. They are working on the local level, and their main frustration is the lack of funds. They could be trusted actually to carry through on a national program. What they lack now is money and the support of the American people.

NEW HAVEN, CONNECTICUT: WHAT ONE CITY CAN DO

Howard W. Hallman

In declaring unconditional war on poverty in America, President Johnson has stated that "we urgently need to bring together the many existing programs—federal, state, local, and private—and focus them more effectively in a frontal assault on the sources of poverty. Most important, we shall encourage and assist communities and regions to develop their own plans of action: to mobilize their own resources as well as those available under federal programs."

With these words the gauntlet has been thrown down to American communities. The challenge has been made. If the President can deliver the resources, cities and regions will have an unprecedented opportunity to take initiative in solving a major problem that confronts the nation. What does a city do if it accepts this challenge? Can a city really take initiative in a federal-aid program? For one answer, the experience in New Haven, Connecticut can be instructive.

New Haven has been engaged in a frontal assault on poverty for the past two years. Blessed with grants from the Ford Foundation and several federal agencies, this city of 152,000 has been able to muster new resources that will total about three million dollars this year. The multi-phased program that is underway corresponds closely with the five keys to better earning power that the President listed in his Economic Report to the Congress: education, health, skills in jobs, community and area rehabilitation, and equal opportunity.

New Haven, Connecticut: What One City Can Do: From *New Haven's Attack Upon Poverty,* Howard W. Hallman (New Haven, Conn.: Community Progress, Inc., March 3, 1964), pp. 1–8.

Howard W. Hallman. Deputy Director, Community Progress, Inc., New Haven, Conn.

From this experience gained so far in New Haven, it seems that there are four essential ingredients in a local program to break the cycle of poverty:

1. Political and civic leadership
2. An effective organizational structure
3. Simultaneous use of a variety of program techniques
4. Sufficient resources.

In New Haven, the program techniques do not turn out to be startlingly new except in their comprehensive application. As a demonstration city, resources have been plentiful. . . . Pulling together the many agencies that must share in the total program has been perhaps the most difficult task, but this has been possible because of the enlightened political and civic leadership found in New Haven.

POLITICAL AND CIVIC LEADERSHIP

New Haven's political leadership is centered in Mayor Richard C. Lee, who has been in office since 1954. When he first became mayor, he called for a "decade of dedication" to rid the city of slums and to rebuild the commercial heart of New Haven. Fortunately, the voters have had the wisdom to keep Dick Lee in office for six consecutive two-year terms. With this continuity of vigorous leadership New Haven has simultaneously tackled redevelopment of the central business district, promoted industrial renewal, embarked upon neighborhood rehabilitation, constructed new housing at all rent levels, and developed a modern highway system.

If this were not enough, public education has been revitalized. As a regular city department, the Board of Education is appointed by the Mayor and its budget is set by the Board of Finance. Lee's appointees to the school board have undertaken a far-reaching program to give to New Haven a modern school system. A building program has started to replace forty percent of the schools within a ten year period. An able new superintendent—Dr. Laurence C. Paquin—was recruited, and under his direction the school curriculum is being broadened and improved.

Lee's insistence upon excellence and dedication has affected every department in City Hall. A municipal staff of high professional competence has been developed.

The Mayor has been in the center of these changes, but he has not stood alone. Throughout this decade the urban renewal program has received the backing of prominent civic leadership, channeled through an advisory body known as the Citizens' Action Commission.

The Community Council of Greater New Haven, which is the planning agency for health and welfare services has worked in close partnership with City Hall. It has been a key source of leadership for tackling the myriad social problems which confront New Haven in common with other American cities.

As these political, civic and administrative leaders worked together, they made progress with one problem only to have another emerge. Redevelopment eliminated many slum dwellings, but it uncovered multi-problem families who had been bypassed by social agencies for years and years. New school buildings could be built, but since the school population was showing an increasing number of pupils from rural backgrounds, a new curriculum would have to be devised. Health and welfare services were mobilized for families in trouble, but the basic problem often turned out to be lack of employment.

Faced with this complex array of problems, the Redevelopment Agency, the Board of Education, and the Community Council entered into a dialogue to strive for solutions. As this was going on, the Ford Foundation dangled before a number of cities the carrot of possible grants for comprehensive programs dealing with the problems of "gray areas." New Haven was in a fine state of readiness, and the three agencies, under Mayor Lee's leadership, put together a program which merited a $2.5 million, three-year grant from the Ford Foundation. The program is aimed at six inner-city neighborhoods which contain three-fifths of the city's population and one-fourth of the population of the metropolitan area.

The Ford grant established the basic framework. It was then possible to obtain funds from several federal agencies for specialized programs. None of these grants would have been made, however, without the initiative of political and civic leadership, which is the starting point for local community action.

ORGANIZATIONAL STRUCTURE

The new program was designed with many elements: employment, education, leisuretime activities, health and welfare services, special youth activities, neighborhood organization, housing. The basic strategy called for the involvement of the key public and private agencies in the city to carry out these various elements, but it was also apparent that there needed to be a coordinating body that could pull them together into a concerted whole. Thus, a new non-profit corporation, Community Progress, Inc., was established.

CPI—as this organization is called in New Haven—is governed by a board of directors with nine members. Its make-up represents the coalition behind the total approach. The Mayor appoints three directors, and one each is designated by the Board of Education, Redevelopment Agency, Community Council, United Fund, Citizens' Action Commission, and Yale University.

This board appointed Mitchell Sviridoff as executive director. A community leader in his own right, Sviridoff was formerly president of the Connecticut State AFL-CIO, and he served as president of the New Haven Board of Education during an important period of change. He possesses a combination of vision, leadership, persuasiveness, skill in negotiation, and a sprinkling of toughness that is needed in so complex an undertaking.

With the money in hand, the new organization chartered, and the executive director and other staff on the job, New Haven went about the task of building a workable structure. Although there was no grand design in the beginning, it is possible after two years of operation to describe the approach that has developed.

CPI and the other members of the New Haven coalition have realized that poverty and related social problems stem from a complexity of interrelated causes. Persons are trapped in these conditions because something is not working properly in the social system. To get at these causes, to open opportunities for people to help themselves, it is necessary to make corrections in the social system, that is, to bring about institutional change.

With this as a starting point, it is then possible to look upon the city as a network of interrelated systems. There is an educational system, an employment system, a system of health and welfare services, and so on. Each system is organized differently, but it usually includes both public and private agencies and it involves not only local governmental agencies, but also state and national agencies. When a system is functioning effectively, it will respond to new problems as they emerge ánd make necessary adaptations. But the existence of mass poverty in an affluent society suggests a serious lack in one or more functional systems.

Take the problem of unemployment, for example. Responsibility for dealing with it is badly fragmented at the local level. In Connecticut the State Employment Service provides testing and placement and administers unemployment compensation. The state and local welfare departments provide relief for the destitute unemployed. The State Division of Vocational Education operates regional high schools for vocational education. The local Board of Education prepares people for employment through the high school and adult education courses. Employers and unions are in the center of the hiring process.

In New Haven the first step was to pull this system together at the policy level. This was done by establishing the Mayor's Committee on Manpower Resources and Employment, which Mayor Lee chairs himself. On it are representatives of the State Department of Education, State Employment Service, New Haven Board of Education, Chamber of Commerce, Central Labor Council, CPI, and United Fund. CPI's manpower director serves as executive secretary.

On the working level, a joint manpower staff has been assembled at CPI headquarters. It includes persons on the payroll of CPI directly and persons assigned by the Central Labor Union, State Department of Education, and the New Haven Board of Education. A representative of the State Employment Service will join them soon. This team acts as a permanent working committee to design and carry out various manpower programs to serve the unemployed. In addition, three neighborhood offices have been established in the inner city, and they are jointly staffed by the State Employment Service and CPI.

The effectiveness of this approach was dramatically illustrated in January [1964], when the Winchester Division of Olin-Mathieson, New Haven's largest employer, announced that it would be laying off 500 workers by June because the Defense Department had cancelled a contract for the M-14 rifle. The next day the Mayor's Committee met. Fortunately, just four days earlier the working team had agreed upon twelve training programs for 446 people. Olin could add to that number by examining needs in other sections of the plant. Since the processing route from New Haven to state offices in Hartford to regional offices in Boston to Washington and back again was well known, it was decided to contact the key federal officials to speed the processing of funds for the training programs. So the team rolled into action.

The employment system offers the most dramatic example of the New Haven approach because it was so loosely organized and because great progress has been made. But the same strategy applies with other functional systems.

In the field of education, primary emphasis has been upon the New Haven Board of Education, one of the original partners in the program. With a staff of over one thousand it represents a subsystem by itself. In addition, the State Department of Education is playing an important role in training related to employment. The New Haven Public Library has on the drawing boards a plan for a store front library that would be closely related to nearby public schools.

The Community Council, another original sponsor, has been the traditional coordinator of health and welfare planning, and it continues to play that role. CPI has added the resources of neighborhood coordinators in each of the six inner-city neighborhoods where the program operates, and this has enhanced coordination on the worker level. The existence of demonstration funds has meant that new techniques could be utilized. Moreover, the relations with state and federal agencies concerned with health and welfare services have been strengthened.

The City's Development Administrator and the Redevelopment Agency, the third of the original partners, have long had the responsibility for pulling together the private and public resources, including state and federal, that relate to housing and city development. CPI has supported this effort where appropriate.

In a similar manner other systems have been drawn into the program: leisure-time (public recreation, after school activities, private group work agencies), legal (police, legal aid, public defender), correctional (juvenile court, state correctional institutions).

CPI acts as a catalyst to assist each functional system in embarking upon changes that will mean more effective services to the poverty group. It serves as a coordinator so that the functional systems will work together as an integrated network. This is accomplished through the board of directors, which represents key agencies in each system, and through the staff in their relations with public officials and private agency personnel. While much remains to be done, linkages between education, employment, and health and welfare services have been established where they scarcely existed before.

This interlocking network of programs is carried into the inner-city neighborhoods through the Community School. This is a remarkable, new concept and is central to the New Haven program. What it means is that the school serves as a neighborhood institution with many functions: education, leisure time activities, social services, neighborhood organization. These functions are related one to another, and the various agencies that carry out programs in the community school plan together and coordinate their efforts. Leadership for this process is provided by the school principal, the community school coordinator, and CPI's neighborhood coordinator. In this way, families are treated as a whole. Right on the front line, programs seeking to remove the causes of poverty are integrated into a meaningful whole.

PROGRAM ACTIVITIES

What are the specific elements that make up New Haven's attack upon the causes of poverty? Altogether there are over fifty separate activities, falling into the main categories of education, employment, health and welfare services, leisure time activities, legal services, housing, and neighborhood organization. Here are some of the highlights.

The employment programs are designed to take maximum advantage of available opportunities in the New Haven area. A 1962 survey revealed that while there were 6500 unemployed, 3500 jobs were open because of the lack of skilled applicants. Although some of these jobs were highly skilled occupations, such as engineering, many of them required skills that could be developed through short-term training. Examples are draftsmen, laboratory technicians, machine operators, cooks, typists.

Therefore, specific skill-training programs are devised by the working team of CPI, state and local education, employment service, management and labor. Usually jobs are committed in advance so that motivation is high. Recruitment is done through the central employment service and neighborhood employment centers.

In 1963 about 300 persons went through such training and nearly 90 percent of them went into jobs. This number will be more than doubled in 1964.

These skill training programs are being supplemented by other activities. Out-of-school youths are assigned to work crews, and the tasks they perform in parks, neighborhood centers, and other community service projects help them to develop work habits and attitudes. At the same time they are provided with remedial education and are taught how to apply for a job. Thirty youths are now involved, and this will be doubled or tripled when more funds are obtained.

A program of basic education is being designed for adults who have been unemployed for a long period. Many of them are on relief. Training up to 72 weeks in duration will begin with basic education in reading, writing, and arithmetic, and will move to instruction in specific skills. This program will serve about 400 each year.

Two types of in-plant training are being planned. One is vestibule training, where the trainee is paid a training allowance but is trained at the place of employment. The other is on-the-job training, where the trainee is paid a wage by the company and performs production work while learning. It is anticipated that several hundred persons a year can receive such training.

Closely related to employment opportunities are the educational programs, which range from pre-kindergarten to adult literacy.

A pre-kindergarten program serves over 200 three- and four-year-old youngsters to help them prepare for school. Stress is upon language patterns and other skills needed to promote success in school. The children's parents attend a complementary program.

Reading specialists have been assigned to all of the inner city elementary schools. They work mostly with teachers to improve the quality of reading instruction, but they also give certain youngsters intensive help in learning to read.

Nine helping teachers are working in seven schools, and this number is likely to be expanded. They are experienced teachers who work with other teachers to improve the quality of teaching. This reverses the usual trend whereby the ablest teachers avoid the inner city schools.

A higher horizons program is operating in fifty classrooms. Its purpose is to provide wider social and cultural experiences and to increase motivation for learning. Among the activities are creative dramatics; visits by businessmen, authors, artists, musicians, and scientists; performances of dance, music and drama; a junior great books program; field trips; and an experiment with bilingual instructions for *all* pupils in one class that has a sizable number of Puerto Rican children.

A series of programs is getting underway for the intermediate school years, grades five to eight. The common focus will be upon dropout prevention through remediation of educational deficiencies before it is too late. Last September a start was made with a modified curriculum for 60 seventh and eighth grade boys who have had a history of non-conforming behavior in school; the idea is to change the curriculum to serve the needs of these youths instead of forcing them to adapt to the traditional classroom situation. Also started is an individualized curriculum at one junior high school, with the aim of doing away with the rigid college-commercial-general labels; this will enable the bright youngster who is not going to college to take such courses as advanced mathematics that will prepare him for a good technical job. Several other related programs will start this spring.

At the secondary level the stress is upon work-related learning so that, as far as possible, every high school graduate will be employable and those who might otherwise drop out will find a reason to stay in school. A ninth grade work-study program is underway with twenty-four participants. Twenty boys and twenty girls who applied but were not admitted to the regional vocational school will be given three years of pre-vocational training related to marketable skills. A business education program will stress data processing. A curriculum is being planned that will prepare youth for middle technical occupations. Each of these is starting as a small pilot program but will be expanded if the initial experience is successful.

Substantial improvements are being made in guidance counseling, with greater stress on occupational guidance for youth who will terminate their formal education with the completion of high school. Study clinics have been organized. And to break away from the traditional educational mold a special volunteer summer school was conducted last summer with 1800 youth from grades four to twelve in attendance.

Courses ranged from remedial reading and refresher math to speed reading and ideas of modern math. Teachers were given the opportunity to try new ideas and new teaching techniques. The response of both students and teachers was enthusiastic, and now city funds have been appropriated to repeat and expand it in the coming summer.

For adults, a literacy program has been organized. Attendance has grown from the six who first came last June to a current enrollment of over two-hundred. One store front minister brought fifteen members of his church. Especially appealing is the opportunity to move from a literacy class into skill training programs, which have been described earlier.

In the field of health and welfare, the aim of the New Haven program is to provide the inner city with a wide roster of community services that are excellent in quality, sufficient in quantity, and effectively coordinated. The first effort has focused upon coordination, and CPI neighborhood coordinators in the six inner-city neighborhoods are working to build teams of welfare workers, visiting nurses, school social workers, probation officers, and others. They are assisted by neighborhood workers, who are indigenous nonprofessionals. The neighborhood coordinators are also responsible for neighborhood organization.

At the same time, several demonstration programs have been developed to try new methods of service. In one neighborhood school nurses and visiting nurses have been combined into a single community nursing team that serves the family as a whole. An effort is being made to provide a coordinating family worker for some large families who are living in private housing with subsidized rent as part of a housing demonstration program.

The most ambitious undertaking, which is still in the planning stage, is an effort to provide a full array of services to all families living in an 855-unit public housing project. Sponsored by a Federal Task Force on Concerted Services, this demonstration will have a family centered service unit, a full time public health physician, community nurses, a vocational rehabilitation team, home-making services, and a day care center. It would tie into the employment, education, and recreation programs already available in the neighborhood.

Leisure time services are developed and supervised by a team of four: CPI's coordinator, the community school coordinator, a public recreation supervisor, and a private groupwork supervisor. They develop their plans with neighborhood residents and hire part-time activity leaders to conduct programs.

All fifty of the programs have not been mentioned, but this gives the essence. Two points remain to be stressed about the total program.

First, the concept of equal opportunity runs through the entire program although only two programs—grants to the Human Relations Council for an equal housing program and to the Urban League for employment activities—are aimed exclusively at equal opportunity. The employment program, which serves all unemployed in the inner city, has given minority persons the skills they need to obtain employment, and the advance commitment of employers assures placement. An interesting sidelight has been individual placement that has so far assisted about seventy-five Negroes to get into approximately twenty-five occupational categories where they had not been previously employed in New Haven. The educational programs have improved the quality of education so that Negro and Puerto Rican youth will be able to compete in the job market. Meanwhile, the Board of Education is developing a plan, to be implemented next September, "to provide intermingling of pupils from a broad spectrum of racial, as well as social and economic backgrounds."

Second, the community school is the central, neighborhood institution for carrying out the various activities. The educational programs and most of the leisure time programs are conducted in schools. The community school is used as a center for community services and neighborhood organization, and the CPI neighborhood coordinator has an office there. The neighborhood employment centers would have been in community schools had space permitted, but they are located nearby and are supervised by the neighborhood coordinator to assure program integration.

RESOURCES

A program of this breadth costs money. The three million dollars of new money that will be spent this year in New Haven comes from a variety of sources: Ford Foundation; President's Committee on Juvenile Delinquency; U.S. Labor Department; Housing and Home Finance Agency; New Haven Redevelopment Agency; City of New Haven; and New Haven Foundation. In the concerted services project negotiations are underway for grants from several constituent agencies of the Department of Health, Education and Welfare, including the Bureau of Family Services, the Public Health Service, and the Vocational Rehabilitation Administration. Undoubtedly a request will be made for a grant under the Vocational Education Act of 1963.

The first grant—from the Ford Foundation—was the hardest to obtain, for it meant putting together the prerequisite coalition of forces and formulating the ideas for a total approach. This grant not only paid for the initial programs but it also established the basic staff, which could then develop other new programs and seek additional sources of financing. Since most of the other grants have been for specialized programs, it has been essential to have the Ford financing for general administration.

If the Johnson poverty program is to succeed in its aim to "encourage and assist communities and regions to develop their own plans of action," a necessary first step will be to make funds available for the establishment of the local instrument. With such a coordinating body in existence, it becomes much more feasible to pool the available local, state and national resources in a total assault upon poverty.

In America we may not yet know how to eliminate poverty entirely, but we certainly know more techniques than we are now applying. We have hopes that adequate resources will be forthcoming so that these techniques can be put into action. It remains to be seen whether national and local political and civic leadership can work together successfully or whether communities can effectively organize to utilize all the available techniques and resources.

If these elements of leadership, organization, techniques, and resources come together, can we really expect to make a substantial reduction in poverty? The New Haven experience provides grounds for cautious optimism.

Poverty in Perspective

Harry Martin: The Dreams of a Six Year Old

"I'm going to be a lawyer," said Harry, aged six. "Lawyers make good money. I'm going to keep my money."

"I'm going to be a doctor," said his seven-year-old brother firmly, "and I'm going to take care of my family."

Their eight-year-old sister announced serenely, "I'm going to be a nurse in a big hospital and wear a real uniform and help people."

The sweet optimism of youth could have been heard in millions of American homes, but this home was rather special.

Though it was midafternoon, the tenement was dark. Gray plastic sheeting was tacked to the insides of the windows. Plaster was off part of the ceiling and walls, and strands of hair on laths trembled with the passing wind from outside. Double doors opened onto the kitchen, which was almost invisible. Its windows, too, were sealed with opaque plastic, presumably to preserve heat. But the darkness was thickened by a crisscross of clothes-lines that filled the room with hanging rags of clothes. In one corner of the kitchen was a table with three legs and one chair. In another was a stove bearing a pan of cold soapy water with clothes soaking, next to it a pan of cold beans and beside that a crusted frying pan bearing one single short rib congealed with fat. Through one kitchen door was a bathroom with the toilet boarded over; it had frozen and burst in the winter cold. Through another door was "the kids' room," two beds for seven children. Neither bed had a mattress; the children slept on the springs.

"Look at this book I got from school," Harry said. "Want to hear me read?"

Harry read about Dick and Jane and their dog, Spot. Dick and Jane were clean-cut, well-dressed Anglo-Saxon children who lived behind a white picket fence in a red-roofed cottage with geraniums in the window. Their mother was a smiling blonde with clear, square teeth. Their father wore a snap-brim hat, a conservative suit, and carried a briefcase. And they all lived happily in a schoolbook called *Friends and Neighbors.*

Little Harry might as well have been reading science fiction. His own family had never in his memory eaten a meal together—there

Harry Martin: The Dreams of a Six Year Old: From "The Invisible Americans," Ben Bagdikian, *Saturday Evening Post,* December 21–28, 1963, pp. 37–38.

were not enough chairs, dishes or forks. The mother's role or the oldest daughter's at mealtime was to watch as each child took a portion of the pot on the stove to make sure no one took more than his share.

But Harry was still eager to please. He had not yet learned that other people expected him to be like Dick and his sister to be like Jane, to have parents like Dick and Jane's, to live in a house like Dick and Jane, and that as a Negro slum kid all of this was as remote to him as the canals of Mars. And unless he were uncommonly lucky, this book and the school would soon seem as remote.

The Martins—a fictitious name—are living off welfare. They came from McCrory, Ark., six years before, and Martin got a job at $84 a week in a meat-packing plant. Last year the plant moved away, and the family went on welfare. Last winter a newborn child whose crib was a supermarket basket died of pneumonia. Martin began drinking and has been more or less drunk ever since.

Mrs. Martin looks weary and bewildered, huddling in the perpetual twilight of their tenement, fearful of the outside world. She was hard to picture as a young woman entering a new city with excitement—until I asked when she had last bought a dress. She stared blankly and then for the first time her eyes lost their emptiness and she smiled. Her voice had a kind of life it had not had before, so much so the children stopped talking and listened in amazement.

"It was six years ago. We was making good money at the meat plant and he took me out to a dress shop. When he saw how much I liked that dress, he said, 'Honey, you get it.' It cost thirty dollars. Oh, that was a dress. I mean it really *was* a dress. It was pink, and it was cut a lot lower than this one and it had sequins all over, and they shined and shined and the pink was so pretty."

The girl from McCrory, Ark., was for the first time identifiable as a woman with a range of emotions. Then the face began to sag again. She wiped her hands automatically on the side of her stained dress, and one could see that her slip was held up with pieces of knotted twine.

Outside, Sister Mary William, the young, tall, indomitable Irish nun who strode through Chicago's West Side, looked down the endless line of row houses, at the trash barrels lolling on their sides, the broken glass laid like a glistening carpet as far as the eye could see. It was the sight her own father had looked at when he first visited from St. Louis and asked his daughter in dismay, "What was it you did that was so bad they sent you here?"

She crunched the broken glass under her awkward black shoes and said, "You figure out what's going to happen to Harry Martin when he finds out he's never going to be a lawyer. And his brother's never going to be a doctor. And his sister's never going to be a nurse. The worst most of us have to resign ourselves to is that there's no Santa Claus. Wait until this hits those kids."

THE HUNGRY WORLD

Royal Bank of Canada

The United Nations Declaration of Human Rights, adopted in 1948, says: "Everyone has the right to a standard of living adequate for the health and well-being of himself and of his family."

To have a good standard of living does not mean becoming encumbered with western world impedimenta. It does mean not having to eat grass, as women have been seen to do near the Persian Gulf; it does mean that the emaciated labourer in China does not have to go for a day on scraps of food that contain only 200 calories while his Canadian counterpart has a regular 2,500-calorie intake.

Owen D. Young said at the University of California: "Let no man think that the living standards of America can be permanently maintained at a measurably higher level than those of the other civilized countries. Either we shall lift theirs to ours or they will drag ours down to theirs."

• • •

One thing is certain: The import of food from the wealthier to the less wealthy regions can never provide more than a small part of what is needed. We cannot feed the underdeveloped countries by scraping our bins, borrowing on next year's crops, shipping dried eggs, lard or milk. Pearson and Paarlberg point out in their book *Starvation Truths, Half-Truths, Untruths:* if all feeding of wheat to live-stock in Canada and the United States were prohibited, and the consumption of wheat by human beings reduced by 25 percent; if the acreage of corn and oats were reduced by 25 percent and planted to wheat; we could produce about 1,000 million additional bushels of grain for human consumption. On the

---

The Hungry World: From "The Hungry World," *Monthly Letter,* Royal Bank of Canada, June 1964, pp. 1–4.

Chinese standard, this would feed about 80 million people for a year. As has been estimated by the United Nations, more than 1,500 million people have to be fed.

. . .

So basically influenced are human beings by the need for food that peace and war, international understanding, and the whole fabric of human social life are profoundly affected by it. Prince Philip said in an address to Canadian engineers and scientists in Toronto: "It is recognized that an explosive situation will inevitably develop if the gap between the 'have' nations and the 'have-not' nations grows too big."

The statistics of misery is not, then, a remote economic and technical affair, but one bound up intimately with social policy. Statesmen who are realists will give a high place in their thinking to the elimination of hunger and squalor in all parts of the world as a means to protecting and enhancing the lives of people in their own countries.

Aldous Huxley said in a paper for the Fund for the Republic in 1963: "By shifting our attention from the now completely irrelevant and anachronistic politics of nationalism and military power to the problems of the human species . . . we shall be . . . reducing the threat of sudden destruction by scientific war and at the same time reducing the threat of more gradual biological disaster."

From disappointment, through resentful frustration, to widespread social unrest the road is short. Shorter still is the road from social unrest, through chaos, to dictatorship, possibly of the Communist party, more probably of generals and colonels.

The restlessness in Asia, the Middle East and Africa means among other things an increasing consciousness of the disparity between their people's present living standards and the standards common in more affluent countries. Of democracy they know little, but of hunger they know much.

Since the end of the second world war more than 800 million people in various parts of the world have seized independence, hopefully seeking to become masters of their own destiny in order to escape from poverty. Almost all of them are abysmally poor, with weak capacity for self-sustained economic growth.

Dr. [H. L.] Trueman [Secretary of the Canadian Freedom from Hunger Committee] warns that we must not allow our attention to what is going on in the major part of the world, affecting two-thirds of the world's population, to be distracted by the banging of fists on conference tables, the blast of rockets from launching pads, and the building of walls dividing nations. "What I hear," he says, "is the babble of millions of children's voices in schools where no schools previously existed; the lapping of water in new irrigation channels; the sound of millions of better ploughs moving through the good earth, and the lowing of healthier cattle on a thousand hills."

The common man throughout the world is not seeking Utopia, but a little alleviation of his lot today and that better tomorrow about which Dr. Trueman speaks. Hundreds of millions whose forebears patiently accepted lives of misery are involved in what has been called "the revolution of rising expectations." What has been, up until the past quarter century, a distant dream has now become a passionate demand.

Historian Arnold Toynbee has expressed the hope that this age will be remembered because it is the first generation in history in which mankind dared to believe it practical to make the benefits of civilization available to the whole human race.

DOMESTIC WELFARE *VERSUS* DEFENSE SPENDING

John W. Fulbright

The Constitution of the United States, in the words of its preamble, was established, among other reasons, in order to "provide for the common defense, promote the general welfare, and secure the blessings of liberty." In the past generation the emphasis of our

Domestic Welfare *versus* Defense Spending: From "The Cold War in American Life," a paper given by Senator John W. Fulbright at the University of North Carolina 1964 Symposium, "Arms and the Man: National Security and the Aims of a Free Society"; reprinted in *Congressional Record*, Vol. 110, No. 65 (April 7, 1964), pp. 6873–77.

John W. Fulbright. U.S. Senator from Arkansas.

public policy has been heavily weighted on measures for the common defense to the considerable neglect of programs for promoting the liberty and welfare of our people. The reason for this, of course, has been the exacting demands of two World Wars and an intractable cold war, which have wrought vast changes in the character of American life.

.   .   .

Overriding all these changes, however, good and bad, has been the massive diversion of wealth and talent from individual and community life to the increasingly complex and costly effort to maintain a minimum level of national security in a world in which no nation can be immune from the threat of sudden catastrophe. We have had to turn away from our hopes in order to concentrate on our fears and the result has been accumulating neglect of those things which bring happiness and beauty and fulfillment into our lives. The "public happiness," in August Heckscher's term, has become a luxury to be postponed to some distant day when the dangers that now beset us will have disappeared.

This, I think, is the real meaning of the cold war in American life. It has consumed money and time and talent that could otherwise be used to build schools and homes and hospitals, to remove the blight of ugliness that is spreading over the cities and highways of America, and to overcome the poverty and hopelessness that afflict the lives of one-fifth of the people in an otherwise affluent society. It has put a high premium on avoiding innovation at home because new programs involve controversy as well as expense and it is felt that we cannot afford domestic divisions at a time when external challenges require us to maintain the highest possible degree of national unity. Far more pervasively than the United Nations or the "Atlantic community" could ever do, the cold war has encroached upon our sovereignty; it has given the Russians the major voice in determining what proportion of our Federal budget must be allocated to the military and what proportion, therefore, cannot be made available for domestic social and economic projects. This is the price that we have been paying for the cold war and it has been a high price indeed.

At least as striking as the inversion of priorities which the cold war has enforced upon American life is the readiness with which the American people have consented to defer programs for their

welfare and happiness in favor of costly military and space programs. Indeed, if the Congress accurately reflects the temper of the
country, then the American people are not only willing, they are
eager, to sacrifice education and urban renewal and public health
programs—to say nothing of foreign aid—to the requirements of
the Armed Forces and the space agency. There is indeed a most
striking paradox in the fact that military budgets of over $50 billion
are adopted by the Congress after only perfunctory debate, while
domestic education anl welfare programs involving sums which
are mere fractions of the military budget are painstakingly examined and then either considerably reduced or rejected outright.
I sometimes suspect that in its zeal for armaments at the expense
of education and welfare the Congress tends to overrepresent those
of our citizens who are extraordinarily agitated about national
security and extraordinarily vigorous about making their agitation
known.

It may be that the people and their representatives are making a
carefully reasoned sacrifice of welfare to security. It may be, but
I doubt it. The sacrifice is made so eagerly as to cause one to suspect that it is fairly painless, that indeed the American people prefer military rockets to public schools and flights to the moon to
urban renewal. In a perverse way, we have grown rather attached
to the cold war. It occupies us with a stirring and seemingly clear
and simple challenge from outside and diverts us from problems
here at home which many Americans would rather not try to solve,
some because they find domestic problems tedious and pedestrian,
others because they genuinely believe these problems to be personal
rather than public, others because they are unwilling to be drawn
into an abrasive national debate as to whether poverty, unemployment, and inadequate education are in fact national rather than local
or individual concerns.

The cold war, it seems clear, is an excuse as well as a genuine
cause for the diversion of our energies from domestic well-being to
external security. We have been preoccupied with foreign affairs
for 25 years, and while striking progress has been made in certain
areas of our national life, the agenda of neglect has grown steadily
longer. We can no longer afford to defer problems of slums and
crime and poverty and inadequate education until some more
tranquil time in the future. These problems have become urgent
if not intolerable in an affluent society. It is entirely reasonable to

defer domestic programs in time of an all-out national effort such as World War II, but in the present cold war it is not reasonable to defer our domestic needs until more tranquil times, for the simple reason that there may be no more tranquil times in this generation or in this century.

Many Americans may regard huge military and space programs as the only truly urgent requirements on our national agenda, but it is difficult to believe that this enthusiasm is shared by the 4.2 million Americans who are unemployed or by the 30 million Americans who have incomes of less than $3,000 a year.

While the cold war and our enormously costly national security programs preempt so much of our time and attention and national wealth, the most important resources of our country—its human resources—are being extravagantly wasted and neglected. . . .

The statistics of poverty, though striking, are antiseptic compared to the actual misery and hopelessness of being poor. The real meaning of poverty is not just losses of learning and productivity, but thousands of angry and dispossessed teenagers who make our city streets dangerous for "respectable" citizens; 350,000 youngsters across the Nation who form what the Secretary of Labor has described as an "outlaw pack" because they have stopped looking for work, are unemployed today, and will remain so for the rest of their lives; children in a blighted mining town in eastern Kentucky who are potbellied and anemic from lack of food; sharecroppers, white as well as black, living in squalid shacks and working for a few dollars a day—when they can find work at all—anywhere in a crescent of rural poverty that extends from southern Virginia along the Coastal Plain across Georgia and Alabama into the Mississippi Delta and the Ozarks.

Poverty in America has a radically different moral connotation from poverty in underdeveloped nations. The poor countries of the world have the excuse, for what it is worth, that the means of feeding, housing, and educating their people simply do not exist. In America the means do exist; the failure is essentially one of distribution. The children who go to bed hungry in a Harlem slum or a West Virginia mining town are not being deprived because no food can be found to give them; they are going to bed hungry because, despite all our miracles of invention and production, we have not yet found a way to make the necessities of life available to all of our citizens—including those whose failure is not a lack of personal industry or initiative but only an unwise choice of parents.

. . .

Whether truly radical measures will be required or not, there is no question that if our national war on poverty is to come anywhere near the goal of total victory proclaimed by President Johnson, it will require enormous public effort and a great deal of public money. To those who shrink from such a commitment in the name of economy, I would emphasize that the elimination of poverty and inadequate education are at least as important to the security of our country in the long run as the maintenance of a strong defense establishment and a good deal more important than a voyage to the moon. I commend to them the words of Edmund Burke, that "Economy is a distributive virtue, and consists not in saving but in selection. Parsimony requires no providence, no sagacity, no powers of combination, no comparison, no judgment."

The cold war has diverted us from problems both quantitative and qualitative. The quantitative problem is essentially to devise ways of elevating the one-fifth of our people who live in poverty to the level of the four-fifths who live in greater material abundance than any other society in human history. The qualitative problem is to find ways of bringing meaning and purpose and standards of excellence into the lives of a people who, because of their material affluence, are free, as no people have ever been before, to shape a spiritual and intellectual environment of their own choice.

. . . .

If there is any validity in this analysis, then it follows that the first thing we must do toward raising the quality of American life is to turn some part of our thoughts and our creative energies away from the cold war that has engaged them for so long back in on America itself. If we do this, and then let nature take its course, we may find that the most vital resources of our Nation, for its public happiness and its security as well, remain locked within our own frontiers, in our cities and in our countryside, in our work and in our leisure, in the hearts and minds of our people.

INCOME WITHOUT JOBS:
A NEW UTOPIA?

Ad Hoc Committee on the Triple Revolution

As a first step to a new consensus it is essential to recognize that the traditional link between jobs and incomes is being broken. The economy of abundance can sustain all citizens in comfort and economic security whether or not they engage in what is commonly reckoned as work. Wealth produced by machines rather than by men is still wealth. We urge, therefore, that society, through its appropriate legal and governmental institutions, undertake an unqualified commitment to provide every individual and every family with an adequate income as a matter of right. This undertaking we consider to be essential to the emerging economic, social and political order in this country. We regard it as the only policy by which the quarter of the nation now dispossessed and soon-to-be dispossessed by lack of employment can be brought within the abundant society. The unqualified right to an income would take the place of the patchwork of welfare measures—from unemployment insurance to relief—designed to ensure that no citizen or resident of the United States actually starves.

We do not pretend to visualize all of the consequences of this change in our values. It is clear, however, that the distribution of abundance in a cybernated society must be based on criteria strikingly different from those of an economic system based on scarcity. In retrospect, the establishment of the right to an income will prove to have been only the first step in the reconstruction of the value system of our society brought on by the triple revolution.

The present system encourages activities which can lead to

Income Without Jobs: A New Utopia?: From *The Triple Revolution: An Appraisal of the Major U.S. Crises and Proposals for Action* (New York: Ad Hoc Committee on the Triple Revolution, March 22, 1964), pp. 16–18.

private profit and neglects those activities which can enhance the wealth and the quality of life of our society. Consequently national policy has hitherto been aimed far more at the welfare of the productive process than at the welfare of people. The era of cybernation can reverse this emphasis. With public policy and research concentrated on people rather than processes we believe that many creative activities and interests commonly thought of as non-economic will absorb the time and the commitment of many of those no longer needed to produce goods and services. Society as a whole must encourage new modes of constructive, rewarding and ennobling activity. Principal among these are activities such as teaching and learning that relate people to people rather than people to things. Education has never been primarily conducted for profit in our society; it represents the first and most obvious activity inviting the expansion of the public sector to meet the needs of this period of transition.

THE ETHICS OF POVERTY

John C. Bennett

In assessing the basic attitude of the Church to the problems of involuntary poverty, I think that we should put major stress on the tendency to see God as concerned for the victims of society, often the economic poor, and to see the response of the Christian to the needs of these victims as an acid test of discipleship, of the reality of love for the neighbor. . . .

In one of the earliest layers of the ethical teaching of the Old Testament you find this remarkable injunction:

If you lend money to any of my people with you who is poor, you shall not be to him as a creditor, and you shall not exact interest from him. If ever you take your neighbor's garment in pledge, you shall

The Ethics of Poverty: From "The Ethics of Poverty," *The Churches and Persistent Pockets of Poverty in the U.S.A.,* John C. Bennett (New York: National Council of the Churches of Christ in the U.S.A., 1962), pp. 3–8. John C. Bennett. Dean of Faculty, Union Theological Seminary.

restore it to him before the sun goes down; for it is his only covering, it is his mantle for his body; in what else shall he sleep? And
if he cries to me, I will hear, *for I am compassionate*.

This is imbedded in a primitive but remarkably humanitarian code
of laws known as the "Book of the Covenant" in Exodus (22:
25–27).

From there we may move through the prophets—whose emphasis upon the religious and ethical concern for the poor is so familiar
—with Amos's condemnation of Israel—"because they sell the
righteous for silver, and the needy for a pair of shoes—they that
trample the head of the poor into the dust of the earth" (2: 6–7)
to such familiar words of Jesus as the Lukan version of the Beatitude: "Blessed are ye poor" (6:20) which needs to be seen in the
light of the woe against the rich a few verses later: "But woe unto
you who are rich, for you have received your consolation" (6:24),
or the words in Matthew's story of the last judgment in which
Jesus says "Truly I say to you, as you did it to one of the least of
these my brethren, you did it unto me" (25:40), and to the later
words of the Epistle of James which were intended to debunk pious
evasions of responsibility for the poor: "If a brother or sister is ill-
clad and in lack of daily food, and one of you says to them, 'Go
in peace, be warmed and filled,' without giving them the things
needed for the body, what does it profit?" (2:16)

The spiritualizing of the problem created by poverty came early
in the life of the Church. It may have come when Matthew
rendered the beatitude: "Blessed are the poor in spirit" (Matthew
5:3). Of course there was no teaching in the New Testament about
dealing with the problem of poverty by changing social institutions.
Even slavery was taken for granted. Jesus' own words: "for you
always have the poor with you" (Matthew 26:11) have always
been a comfort to those who do not want to change institutions but
these words at the time were no more than a common sense obser-
vation about the world as it was.

There is a contrast of enormous importance for Christian ethics
between the situation when poverty seemed to be the inevitable
lot of almost all humanity, and the situation in which we now live
in which poverty can be overcome by political and economic
changes in the social structure. I think that this point was put in
a very clear and indeed definitive way by the report of the Oxford
Conference in 1937—one of the most significant of all corporate
statements of Christian ethical teachings:

The abolition of such poverty now seems to depend on the human organization of economic life, rather than on favors given in nature or on what might be called the inevitable constitution of every economic order. But the possibility of economic 'plenty' has this moral importance, that to an increasing extent it makes the persistence of poverty a matter for which men are morally responsible. This possibility marks off our time from the period of the New Testament and from other periods in which Christian thinking about economic life has been formulated. In the light of it the direction of Christian effort in relation to the economic order should henceforth be turned from charitable paternalism to the realization of more equal justice in the distribution of wealth—*The Oxford Conference Official Report*, p. 87.

There is a revolutionary bias in Christianity in favor of the poor. It has been hidden by many forms of accommodation to the actual situation and one would often not guess that it was there, so much has Christianity been the religion of the rich and the powerful, but it does not take long to uncover this bias. Indeed you often notice it in Church when the congregation sings: "He hath put down the mighty from their thrones, and exalted those of low degree; he has filled the hungry with good things, and the rich he has sent empty away" (Luke 1: 52–3). How many times have those words been sung at the centers of power and privilege and how many times have they been unnoticed as part of the poetry of worship, and forgotten?

In the past half century we know that emphasis upon this revolutionary aspect of our faith has come into its own, partly because we now know that poverty is not inevitable, partly because many groups of the poor have gained a voice and can remind us of their plight and have gained power and can push us until we see the world to some extent from their point of view.

I shall now speak briefly of two issues which should be in our minds as we think of those poor who have not yet acquired a strong enough voice or enough power to press us.

OLD RATIONALIZATIONS VERSUS TODAY'S REALISM

The first is that we should be realistic about the effect of poverty upon people and counter within the Church the remnants of the old rationalizations which have caused Christians from about the year

50 A.D. to be complacent about poverty. There is still some tendency to moralize concerning the problem of poverty and regard it as chiefly a punishment for moral weakness in individuals. You may remember the ironic title of the book, published when there were ten or more million unemployed in the '30's—*"Some Folks Won't Work."*

The Christian concern for the poor has in some of our traditions been overlaid by the idea that poverty is deserved. This keeps coming up when anyone advocates a purely individualistic method of dealing with poverty, often in the context of relief. One obvious difficulty with this is that even when the male breadwinner may be shiftless, the mother of the family may work over-time and the children are the victims. When we see the family unit as the most significant unit of the problem we can afford to dispense with some of our individualism and moralism.

Of course there are problems here that have to do with social disciplines and the encouragement of initiative, but the first consideration must be the effort to counteract disastrous effects on children. This leads me to another way in which people often dodge the full force of the problem.

They spiritualize it and point to the danger of emphasizing too much the economic factor in the environment and the danger of succumbing to a form of economic determinism that overlooks the capacity of the spirit of man to overcome all kinds of hardship and indeed to be stimulated by hardship to find constructive compensations for it. I agree that we can take too simple a view of these matters and I have warned against the tendency to suppose that poverty is the basic human evil. We know how false this is when we contemplate those who are not poor, including ourselves.

I do not know at what point economic hardship ceases to be a stimulus but injures the spirit. I do not know the relationship between the factor of economic deprivation and the vulnerability of a family to the most destructive anti-social temptations, such as delinquency and dope addiction. But there do seem to be situations in which even the more or less spiritually healthy family ceases to be an effective buffer for its members in a slum, but is overwhelmed by conditions where young people seem to inherit the worst of everything, and while this situation is not entirely a matter of poverty, the factor of poverty makes it most difficult for the family to neutralize the worst conditions. Today we have it brought home to us that this same complex of conditions may drag the schools down so that they *reflect* more than they *counteract* the situation.

Under these conditions it is almost a miracle for young people, even when they do not become anti-social, to develop their real capacities. Housing, school, the ethos of the streets, general expectations—all these are against them. And then on top of these handicaps, there is the handicap of race, and then of unemployment, or partial employment that helps little to organize life constructively. By this process unemployables are made, and this becomes a kind of mundane damnation.

We do these things daily to our neighbors—to the children of our neighbors, and we boast of our economic institutions for the world's benefit.

I am not arguing for a complete environmental determinism. I am not saying that poverty always does this but poverty is one highly important factor in a complex of conditions which produce such results. A man is not a disembodied soul. Not only must he eat to live but he is affected in his deeply personal life by forces that injure his body and that undermine his material welfare. And when this happens to children and young people and when various neutralizing institutions such as schools are themselves distorted by these same conditions, their chance of developing their human capacities is very limited. The formative period of life is the very period when we are most vulnerable to these destructive forces in the environment.

Let us not sentimentalize or spiritualize poverty and be led by notable cases of the strong person who has risen above it, moving from selling papers to such a high point that he may be a great executive or even one of us, to obscure the effect of this complex of conditions upon the many victims.

UNEASINESS ABOUT GREAT INEQUALITIES

A second issue that I shall only present to you as something for a future agenda has to do with the relationship between our concern to overcome poverty with the uneasiness that we may feel about great inequalities in society. I noticed in the course of the National Council studies of the ethics of economic life that the economists were so much concerned to overcome poverty that they were not much troubled about inequalities. There was a difference of emphasis between economists and theologians. They often spoke of having so large a pie that everyone would have enough even if some seemed to get large pieces which were all out of proportion.

And I notice that in our public life the eye of the needle does not seem to have political significance and in the personal cases that come to our minds I do not criticize this. Indeed wealth seems to have some advantages in removing conflicts of interest in the second or third generation, and in giving a kind of independence of the competitive pressures that create hardness toward the poor. But we ought not to forget the injunctions in our tradition about wealth as well as its concern for the poor.

There may be no situations today in which any realistic dealing with poverty would not be of considerable cost to the rich. Willingness to accept higher taxes for social purposes will often be the mark of social responsibility among those who are in the higher income brackets. I am not suggesting any form of Christian legalism that would prescribe some maximum of income as well as a minimum. I am only suggesting that we need to look at the possibility that even the overcoming of poverty may leave us with a chasm that is too great between the lavishness of the rich in our society and the way of life of the moderately poor. When I read of the death of R. H. Tawney the other day I was reminded of the passage in his book, *"The Acquisitive Society,"* which helped to form the minds of many of us who are now in the class of the aging—(I was reading in an editorial coming down on the plane that Archbishop Temple said, "There are no men like Tawney")—

> It is said that among the barbarians, where wealth is still measured by cattle, great chiefs are described as hundred-cow men. The manager of a great enterprise who is paid $400,000 a year, might similarly be described as a hundred-family man, since he receives the income of a hundred families. It is true that special talent is worth any price, and that a payment of $400,000 a year to a head of a business with a turnover of millions is a bagatelle. But economic considerations are not the only considerations. There is also 'the point of honor.' And the truth is that these hundred-family salaries are ungentlemanly (p. 178).

I know that this is not popular doctrine in this country at the present time, but I think that the moral health of our society—not only from a Christian standpoint but also from the standpoint of a broader moral sensitivity—will depend in the long run on the recognition of the truth in it. Perhaps one way in which we do recognize it is the common assumption that great wealth should be turned back to the public by way of graduated income taxes and by philanthropy on an immense scale. But suppose that with the great reduction of the expenditure for armaments, there were an unwillingness to retain high taxes for social purposes and suppose the philanthropic impulse should atrophy—we would then need to face directly the need of keeping our ideas of social and economic justice under the continuous criticism of the idea of equality.

. . .

Let me conclude with two brief quotations which bring us back to the central point again—one a quotation from St. Ambrose in the fourth century that was given a prominent place by Thomas Aquinas in the 13th century—the second from the greatest living Protestant theologian, Karl Barth.

Thou then, who hast received the gift of God, thinkest thou that thou commitest no injustice by keeping to thyself alone what would be the means of life to many? It is the bread of the hungry that thou keepest, it is the clothing of the naked that thou lockest up; the money that thou buriest is the redemption of the wretched.

The Church is witness to the fact that the Son of man came to seek and to save the lost. And this implies—casting all false impartiality aside—the Church must concentrate first on the lower and lowest levels of society. The poor, the socially and economically weak and threatened, will always be the object of its primary and particular concern, and it will always insist on the State's special responsibility for these weaker members of society.